Modern Day Surveillance Ecosystem and Impacts on Privacy

Ananda Mitra
Wake Forest University, USA

A volume in the Advances in
Information Security, Privacy, and
Ethics (AISPE) Book Series

Published in the United States of America by
    IGI Global
    Information Science Reference (an imprint of IGI Global)
    701 E. Chocolate Avenue
    Hershey PA, USA 17033
    Tel: 717-533-8845
    Fax: 717-533-8661
    E-mail: cust@igi-global.com
    Web site: http://www.igi-global.com

Library of Congress Cataloging-in-Publication Data

Names: Mitra, Ananda, 1960- author.
Title: Modern day surveillance ecosystem and impacts on privacy / by Ananda
  Mitra.
Description: Hershey : Information Science Reference, 2021. | Includes
  bibliographical references and index. | Summary: "This book offers the
  readers an understanding of the current state of public surveillance we
  face today, the rationale of surveillance (security, commodification,
  perversion and control), discussing the critical consequences of
  pervasive surveillance and some future projections on the topic"--
  Provided by publisher.
Identifiers: LCCN 2021018332 (print) | LCCN 2021018333 (ebook) | ISBN
  9781799838470 (hardcover) | ISBN 9781799881346 (paperback) | ISBN
  9781799838487 (ebook)
Subjects: LCSH: Electronic surveillance--Social aspects. | Privacy, Right
  of.
Classification: LCC HM853 .M58 2021 (print) | LCC HM853 (ebook) | DDC
  363.2/32--dc23
LC record available at https://lccn.loc.gov/2021018332
LC ebook record available at https://lccn.loc.gov/2021018333

This book is published in the IGI Global book series Advances in Information Security, Privacy, and Ethics (AISPE) (ISSN: 1948-9730; eISSN: 1948-9749)

British Cataloguing in Publication Data
A Cataloguing in Publication record for this book is available from the British Library.

All work contributed to this book is new, previously-unpublished material.
The views expressed in this book are those of the authors, but not necessarily of the publisher.

For electronic access to this publication, please contact: eresources@igi-global.com.

Advances in Information Security, Privacy, and Ethics (AISPE) Book Series

ISSN:1948-9730
EISSN:1948-9749

Editor-in-Chief: Manish Gupta, State University of New York, USA

MISSION

As digital technologies become more pervasive in everyday life and the Internet is utilized in ever increasing ways by both private and public entities, concern over digital threats becomes more prevalent.

The **Advances in Information Security, Privacy, & Ethics (AISPE) Book Series** provides cutting-edge research on the protection and misuse of information and technology across various industries and settings. Comprised of scholarly research on topics such as identity management, cryptography, system security, authentication, and data protection, this book series is ideal for reference by IT professionals, academicians, and upper-level students.

COVERAGE

- Privacy-Enhancing Technologies
- Electronic Mail Security
- Information Security Standards
- Telecommunications Regulations
- CIA Triad of Information Security
- Network Security Services
- Risk Management
- Global Privacy Concerns
- Internet Governance
- Data Storage of Minors

IGI Global is currently accepting manuscripts for publication within this series. To submit a proposal for a volume in this series, please contact our Acquisition Editors at Acquisitions@igi-global.com or visit: http://www.igi-global.com/publish/.

Titles in this Series

For a list of additional titles in this series, please visit: *http://www.igi-global.com/book-series/*

701 East Chocolate Avenue, Hershey, PA 17033, USA
Tel: 717-533-8845 x100 • Fax: 717-533-8661
E-Mail: cust@igi-global.com • www.igi-global.com

Table of Contents

Preface

There is a saying that can be traced back to the early 1600s in British writing that later becomes a part of the corpus of idioms that says, "curiosity killed the cat." Referring to an unfortunate feline, the proverb points towards a fundamental tendency in humans – the need to know. This can be considered one of the tendencies that makes us humans. This book is about curiosity and how we have developed it into a systematic form and the consequence of curiosity. The book is presented in accessible language, offering sufficient theories for the curious to delve deeper and is supported with references to contemporary, at least when the book was written, references from popular culture. This is not meant to be an "academic" book but something that could be useful to a large range of readers. It also presents my perspective on a series of vital issues, thus demonstrating my biases. I hope the readers will disagree with my biases and interpret the information in the way they want to. The information, however, remains sanguine. The structure of the book begins with the notion of surveillance and then concludes with the idea of privacy – the two main topics of the book.

The first chapter presents an overview of curiosity – in this case called "surveillance." It offers a brief history of surveillance and its connection with a more common term – spying. Expanding on the history, I take the readers through an understanding of the various contexts of surveillance, from personal to institutional, to demonstrate the pervasive nature of surveillance. Here I also present the four typographies of surveillance: I2I, I2P, P2I, and P2P. The chapter then offers a review of the principal theories of surveillance beginning with the notion of the panopticon and continuing to the idea of rhizomatic surveillance. I conclude with the invitation to consider the process of surveillance as a communicative moment and examine the process from the perspective that surveillance creates narratives.

The second chapter offers a close look at the notion of narratives. I draw from my existing work on the narrative paradigm arguing that as "narrative beings" we need to find meaning through stories and the process of surveillance is a way to seek narratives connecting the act of surveillance to the creation of numerous tiny narratives – narbs – all of which make up the body of Big Data that becomes the outcome of surveillance. It is this Big Data that is the fountainhead of the narratives, and a large portion of surveillance is collection and management of this data.

In Chapters 3-4, I elaborate on the data collection process. Chapter 3 looks at the various elements collecting the data. These include both private individuals who are the 'watchers' as well as institution such as governments that are engaged in the process of watching and collecting data. The chapter elaborates on the different types of watchers and the watched. In Chapter 4, the focus shifts to the way in which the watching is done from the data collection process to create a representation of the real person to the ways in the real person is observed with elaborate systems of cameras and other tools to keep an eye on the real body. These two chapters offer a review of the way in which surveillance works, opening up the space to examine the motivation to surveil and the current consequences of the surveillance process.

Chapter 5 examines the most popular argument to justify the process of surveillance – offering security. This has been the reason for surveillance in all categories of surveillance from the state watching its subjects to spouses secretly watching each other. The normative rationale for the watching is to offer a sense of safety for the watched – so that the watcher can claim to ensure that the watched is always safe. I examine this perspective on surveillance and then offer evidence for a second reason why surveillance is becoming prolific.

In Chapter 6, I posit that surveillance is also offered as an assessment of the condition of the watched. Within this logic, surveillance is needed to ensure that the watched has a certain set of characteristics that can be considered to be "normal" by the watcher. This relates to the way in which the narratives obtained from the data produces profiles of the watched which in turn can be assessed and even commodified for the benefit of the watcher.

Both Chapters 5 and 6 elaborate the justification for surveillance within the four categories of surveillance. The justification finally leads to an examination of the key consequences of the pervasive form of surveillance described in the book.

In Chapter 7, I offer the first consequence of surveillance – a sense of being controlled by the watcher. Given the level of information that cumulates through the process of surveillance there are numerous ways in which the information can be utilized for controlling the watched. The data offers a reliable basis of predicting the behavior of the watch and thus eventually controlling the behavior in a way that is determined by the watcher in any of the four contexts of surveillance.

Chapter 8 offers an overview of the second aspect of the book – privacy. The notion of privacy permeates through each chapter and eventually culminates in this chapter, offering a form of a "book end" where I offer different ways in which the idea of privacy needs to be rethought in the face of the surveillance processes that have become persistent in our lives. My primary concern here is on the inadequacy of some of the traditional ways to theorize privacy and I argue that the notion needs an overhaul and redefinition with what the future of surveillance may offer.

Chapter 9 elaborates on the possible future(s) of surveillance. Extrapolating from the changes in technology I argue that societal shifts will engage different technologies for the watching process. In all such cases there could be further erosion of the notion of privacy and greater control offered to the watchers. However, given the justifications for surveillance that have been accepted by the watched, there are good reasons to believe that surveillance will be a part of our future lived experience.

The final chapter offers a set of strategies to cope with a surveillance society. Here I focus on the principles of the surveillance process – the creation and maintenance of personal narratives – and offers some directions about managing this narrative. I offer the consequences of not being mindful and the benefits of being cognizant of the surveillance processes and the goals of surveillance.

Books like this often get "dated" rapidly because of the rapid advances in technologies or momentous events in human society. For instance, the pandemic of 2020 that continued in 2021, was the backdrop of authoring this manuscript. As such many of the pragmatic aspects of surveillance changed in this time period. However, what remained unchanged was the need to create narratives. The lasting value of this book lies in the unique juxtaposition of narrative theories and the processes of surveillance. That connection would most likely continue in spite of the changes in technologies and societies.

Chapter 1
The Essentials of Surveillance

ABSTRACT

The process of surveillance has been around for a long period. Different theories of surveillance such as the notion of the panopticon were suggested to explain the ways in which surveillance can create a more controlled society. This led to the notion of the docility and surveillance where the knowledge of surveillance can create a docile society. With the availability of newer tools, surveillance becomes more widespread, which leads to a networked surveillance. All of this eventually builds up to a process of surveillance of the life story of institutions and people.

INTRODUCTION

It was a winter day in the state of North Carolina in United States when my son had turned nineteen years old and was the proud possessor of his first car. It was a relatively old Ford Mustang, a car that he had dreamed of for some time and I was able to obtain at a price I could afford. The possession of a car in America is a rite of passage that teens in the USA await with great anticipation and the guardians dread. Now, there was no holding back a young person from being able to go wherever the person wished and most teens would happily exercise the rights that the freedom and possession offered. For the guardians, it was an immediate loss of control on the life of a young loved one. It became immediately apparent to my wife and me that our only child could now roam freely the highways of North Carolina, and perhaps even further. This, for many, is a moment of panic. The secure bubble that the youngster lived in suddenly disappeared. This was no longer the case that I would be driving him to his next music concert or to a friend's place. Now he could go alone, and we would never know where he was, and until he returned we would be holding our breath. We had lost control, and we were desperately curious to know how our child's life would change with the freedom that the Mustang heralded. In speaking to many other parents, we realized that within the confines of small-town USA, my wife and I were not alone in our curiosity and anxiety.

I needed to find out. There must be a way, I argued, by which I could know how the life of the youngster was altered by the car. I also needed to know what new relational challenges would be presented with the new freedom. We wondered if our relationship with our child would be altered because now, we would not always know everything about his life. He could be at one place, but he may choose not to disclose where he is. In the past, we always knew his location, because we would take him to a place, and we would collect him from the place. In cases he would travel with others, there would always be an "adult" involved and we could check-in with the person he was with. We were now facing a new challenge of uncertainty. The way this matter was resolved was through a credit card that my son used for some of his purchases, which now included paying for the gasoline for the car. I set up a simple tracking system, offered by the Credit Card company, that would alert me whenever the card was used for a purchase. All of a sudden a whole new World opened up. A new story was being constructed as the use of the card showed the movement of a person and the kind of places the person would frequent using the car he possessed. A curious matter happened soon. I no longer had to ask my son where he had been on a weekend evening. I knew because of the alerts, the card was, for instance, used at a convenience store in the downtown of Winston-Salem, or at fast food restaurant in Chapel Hill, or at a music equipment supply store in Greensboro – all towns within North Carolina. Not only was my curiosity fulfilled but it also gave me a sense of comfort in knowing that my son was safe and was using his freedom in a responsible manner and not driving away wherever the road would take him. I realized I was actively surveilling him, using a technology that was not subversive or secret. He would know that his purchases can be tracked and if he would be mindful about it he would know that I would know. Given the relationship of trust within our family this process was not worrisome to anyone. Surveillance became a part of our life thereafter.

Indeed, the fact that surveillance has become a part of our lives is the motivation for this book. We are constantly surveilled, and we have come to accept it as a part of our life. Sometimes we realize that we are surveilled and at other times we do not, but perhaps in the back of our mind we are always aware of being watched. This was aptly stated by a fictional former agent of the Central Investigation Agency (CIA) in the 1998 thriller, *Enemy of the State*, in saying, "Every wire, every airwave. The more technology used, the easier it is for them to keep tabs on you. It's a brave new world out there." While the film represented the tools of surveillance from the late 1990s, the World has changed even more as I would discuss in this book.

In this chapter I elaborate on the history of the process of surveillance tracing its roots from the act of spying. I then offer the four contexts of surveillance that offer a way to categorize the vast contemporary experience of surveillance into systematic parts, followed by the review of some of the key theories of surveillance that have emerged. I conclude with the proposal of engaging narrative theories to understand the way in which surveillance occurs.

History

The notion of surveillance and spying are historically connected. Human history has numerous instances of the way in which spying has worked. The key to the process of spying has been collecting information about an entity without the entity having any notion that the entity was being observed. Legend has that spying was actively used in ancient civilizations and there are records of the process of spying and its utility in ancient writings such as the Sun Tzu's ancient Chinese book, *The Art of War*, where the importance of spying was emphasized in stating that, "One who knows the enemy and knows himself will not be endangered in a hundred engagements (Derek, 2014)." Similar records of the importance of spying have been mentioned by other ancient authors such as Chanyaka, in India, when in the 4th Century BC he had mentioned the importance of espionage in his book, *Arthashastra* (Shoham and Liebig, 2016). The fundamental idea of spying was continued through history as different entities, primarily state institutions, have developed elaborate mechanisms of spying and observation. There are numerous references to espionage in historical documents and the fictionalization of famous instances of espionage. An elaborate entertainment industry has existed that focuses on spy novels, and later spy movies and television shows that narrates real and fictional spying events.

Indeed, the history of the modern World would have been different in the absence of specific spying events and infamous real-World spies who have helped shape the face of the World today. For instance, the tide of World War 2 turned in the favor of the Allies when they were able to capture and use a messaging machine called the Enigma that was used by Germans to send encrypted messages to their troops. When such a machine was captured by the Allies, scientists at Benchley Park in UK were able to work out the encryption system and thus spy on the communication of the Germans, and were able to anticipate what the Germans were about to do. Years after World War 2, at the height of the Cold War, Americans were able to fly over Soviet Russia carefully photographing the military establishments of USSR and thus spying on the military capabilities of Russia. Such military spying is a part of the defense strategy of all nations where a nation needs to be able to track the "enemy" so that a nation is not surprised by the enemy. In many cases, spying does not only involve observing the stated enemy, but American satellite technology is able to keep an eye on the entire World to see what the rest of the World is doing. In some cases, such spying is well known to all, and the fact that a nation is being spied upon is not necessarily a secret. Belligerent neighbors such as North and South Korea, Pakistan, and India, are well aware that one is keeping an eye on the other and in a "cat and mouse" game each is trying to outsmart the other. Such "spy vs spy" episodes are part of the fabric of the intelligence organizations across the World.

Within the mainstream World of spying the emphasis has been on seeing what the enemy defense infrastructure is doing. This idea has also been adopted for other kinds of institutions. One of the most important adaptation of military spying has been developed for industrial espionage. Just like nations compete with each other in the military theater, there is economic competition in the sphere of global Capitalism. Multi-national corporations are constantly in competition with each other for market shares, and it is of great advantage for corporations to know and anticipate what the competitor may be planning. The process of spying on the competition does not have any national security implications but still uses strategies similar to the ones used by states and militaries to construct specific narratives of the competition to gain strategic business advantages. This form of spying has ranged from learning proprietary know-hows to outright stealth of technology and means of production. An infamous example of this form of espionage goes back to the 1800s when Scottish botanist Robert Fortune smuggled out tea plants from China and re-planted them in the Darjeeling region of the Himalayan foothills starting the tea industry on behalf of the British East India Company. This effectively wiped out the tea monopoly of China and established the Indian Sub-Continent as the leading producer of tea. Instances such as this demonstrates that industrial espionage uses elaborate methods to not only steal competing technology, as in the case of tea, but there are also instances where corporations would duplicate the competition's business narratives to duplicate them. Consider for instance the case of the stealth of an entire business concept when the well-known Hilton group of properties were able to duplicate a specific line of luxury hotel products from the competing Starwood group of hotels (Guardian News Media, 2009).

Another aspect of spying has involved historic social inequities where the "powerful" in societal hierarchies have spied on the "powerless" to ensure that the powerless are kept in their place. Such social injustice has not always needed an overt state approval but has created a theater of imbalance that has been supported by the spying apparatus. Consider for instance, the relationship between race and surveillance in America;

the way in which citizens spy on each other in America in the early Twenty-First Century or the historical treatise on surveillance in America. It should be noted that these instances deal primarily with the tradition of spying in the United States, but any place which has experienced systemic harsh hierarchies can find such histories of spying which do not neatly fall into either state sponsored spying or industrial espionage but belongs to the arena of people sponsored spying because some people are able to wield power (Simon Browne Joshua Reeves Christian Parenti).

All these histories have had one similar trait – the process of "watching" was often initiated by an institution such as a corporation or a nation and the object of observation was another institution. In many cases, the actual observer might be an iconic individual, or a small group of individuals trained in the process of observation as in the case of well-known spies such Major John Andre (the iconic individual) who spied for the British during the American Revolutionary War for Independence to Mata Hari who spied for the German. These individuals represented nations and then spied on other nations, often represented by specific individuals, but in all these cases the object of observation was rarely a specific individual but often another institution who could be represented by an individual. The notion of surveillance is somewhat different from this conventional process of spying.

Surveillance

The key to surveillance is observation. Tracing the English word "surveillance" to its roots one encounters the Latin word *vigilia* which loosely translates to being wakeful and watching. When connected with the French preposition *sur* which translates to "on" the origins of the term surveillance leads to the notion of watching on or watching over some entity. Thus, the notion of surveillance is not very different from the way spying worked, which also involved watching over something, but the process of surveillance could be much wider. Unlike espionage which was often restricted to watching over nations, militaries and corporations, surveillance, as a process and a concept, could apply to any instance of watching conducted by any entity, from a nation to an individual, over any other entity, from a nation to an individual. Although this might appear to be merely a semantic difference allowing the word surveillance to widen the scope of watching, it also opens up the space to re-consider surveillance in a manner that is somewhat different from traditional spying.

The first important difference between traditional spying and surveillance relates to the power relations between the watcher and the watched. In the case of traditional spying the primary actors were institutions. Thus, India would spy on Pakistan and vice versa. Institutions such as the Central Intelligence Agency (CIA) and the Komitet Gosudarstvennoy Bezopasnosti (KGB) of the United States and Russia respectively were legendary rivals and the stuff of many real and fictional events. Such agencies worked for the nations they represented, and the people in the employment of such agencies spied on each other and the countries they worked for. There was a delicate balance of power between these agencies. All through the Cold War following World War II, the balance of power between America and Russia maintained an uneasy peace and disastrous nuclear confrontations were avoided with the knowledge that any imbalance of the power could lead to Mutually Assured Destruction (MAD) of major parts of the World. The same power relation applied to industrial espionage where giant corporation would spy on each other where the watched and the watcher had similar resources available to them.

The relationship between power and resources is of special importance when considering the process of surveillance. In the case of spying each of the institutions could bring to bear similar modes of spying and each was aware that someone was watching them, and each had the resources to combat the act of spying. In the case of surveillance, the matter changes somewhat because surveillance includes the process of institutions watching individuals, as well as individuals watching other individuals. In such cases there is often an imbalance of power and resources between the one who is observing and the one that is being observed. Additionally, unlike the nations and corporations, individuals may not even realize that they are being surveilled. Institutions can wield sufficient deception to hide the process of watching where the people being watched would not be aware that they are being watched and not have the resources to stop the process of watching even if the individual becomes aware of being watched. The power imbalance and the everyday life activities of an individual would automatically make them powerless in the face of surveillance. Consider for instance the simple act of going to a bank to withdraw money or walking up to an ATM to use an ATM card to withdraw money. In both these cases the individual is being watched through cameras, indeed in some cases there is a clear statement that may say that the place is under camera surveillance. However, the individual is powerless to avoid that surveillance because withdrawing cash might be an essential task in everyday life. In 2016, when the Government of India declared that certain currency notes were no longer legal tender, nearly every Indian with a bank account had to either visit a bank or an ATM to withdraw cash in the newly minted notes that replaced the old notes. In such a situation the individual is powerless to avoid surveillance. This imbalance of power leads to the placement of the watched in a "subject" position before the institution, be it the state or a corporation.

The notion of the subject is a particularly vital construct in understanding the relations of power between entities. Scholars such as the French philosopher Louis Althusser (1918-90) have argued that there are numerous mechanisms, often called State Apparatuses, that always place individuals in the position of the subject of an institution (Althusser, 1977). Drawing upon the nomenclature attached to the people in a monarchy as subjects of the king, the term can be extended to people in a modern state where they are placed in the position of the subject of the state through the mechanisms of control via the arms of the state extending from public education systems to the law enforcement systems. The tools of surveillance go on to extend the reach of the apparatuses that are already in the role of placing people in the relatively powerless position of the subject. As I have pointed out earlier, people often have no choice but to be observed by entities who remain beyond the scope of the observation of the one who is constantly being watched. It is as if there is a law enforcement system that cannot be questioned and remains beyond the law.

There is thus a distinct split or differentiation between the watcher and the watched. The watcher can become increasingly more powerful in its act of observation, while the watched becomes increasingly helpless in avoiding the gaze. The tools for observation are becoming so pervasive that it is possible to incorporate the tools in many different everyday aspects of life and the watcher can always watch. Consider for instance the way in which it is being reported that TV sets connected with the Internet are now operating as a tool to watch the people watching TV. The capability of the TV to be doing surveillance has been noted starting around 2015 when TV sets were equipped with cameras (for face recognition) and microphones (for voice control) and the TV was able to "listen" and "watch." This produces a distinct separation between the corporate apparatus that brings the TV to the consumer and the user of the TV who is aware of being watched but sometimes powerless to challenge the process of watching (Shoham & Liebig, 2016). This notion of the split between the subject of surveillance and the watcher is, however, not restricted to the state and corporate apparatuses but can be traced within the many contexts of surveillance. It is thus useful to consider the different contexts of the process of surveillance. In the next section, I present a typography to categorize the different processes of surveillance. These categories will be used all through the book to elaborate the different contexts of surveillance.

Contexts of Surveillance

One of the key aspects of the process of surveillance that has an impact on the split between the watcher and the watched is overall context of surveillance. Later in the book, I will delve further into the various tools used in the surveillance process, but it is useful to consider the situations in which surveillance occurs and the way in which the position of the watcher and the watched keeps switching with implications for the relations of power between the entities.

The most common context of surveillance is the institution(I) on the person(P) which can be called I2P surveillance. In this case, as in the case of the state spying on people, there are a set of *a priori* relations of power which automatically empowers the institution to be able to observe the person or the individual.

A second context of surveillance that is rapidly emerging is a person(P) on person(P) surveillance that can be called P2P surveillance. In this case, also as in the anecdote about my son, the watcher is often an individual who is watching another individual. The relations of power are trickier to pinpoint in the P2P context. It is possible that in certain contexts, such as a parent tracking the activities of a child, there are pre-existing normative relations of power within the parent-child context. Yet, with generational shifts, and with the family structure transforming with time, the "traditional" context of parent-child relationship is open for discussion and transformation. Other P2P contexts, such as relational partners, such as spouses, watching each other bring in far more complicated power contexts that can impact the process and outcome of surveillance. Suffice to say, the P2P context presents certain concerns of power relationships that can become quite complicated, as I will point out later.

A third context of surveillance, which I have suggested is the example of the earliest form of surveillance as spying, is the process when an institution(I) would be watching another institution which can be called I2I surveillance. The contexts of power are simpler to trace in this situation because there could be sufficient information about the power differentials between the institutions. Consider a "weaker" nation attempting to spy on a "stronger" nation. The differences in the access to technologies, infrastructure, personnel could all be factors in determining the power relations in the I2I situation.

Finally, a fourth context of surveillance that needs to be considered is the person(P) watching an institution(I) which can be called P2I surveillance. Consider for instance the way in which individuals are able to keep an eye on institutions by watching the activities of an institution and then presenting the observation in the public sphere that draws attention to the activities of the institution. There are examples of this form of P2I surveillance in many different domains – from customers pointing towards unacceptable business practices to citizens pointing out unethical behavior of representatives of governments. The P2I context is emerging because of the ways in which access to technologies have altered with the individual gaining greater access and consequently altering the relations of power.

The four contexts are important to identify before entering into a more elaborate discussion of the processes of surveillance. At the same time, there has been significant amount of the process of surveillance leading to the development of different theories to understand how surveillance works in societies. It is important to review these theories since the processes and the accompanying theories have shifted with time as the processes have changed.

Theories of Surveillance

The process of watching has been a part of everyday life for a long period of time as different mechanisms of observation has been developed and applied in society. However, a careful analysis of the process, with an effort to offer a theoretical foundation is often traced to a British philosopher and jurist Jeremy Bentham (1748-1832). Although Bentham was trained in law, he did not actually practice law as much as be critiqued the legal systems of 1700s Britain and offered different approaches to the transformation of society for the betterment of the individual. One of his primary contributions was the development of the theory of Utilitarianism with the associated principle of "greatest happiness of the greatest number." The notion of utilitarianism was not necessarily the bastion of the work of Bentham alone, but others before him, especially theological utilatirists suggested that the promotion of human happiness was expected of us because that would be the will of God. Bentham, however, is of special interest to those studying the process and consequences of surveillance because his fundamental position as an utiliarist offered the basis for some of his work on the notion of surveillance, which Bentham approached from a non-coercive perspective arguing that even the process of surveillance, as suggested by Bentham, would produce the greatest good for the most number of people.

The central theme of surveillance suggested by Bentham rested on the idea of the Panopticon. This was an architectural idea that was supposed to change the design of prisons. Bentham had suggested four different kinds of Panopticons, all of which, as the word suggests, had the objecting of watching (opticon) a large group of people (pan) at all times. The prison Panopticon was conceived as a circular space where there would be a central tower in the middle of the circular space and guards would be positioned in the central tower to observe the prisoners who would be free to move around the space while cognizant of the fact that they are being observed constantly. The presence of the central tower was sufficient reason to *believe* that they were under constant watch even if there was no one in the tower. According to Bentham, that belief would be sufficient to attenuate the behavior of the prisoners. Applying the utilitarian approach, Bentham argued that the prison Panopticon offered a better form of reform for the prisoner, for the prisoner's good, than the cruel forms of punishment that was commonplace in prisons in the times of Bentham. The prison Panopticon was not meant to be a new form of punishment, but as stated by Galic and others, "Bentham saw punishment as evil in itself, allowed only if it excluded greater evil. In regard to the prison-Panopticon, the specific architecture thus also served the goal of prisoners' liberation from more overtly coercive forms of institutional violence, which were common at the time (Galič et al., 2016)." However, the idea of the Panopticon became central to understanding the notions of surveillance with the focus being on the prison-Panopticon.

The focus on the prison metaphor, however, deflected attention from the other forms of Panopticon suggested by Bentham. Within the historical circumstances of the times of Bentham, and through to the Twentieth Century, the prison-Panopticon became central in developing theories of discipline through surveillance, but Bentham also suggested that the Panopticon could be used for other institutions such as schools. Bentham continued to apply his interpretation of utilatiarism and argued that, "people may not respond to the actions good qualities — perhaps they don't perceive the good effects. But as long as there are these good effects which are, on balance, better than the effects of any alternative course of action, then the action is the right one (Driver, 2014)." In the school version of the Panopticon the idea was that one teacher could observe hundreds of students as long as the students were in the school ground so that a sense of harmony could be maintained within the school. The utilitarian aspect of this school-Panopticon is evident in the way that Brunon-Earnst describes it: "The plan was based on Bentham's 'scholar-teacher principle', whereby the more advanced pupils taught the less advanced, 'for the greatest improvement of the minds of (Brunon-Ernst, 2016)."

The most consequential impact of Bentham was indeed the proposal of the prison-Panopticon which was rapidly considered to be a disciplinarian process, and the original basis on Utilitarianism was lost. Indeed, even though no such prison was actually built in the time of Bentham, there have been prisons that were inspired by the proposal of Bentham. Prisons like the Pentonville Prison in England and the Kilmainham Gaol in Dublin were inspired by the disciplinary benefits that Bentham's design would offer. Indeed, the following slightly lengthy description connects the prison in Dublin with the specific disciplinary interpretation of Bentham's Panopticon:

The east wing of Kilmainham Gaol opened in 1864, and 'was enthusiastically received with its 'panoptic design'. The design was modelled on that of Pentonville Prison, and like it was a '3 storey high, barrel vaulted space, lined on either side with a network of iron galleries and catwalks. The overall view from the hall demonstrated an ordered vista of salubrious space showing separate confinement from outside of the cell door without the visibility of the human form cornered in the wretchedness of isolation.' Freida Kelly A History of Kilmainhan Gaol: the dismal house of little ease (1998), p. 83.

Here the claim is made because of the 'overall view from the hall'. For Bentham, the method of inspection meant far more than this. He did not invent the 'inspection principle' but his particular architectural solution to the problem of surveillance was original and facilitated uncertainty in the prisoner in a particularly powerful way. Kilmainham, and the other Pentonville clones, are pale approximations (Ucl, 2018). Yet, the disciplinary aspect becomes the central tenet of another influential thinker in the matter of surveillance – Foucault.

Michael Foucault (1926-84) is considered one of the most important thinker, commentator, and author of the Twentieth Century. Hailing from France, his contributions have spanned many disciplines and influenced the way in which specific ways of thinking offered by Foucault have affected policy in a variety of spheres of everyday life. Amongst his many books, the 1957 book called *Discipline and Punishment* is most relevant to the current discussion about surveillance. Foucault drew a strong contrast between the way discipline was maintained in the 1700s to the way discipline needed to be maintained in the 1900s. His principal argument was that the traditional form of discipline, that was often maintained by the monarch on the subject, was often sustained by examples of spectacular punishment where the spectacle of the punishment would be the deterrent to future threats to the system of discipline. The horrific show of power that Foucault offers in the opening of his book where he describes the way in which a criminal is drawn and quartered, exemplified the way in which a monarchial system could maintain discipline.

However, the space for such mechanisms of punishment disappeared with the emergence of the "state," often the product of a democratic ideology, where the monarch has been replaced by a more diffuse form of control and power where the spectacular display of punishment is no longer an option. It is in this condition that Foucault draws upon Bentham's notion of the Panopticon and Foucault suggests that power, and consequently discipline, is now sustained by the process of watching the subject constantly as would be possible in Bentham's Panoptic prison. Much like Bentham, Foucault argues that acquiring control on the prisoner was no longer the product of horrific punishment, but discipline was obtained by making the body "docile" and aware of the fact that the body could be watched all the time. This would produce a disciplined body that would always and already do the "right" thing and be disempowered because of the possibility of being watched. As suggested by Foucault, the Panoptic structure would have "a central point [that] would be both the source of light illuminating everything, and a locus of convergence for everything that must be known; a perfect eye that nothing would escape and a center towards which all gazes would be turned (Foucault & Sheridan, 2020)." It is this central point that would be crucial to the way in which surveillance is conducted.

Yet, in 1975 when Foucault was expanding on the notion of the Panopticon as the alternative to culture of spectacle to maintain discipline, the technologies that could actually create the Panopticon gaze were still in their infancy. There were only a few tools that could actually do what Foucault, and Bentham were suggesting. The ideal Panopticon prison, as designed by Willey Reveley (1760–1799) was never really built and Foucault's central point was still a possibility without operationalization in 1975. Furthermore, both these forms of surveillance relied on the "state" as the key actor who would be the watcher on the tower in the prison, or who would be the point where everything that must be known would converge. In both the work of Bentham and Foucault, power was concentrated in the relatively narrow space of the government which is interested in exercising control on the subjects of the state.

However, as pointed out earlier in the chapter, the contexts of "watching" have shifted wildly from the days of Bentham as well as Foucault and other forms and spheres of surveillance have emerged which have attracted other ways of thinking of the process of surveillance. The traditional I2P context of surveillance that was the focus of the early scholars was quickly being supplemented by the other contexts of surveillance.

To a large degree, the work of Bentham and later that of Foucault had some commonalities that suited the specific I2P context of the periods when they worked. For the more recent work of Foucault the key was creating a "discipline society," expanding on the Panopticon prison to a larger canvas where all subjects of the state would be rendered docile through the process of watching and the very fact that they were being watched would offer a sense of control to the watcher over the watched body. The notion of the body was also critical to the discipline society of Foucault, where the physical body would be watched. This physical body was considered to be relatively stable and often lived within well-defined spatial boundaries making the maintenance of discipline, and control, a function of the watching process. This focus on the interaction between discipline, control and punishment was called into question by a set of scholars who wanted to move away from the Panopticon model to what has been called a "rhizomatic" model of surveillance which seemed more appropriate to accommodate the emerging contexts of surveillance, as in the example of my son and his car where the physical body was no longer in one place.

A rhizome is the part of a plant that is often underground and has many interconnected pieces, just like ginger. This metaphor offers a convenient way to understand the way in which French philosopher Gilles Deleuze (1925-95) and others have suggested that with the changes in technology, Global connectedness, migration, and emergence of a Global public sphere the Panopticon metaphor fails to capture the complexity of the system that began to develop in the latter part of the Twentieth Century. The key argument was that it was no longer the case that a single entity, such as the prison guard in Bentham's prison, was watching over a set of physical bodies to keep them disciplined and docile, but it was now the case that multitude of entities from the Government to the corporations were needing to have a sense of control on the many aspects of the physical body that was beginning to be highly mobile. The discipline metaphor was being replaced by a control metaphor, and the intense desire to discipline was being abandoned, and it was being suggested that it was necessary to control the rhizomatic society and the multi-faceted people who dwelled in this interconnected public sphere. It was becoming clear that creating a disciplined public sphere depended on the level of control that could be exercised on a public without the use of undue coercion.

Furthermore, it was also becoming clear that control was to be exercised on a complex "body" which had presence in multiple spaces. The real flesh and blood body that was the site of the disciplinary action was now also represented in the digital space where the representation itself was worthy of observation and regulation. In some instances, this representation has been called the "data double," as described by Galič Maša, Timan Tjerk and Koops Bert-Jaap in a 2017 article in the *Philosophy and Technology* journal, where they stated, "The data double, however, goes beyond representation of our physical selves—it does not matter whether the double actually corresponds to the 'real' body. The data double constitutes an additional self (Galič et al., 2016)."

It is the combination of the body and its representations that is increasingly being watched by an equally fragmented body of watchers. Just as the watched has become simultaneously fragmented and rhizomatic as the fragments are inter-connected, the locus of the watcher has also changed and moved away from the singular watchers that could be identified in the past Worlds of the Panopticon. This shift has resulted from the transition to control as opposed to discipline. Only certain elements in society are in the business of disciplining, but there are far more elements interested in control. A marketer needs to know the purchase behavior to control future purchase practices. The medical system needs to know the medical indicators of a social group to better control behavior to channel it in what could be considered to be beneficial to the social group. The financial systems need to observe and control financial behavior to limit reckless financial decisions that could be detrimental to an individual and to the financial system in general. In all such cases of the I2P context, there is a move to a fragmented system of observation as stated again by the authors such as David Lyon who offered the idea of the body double as stated in the 2017 article quoted earlier, "it is increasingly difficult to suggest that surveillance serves a single coherent purpose such as social control, or even a limited set of purposes." The process is certainly multi-faceted which moves the theoretical approach towards surveillance in new directions as the context, site and subject(s) of surveillance keeps shifting.

It should be noted that the theoretical perspectives summarized here is a portion of a larger body of literature that has developed over a length of time in the area of surveillance. Different scholars from different disciplines have looked at the same phenomenon from different perspectives and have labelled and interpreted the phenomenon through the lens of their unique discipline. For instance, the work of David Lyon has explored the state of surveillance in a historical way in a set of seminal books that has engaged in the debates related to the process of surveillance. Different terms have been used to describe some of the phenomenon I have highlighted here, such as the P2I process which Steve Mann called "sousveillance," as a contrast to watching from above but watching on level, or even below level. Numerous other terms have been used to describe emerging methods of surveillance that address specific sub-areas of surveillance such as synopticon (Mathiesen), banopticon (Didier Bigo, 2008), dataveillance (or shareveillance). The specific notion of data surveillance will be discussed at length in this book. Other theoretical moves are constantly being made as there are rapid changes in everyday life where fundamental concepts such as those of privacy are re-cast and re-thought. Consider for instance the 2013 work by Zygmunt Bauman and David Lyon on liquid surveillance that attempts to recast the question of surveillance in view of a highly mobile and "liquid" modern life (Bauman & Lyon, 2016).

These theoretical transformations, that often follow the "what is going on?" query about what is empirically observed are important to note. However, it is also important to consider why these theories matter, and why new approaches need to be developed. The objective is to examine the phenomenon and have access to theories that can help explain what is being observed. However, it is phenomenon that is important, and it is useful to consider, in brief, why this phenomenon matters.

As I have explained earlier in this chapter, it is nearly impossible to avoid the condition where a person is not being observed. While the Panopticon prison of Bentham might not have been built and operated quite in the way that he had imagined it, or people may not be overtly disciplined to create the docile subjects of Foucault, the fact remains that every time a credit card is used, a telephone call is made, a picture posted on Instagram or there is a doctor visit, the information about that episode is being captured and stored. Each such incident does not measure up to the Panopticon vision, but these are indeed small but interconnected events that make up the parts of the rhizomatic structure that represents the apparatus of surveillance that we are all immersed in. There is no denying that surveillance is going on, and as individuals we have nearly lost the ability to escape from the process. The tales of "going off the grid" popularized in movies and fiction, are indeed fiction. If one were to live a "normal" life in the developed and developing World, then it is nearly impossible to not have generated some data about oneself that is available to others. It is therefore important to get the proverbial ostrich head from under the sand and begin to understand how to manage everyday life within this surveillance society that we are all a part of.

The rest of this book addresses many of the systems of surveillance that one encounters by elaborating on who the various watchers are, what their tools are, and what the common rationale and outcome of surveillance could be. However, one element that is important and unique is to carefully examine what is being watched. It is easy to claim that the "individual" is watched, which was indeed the goal of the prison of Bentham. However, with the constantly shifting technologies, the different motives for surveillance and the multi-faceted composition of the individual there needs to be a robust understanding of the object of surveillance and what the process of surveillance can say about the object being watched. It is no longer the simplistic aspect of watching prisoners from the Panopticon tower, or watching shoplifters with the ceiling mounted cameras, but a much more complex and inter-connected system of observation is at work and all the information needs to synthesized to construct the individual.

In the next chapter I argue that the process of surveillance has the purpose of formulating a story about the entity being watched over. There may not be any clear strategic advantage that can be immediately gained from the compilation of the story, but the objective of surveillance could simply be to pre-emptively construct a story with the promise of future use. This perspective on surveillance makes the process unique and different from traditional espionage and places the process of surveillance within the realm of narrative theories where the story becomes the critical outcome of the process of surveillance. This book elaborates on surveillance through the lens of narrative theory to not only describe the processes of surveillance but place it within that theoretical framework.

REFERENCES

Althusser, L. (1977). *Lenin and philosophy, and other essays: transl. from the french by ben brewster*. Monthly Review Press.

Brunon-Ernst, A. (2016). *Beyond Foucault: new perspectives on Bentham's Panopticon*. Routledge Taylor & Francis Group. doi:10.4324/9781315569192

Derek, M., & Yuen, C. (2014). *Deciphering Sun Tzu: how to read 'The art of war*. Oxford University Press.

Driver, J. (2014, September 22). The History of Utilitarianism. *Stanford Encyclopedia of Philosophy*. https://plato.stanford.edu/entries/utilitarianism-history/

Foucault, M., & Sheridan, A. (2020). *Discipline and punish: the birth of the prison*. Penguin Books.

Galič, M., Timan, T., & Koops, B.-J. (2016, May 13). Bentham, Deleuze and Beyond: An Overview of Surveillance Theories from the Panopticon to Participation. *Philosophy & Technology*. https://link.springer.com/article/10.1007/s13347-016-0219-1

Guardian News and Media. (2009, April 17). Starwood sues Hilton for 'stealing trade secrets'. *The Guardian*. https://www.theguardian.com/business/2009/apr/17/industrial-espionage-hotel-industry-lawsuit

Shoham, D., & Liebig, M. (2016). The intelligence dimension of Kautilyan statecraft and its implications for the present. *Journal of Intelligence History*, *15*(2), 119–138. doi:10.1080/16161262.2015.1116330

UCL. (2018, May 17). *Kilmainham Gaol, Dublin: a 'panoptic' prison?* Bentham Project. https://www.ucl.ac.uk/bentham-project/who-was-jeremy-bentham/panopticon/kilmainham-gaol-dublin-panoptic-prison

Your smart TV may be spying on you - and stopping it is against the law. The World from PRX. (n.d.). https://www.pri.org/stories/2015-02-13/your-smart-tv-may-be-spying-you-and-stopping-it-against-law

Chapter 2
Reading the Stories

ABSTRACT

The life stories of the surveilled are contained in the digital representation and their analog presence. These stories make up the narrative bits—narbs—that eventually create the profiles of institutions and people. These narbs eventually become the big data that offer the information that the watchers seek.

INTRODUCTION

A story that I have often used in my classes and lectures deals with the time period of 2009 when the digital network, Facebook, was quite popular among the teenagers in the USA. Simultaneously, there was not much concern about protecting the information from prying eyes. Thus many youngsters would present significant amount of information on Facebook and would be unconcerned or unaware of the amount of information or the details that were available.

As such, in 2009, I faced a situation where I had to rely on my own abilities to explore information about different people only through what was available in the "public domain" in the digital space. The notion of public domain referred to what was not explicitly protected, to keep information private, by an individual or on behalf of an individual. These explorations into the data made it clear to me, and others who were doing similar work, that there was sufficient data in the public sphere about individuals that it was possible to construct a brief narrative of the person's life. Indeed, Facebook invited people to tell their life stories. This phenomenon only underscored an important aspect of everyday life – stories are important in our lives and we live by stories and sometimes make important decisions based on the narratives we hear.

This led to my 2014 book, *Digital DNA: Social Networking and You,* where I elaborated on the way different ways in which narratives take on a significant role in how we live our lives on digital networks and virtually lay out our genes in the digital space. In this chapter, I draw liberally on my book. Here I lay out the importance of narratives in our lives pointing to the theories that frame the discussion of narratives, then I propose the notion of short narratives in the digital space and finally connect the process of digital narrativizing with the development of representations of people and institutions. Given, the significant reliance on theories, this chapter is a little different in tenor from the other chapters but offers the foundation to make the connection between surveillance and narratives.

Narratives

In laying out the digital DNA of an individual I had made the argument that any person can be constructed around a set of narratives. This idea draws from the work of American communication scholar Walter Fisher (1931-2018) who introduced the notion of the narrative paradigm. In most analysis of human activity, the traditional approach towards understanding human behavior, particularly in terms of the way people make decisions, has been analyzed from two broad traditional perspectives. Some have argued that humans are rational beings and make decisions based on reason. Thus, one may decide to carry an umbrella if there it is a cloudy day because a "cause-effect" relationship is established. Children are acculturated around this model where they are taught that good behavior may result in rewards whereas bad behavior will be punished. Within this rational model it is possible to bring "reason" into the decision-making process and understand why people would behave in a particular fashion. A second way in which people may make decisions relies on the persuasive appeal of a message urging the listener to make a decision. This appeal need not be rational, but as a "rhetorical being" individuals could be swayed by the emotional or ethical appeals or simply by the eloquence of the appeal. At such moments there may not be reliance on the "rationality" of the decision, but the rhetorical power of a moment is sufficient to explain the behavior of individuals and people. This has been used to explain why large groups of people, such as in Germany before the beginning of World War II were convinced by their genocidal leader Adolf Hitler to blame all the woes of Germany on Jews or the way in which the base of supporters of American President Donald Trump would blame all the woes of USA on immigrants. Such moments, which are not necessarily supported by reason, are called rhetorical moments when rationality is abandoned.

Walter Fisher suggested that people also act as narrative beings. This approach to understanding the behavior of people and groups emphasize the importance of narratives in our lives. This is commonly called the narrative paradigm, suggesting that looking at behavior, emotions, and their outcomes through the lens of narratives offers a completely new way – a new paradigm – to understand everyday life. This paradigm shift is especially important to understand the way in which the different contexts to surveillance operates. A careful examination of the narrative paradigm would be instructive in getting closer to the answer to the question asked in Chapter 1 – what is being watched?

The Narrative Paradigm

I begin to answer the question by suggesting that the purpose of surveillance is to construct a narrative, or a story, about the object. And the theoretical basis of the narrative paradigm allows for focusing on stories as an integral part of our lived experience. The notion of the narrative paradigm was proposed in the early 1980s. The theory focuses on the importance of story-telling and narratives in the process of making meaning of everyday life as people operate within the cultural and social spaces that they occupy (see, e.g., Andrews, 1982; Gadamer, 1982; MacIntyre, 1981; Ricouer, 1977, 1983, 1984; White,

1984). In setting forth the notion that human beings operate not only as a rational and rhetorical being, Fisher suggested, people can also operate as a narrative being where the act of creating and articulating a coherent and rational narrative becomes a part of being human. In doing this, the narrative paradigm offers a different way of analyzing and understanding communication, and the way in which people act. The narrative paradigm of Fisher is best considered by examining Fisher's own description:

The narrative paradigm is a fabric woven if threads of thought from both social sciences and humanities. It seeks, like any other theory of human action, to account for how persons come to believe and behave. It differs from social scientific and humanistic theories in that it projects narration not as an art, genre, or activity but as a paradigm. It goes beyond these theories in providing a —new‖ logic, the concept of narrative rationality, which is applicable to all forms of human communication (Fisher 1985a, p. 357).

Fisher provides an opening to consider other forms of data – the narratives – as a way of understanding everyday life. The narrative paradigm suggests that it is possible to examine a story to seek internal coherence and fidelity of a story. Coherence refers to the internal logic of the story to see if indeed all the elements connect in a coherent fashion and fidelity refers to the believability of the story in terms of its truth value. Stories that demonstrate high coherence and fidelity could provide insights into the story and its author. This theoretical assertion about coherence and fidelity was used to analyze different kinds of stories by different professional authors to unravel the point of view of the author. The objective of narrative analysis, when couched in the narrative paradigm, was to somehow discover and expose the role that those specific stories by——professional authors play in shaping human belief and behavior. This presumption was tested by the analysis of stories by well-known authors. For instance, some scholars examined famous speeches (&&Bass, 1985), and famous novels (&&see, e.g., Bennett, 1978; Fisher and Filloy, 1982) telling stories with far reaching consequences on large portions of the global readers. The focus on institutional authors seemed sensible since there were not too many other authors. The analysis also demonstrated that stories, even if it were fiction, did reveal the perspective of the author and the analysis could offer a glimpse into the life of the author. However, the fact that narrative analysis offers an idea about the author was not a part of the focus in the early days of the development of the paradigm. Consider for instance the analysis that Fisher provides of the conversation between Socrates and Callicles, Fisher offers conclusions that relate to the ways in which a narrative analysis of this conversation throws light on how societies operate, and how the stories remain in fidelity with the reality of some societies. It is only in passing does Fisher focuses on precisely what the storyteller was thinking when telling the story. In this case the storyteller would be Plato because it was the works of Plato that Fisher uses to draw conclusions about the role of the stories in society. At the end of the analysis, Fisher claims, ——There can be no doubt that Plato's concern about rhetoric was pervasive – how it distorted education, corrupted politics, and failed as philosophy and a way of life (p. 364). In making these statements Fisher provides the opening to fill in the missing element related to the author of the story. Once that gap is filled, it could be possible to draw conclusions about any individual who chooses to express himself or herself, just as Plato did, as long as it is possible to access the narratives authored by an individual or a community of individuals.

When connected with the process of surveillance, these are stories that are voluntarily and involuntarily told by individuals who may be under surveillance. These would be stories, much like other stories, are made up of a set of immutable facts about the individual, and some points of view the storyteller adopts in telling the story. The first part of these two components deals with the undeniable facts about the storyteller. For instance, in the case of Plato of Fisher's analysis, there are certain facts about Plato one needs to know to be able to understand the story. The fact that Plato was a privileged male within the social system he lived in impacts the stories he tells. In the realm of literary analysis it is commonplace to learn about the storyteller's life in order to understand the narrative qualities of the story being told. Those facts offer the context of the story and the story itself deals with the second component – the perspective from which the story is told. The fact that Plato believed in certain things shapes the story that is told, and analyzing the story, in turn, can offer insights into the mind of the storyteller. Narrative analysis is not only concerned with the aesthetics of storytelling but is equally concerned with the attitudes, opinions, and beliefs of the author. In the World of surveillance, the analogy with Plato is that any individual who creates and distributes stories, much like Plato and Fisher, is now available for probing by a careful analysis of the stories authored by the individual. Consider the fact that a social media database such as Facebook could contain over 200 different attributes of every dweller in the Facebook space. This gives a vast amount of information about the storyteller. At the same time, in databases such as Facebook, there is a vast amount of information about the mind of the author since a large portion of the members of the social media ecologies also speak about themselves by using their own voice to tell things about themselves. In such spaces, each individual becomes a ——storytelling being, in the manner suggested within the narrative paradigm of society. Consequently, using the paradigm, it is possible to understand how people believe and behave by systematically analyzing the stories that are being told. In the case of social media systems these stories appear as collection of narbs that are made up of the different ways people express themselves – from simple status updates to the elaborate process of offering visual information that makes up the elements of the narrative. The object of surveillance is then the narrative which is composed of narbs as discussed in the next section.

Narbs

I propose a specific strategy for making sense of the digital expressions by arguing that this data can be parsed into narrative bits – narbs – that become available for analysis and interpretation through the lens of narrative theories (&&Mitra, in press, 2013, 2012a, 2012b, 2011, 2010). This process begins with categorizing narbs and using that as an alternative way of understanding people and groups. Narbs include all the different digital discourses that a person or institution produces within the digital environment in which a person or institution resides.

Thus, a status update on Facebook becomes an example of a narb just as micro-blogs on Twitter would be considered a narb as well. With the increasing variety of digital data – from text to complex combination of video and texts – it is important to consider the different kinds of narbs that make up the corpus of data that is the basis of the narratives discussed earlier.

A starting point for narb categorization begins with the question of authorship: Who creates a narb? Generally, there are two options; either the narb is created by the person whose story is being told, or it is created by someone else but contributes to the creation of the story of a particular person distinct from the author. In the case of the former it becomes a "self-narb" where power of authorship is retained by the person whose narrative is being told, whereas the other option produces the "other-narb" where the person whose narrative is produced has marginal control on the narrative. For the watcher both kinds of narbs offer valuable information. If the person voluntarily discloses information then it can become a part of the corpus of information that a watcher can hope to rely on, assuming the narber is speaking authentically. However, an other-narb could be even more powerful, as in the case of a letter of recommendation, where the other could offer information to the watcher that the watched might not want to be revealed. Narbs thus become powerful elements for process of surveillance.

Having placed narbs in these two primary categories it is possible to consider both kinds of narbs from the perspective of the content of the narbs and what role content plays in creating the story of an individual. To begin with, the content-based categorization offers a starting point to systematically classify narbs that use specific symbolic strategies to create narrative content and meaning – the stuff that makes up the story that the watcher needs to analyze.

The most common category of narb is the "text narb." This is essentially a simple statement that tells a tiny story about a person. Independent of whether the narb is a self-narb or an other-narb, these textual pieces are usually small in size. A good example of a text narb is a simple status update that a person might post to a digital social network. These narbs are relatively easy to produce, and can be done with a variety of tools, from a computer to a smartphone. Following the text narb perhaps the most common category of narbs are "picture narbs." These are made up of a still picture that is added to the profile page of a person's presence in a digital social network. The picture could come from many different sources and could serve both as a self narb and other narb. One of the most interesting aspects of picture narbs is the ability to not only place a picture on the digital network site but also provide an accompanying text narb that explains the picture and provides qualifying information accompanying the picture. A picture narb thus often works in conjunction with a text narb. The picture narb also allows for the addition of meta-information in the form of tags. As most users know it is possible to annotate the picture with specific names of people who might be in the picture. Indeed, the process of naming the people in a picture is a part of the technology offered by some platforms that offer digital social networking opportunities. For example, starting in June 2011 Facebook developed a semi-automatic tagging option where users would have their picture narbs tagged by the Facebook computing system based on the history of tagging. Much in the way that the picture narb has become popular because of the existence of cameras on cell phones and applications such as Instagram, it is possible to use smartphones to also capture digital video and quickly place that on a social media site. The "video narb" is thus the third category of narbs. The process of creating and using a video narb is not dissimilar to the way in which a picture narb would be used – a caption and a description in text would accompany the video narb.

The content-based categorization has to be coupled with one more analytic criteria to complete the categorization of narbs: the functional categorization, where narbs of all kinds can also be considered from the specific function they perform in creating the narrative of a particular individual. The idea of function is quite traditional to understanding narratives. Most stories have characters and segments of the story that serve different purposes. There has been extensive consideration of the way in which narratives can be analyzed in terms of the codes that can be discovered in every narrative, discourse, or text. Consider for instance, the five narrative codes suggested by Barthes (1975) where he as has also argued that all texts first fall into an 'open' or 'closed' category referring to the openness of the text to multiple meanings, which then is contained within the five codes. Amongst Barthes's codes there is the suggestion that a text contains codes referring to action, deeper meaning, and external bodies of knowledge. Analysis of text can be performed by seeking these codes in the text and then interpreting the way the codes are used and how they function to produce meaning. At the same time, scholars such as Tzvetan Todorov (1977) and Vladimir Propp (1968) have suggested that different elements of a story can be analyzed based on predictable narrative structure and repeated function of different elements of a story in advancing a narrative. In the case of Todorov, the idea of a narrative structure is particularly important; he argues that the construction of narratives go through a structured process, starting with a state of equilibrium, followed by a crisis, and then the re-establishment of a desirable equilibrium. Indeed, the analysis of narbs is well served by this approach since it is now possible to test the various stages of the narrative structure of the stories created by different combination of the categories of narbs. When the idea of narrative structure is combined with the notion of narrative function suggested by Propp, it is possible to claim that a narrative is built through the 31 functions that Propp identifies. These functions are the most fundamental elements of a tale and they tend to follow each other to help build the structure of the narrative. For instance, in the analysis of the folklore which was the focus of the work of Propp he suggests that "trickery," when a villain tries to deceive his victim always precedes, "complicity," when the victim submits to the trickery. In this manner, Propp builds a lexicon of functions which focus in on minute details of narratives. It is the case that Propp was working with the specific genre of folk tales, but his identification of the functions has been found to be useful for analysis of other kinds of texts particularly film narratives. As such, even though the functions were based on a small corpus of texts, the notion of functions is useful to bear in mind in the categorization of narbs.

I use these approaches to narrative analysis to argue that narratives produced by narbs also follow a structure, albeit less systematic as in the case of fiction, and the structure is composed of codes and functions, again less elaborated than in the case of fiction. Consequently, in the analysis of narbs, it is possible to divide them into specific functional categories. The first set of functional categories would deal with the "spatial narb" that offers specific information about the real-life spatial location or spatial attributes of an individual. In the case of narbs that are self narbs this could be an important indicator about the background of a specific developing narrative about an individual. The second functional category can be referred to as "temporal narb" that offer specific chronological information about a person. Every narb has temporal information connected to it because the narb is usually stamped with time information. It is possible to extract information about the time of a posting from the temporal narb. This kind of information can allow an observer to get a better sense of the flow of the identity narrative of an individual. In this case the narbs provide the information that shows when the person has been born, perhaps how old the person is, and how the person's narbs are dependent on the specific point in one's life. A third functional category is the "causal narb" which offers information about the fundamental attitudes and opinions of a person that shape the identity narrative of a person. These could be text narbs, picture narbs, or video narbs and are most frequently self-narbs where a person would update the status by making a statement that specifically expresses an opinion about a matter. Many narbs serve this function including narbs that an individual would share on a profile page to demonstrate his/her specific opinion about a matter. Sometimes these narbs can take on collective power as a narb used by one individual connects his opinion with thousands of other people who might feel the same way. First, these narbs, over time, can shed light on the opinions of a particular individual. Such information can be extremely useful in creating the identity narrative of a person by understanding what a person feels about a range of issues. It does not matter what type of a narb it is, as long as a specific feeling is expressed. Secondly, the collection of narbs that serve the causal function can also tell the story of a collection of individuals. In that situation entire groups of people who post the same narb express a unified opinion about a matter.

The fourth functional category focuses on the specific activities that a person does and is called the "activity narb." In this case a person explicitly states what the person is doing. The activity function can be served by both self-narbs and other-narbs. An individual can state what she is doing just as the friends of a person can state what he is doing.

It is always the case that while the different kinds of narbs can be parsed into categories such as the ones described here, the function of narbs in analysis is to offer a mechanism to consider how narbs provide a way of looking at an individual in terms of the different narbs generated by a person. It is possible for an individual to create the different kinds of narbs using the digital tools available to the person that range from posting a picture of the self to a digital social network to making statements about political matters in micro-blog spaces. An individual has the opportunity to create the different kinds of narbs, sometimes perhaps inadvertently, and in summation the narbs offer an image of the person.

At the same time, narbs about a person are also generated by systems that the individual might have little control over. Most people who live in contemporary social systems have to interact with the social, political, financial, and cultural systems that surround us. These are simple activities – going to the store to buy some things, going to the doctor when ill, using a bank to do a financial transaction or going to a school for education. In each situation an individual is creating narbs and narbs are being created for the individual. Consider the simple act of traveling across national borders by legally entering a country through an airport. Nearly all nations require that one goes through some form of a barrier, either electronic or one where a person would interview the traveler. Nearly every such barrier has a mechanism of capturing the digital image of the face of the person. This is a visual narb that also serves as an activity narb and the individual has no choice other than to offer that narb to the government of the country that the person is visiting. These narbs are increasingly crucial for everyday existence and increasing facets of everyday life is being digitized to make everyday life more convenient. The production of a digital representation of an individual is constantly becoming valuable to negotiate the activities of everyday life where a single digital representation encapsulates a narrative of the individual that can be accessed and utilized to know more about the person.

The increasing digitization of the life story of an individual offers a way of knowing a person which supplements the story of the flesh and blood person who is represented by the narbs. The existence of the digital being obviously does not invalidate the real person. The real person also carries narratives that may not be captured in the digital data. The real person may behave at any moment in a way that the narb-based narrative might not be able to accurately predict. The real person provides another part of the narrative about the individual which needs to be understood as well. I offer myself as a unique data point. My first name is spelt "Ananda," which is a common first name for a male in India. This name is dangerously close to another name that is spelt "Amanda," which is a common first name for most of the West, such as Western Europe and North America. At the same time, the spelling "Ananda" is also commonly used for the name of women in Brazil. On a trip to Brazil my taxi drivers were constantly amused by the face that their digital system showed them that they were picking up a person whose name suggested that the passenger would be a woman, whereas the person they were picking up was a male. This might be an unusual story related to the connection between the digital and the real, but it goes to show that the narrative of an individual is produced through the combination of the digital and analog narratives that can be created about the person. It is in the combination of stories that most people live their lives and become who they are in the view of the rest of the World. Indeed such stories are now available for the majority of the population of the World.

Surveillance and Narbs

The process of creating the narrative therefore becomes a twofold mechanism where first there needs to be a robust way in which the gather the narrative to make it as complete as possible and secondly there needs to be a way to analyze the narrative to be able to predict how the narrative may progress.

The first part of the process is indeed the process of modern-day surveillance where the objective is to create the narrative using the information about the digital and the analog self. These narrative elements are made up of numerous pieces, some of which are enumerated below based on who can access the data about the individual. To begin with, there is a significant amount of data that relates the *physical and mental health* of the individual. This is typically what would be considered medical data about an individual that we all have to offer whenever we have to see a medical professional. This data is held by the medical institutions. A second set of data is about the *legal standing* of the individual in terms of whether the individual is considered to be a law-abiding person who has the correct permissions to do the things the person does, such as drive a car or legally cross a national border. This data in made up of information stored in a driver's license card or in a passport. This data is typically held by the governments that would issue the specific permits such as the permission to drive. A third corpus of data deals with the *financial status* of the individual. This tells the story of how an individual makes and spends money. Such financial data also becomes an indicator of the level of responsibility a person has with respect to fiscal matters. Such data is stored in a variety of places that include financial institutions and financial record keeping agencies such as those institutions the level of financial risk a person poses. A fourth set of data addresses different kinds of *behavior* displayed by an individual. This could include elements such as commercial behavior, travel, education, religion, exercise, and a plethora of data about the things a person does. Such behavior data is vital in creating the narrative of an individual because we are what we do. Our everyday actions display who we are, and this data is important to create the narrative. A fifth kind of data deals with the *beliefs and opinions* of the individual. Every utterance made by an individual can display what the person believes in. To be sure, it is possible to infer beliefs by observing and measuring behavior as has been done by many marketing and polling institutions. However, in a public sphere where people feel the freedom to speak honestly, it is possible to gather a sense of the beliefs of an individual by listening to the person speak. The narrative about the individual becomes especially powerful when the aspect of belief is brought into creating the composite narrative. This data is also distributed in a variety of places – from the private journal of an individual to the public pronouncement made by an individual within social networks.

The narrative of the individual lies in the combination of these different elements of data. Once the data can be gathered by different means of data collection – surveillance – then narratives can be produced about the individuals as well as the collectivities that the individuals represent. Therefor the unit of data collection is the P (person) in the nomenclature offered earlier, and the collection of the Ps help to create narratives of the I (institution) as well.

The challenge in the process of surveillance results from the sophistication in the processes of data collection that make up the rest of the book. Data about individuals can be collected in a variety of ways and that data can then be parsed in many different ways to create data sets that might refer to many different units of analysis, from a specific individual to a group of people to entire sub-populations. This data is vast and has often been called "Big Data."

Surveillance and Big Data

There is some degree of confusion regarding the exact meaning and definition of the term Big Data. For the purpose of the discussion in this book, the data of "Big Data" is the combination of all the information, including narbs, that can potentially be gathered about a person or an institution. This is not different from the different descriptions of Big Data that has been used within different disciplines.

Some commentators have pointed out that the term first came into existence within the Silicon Graphics Corporation in the 1990s an internal term (Diebold, 2012). The term has also been used in discussions of large data set analysis in computer science (Weiss and Indurkhya, 1997). The term Big Data started to become commonplace in 2012 and has gained institutional status with inter-disciplinary conversations about Big Data, as demonstrated in many different forums dedicated to advance a better understanding of the ways in which large amounts of data can be manipulated and then used for different purposes. This process has gone on even though the term Big Data has been adopted without an accepted definition that captures all the elements of what Big Data could stand for.

Much of the attention on big data has focused on the two key components: (1) gathering the large amounts of data and (2) quantitatively analyzing the data to obtain both personal-individualized information as well as information about different groups of people. The data can be broadly divided into two categories for the sake of analytic tools that can be used to look at the data. One significant portion of the data is the structured numeric data which refers to quantifiable elements of the data, which for an individual are things like, gender, age, education, income, and other stable and easily measured and quantified attributes. Such data is amenable to numeric analysis, which is the forte of computers, to produce specific statistics about an individual or cluster of people. It is the second component of the data - unstructured - that becomes more challenging to analyze and interpret. There are only exploratory and proprietary numerical tools that can extract meaningful statistics from thousands of messages sent, for instance, via Twitter, or the millions of lines of status updates that are produced by the nearly one billion users of Facebook. This is what I call narbs earlier. It is Big Data that offers the narbs, and this unstructured data needs to be considered more carefully to understand the narrative of a person. Narbs serve as the repository of personal and communal narratives that need to be extracted from the data to offer a better understanding of the persons and groups represented by big data. The premise here is not necessarily new; indeed, it has been argued that analysis of the material available on the Internet is indeed a process of discursive analysis (Mitra, 1999; Mitra and Cohen, 2012).

Big Data also possess a set of characteristics that make is especially attractive for the creation of the narrative. As suggested earlier, the narrative of the analog being changes with time. People simply change with age. Their physical characteristics change, men with thick black lush hair become bald, physiological systems become weaker, and age stamps itself on the physical self. Life events happen to the analog being – marriage, childbirth, divorce, job changes – all of these become the part of the narrative of the analog body. Some of these changes happen at a slow pace, others could be massive changes that happen in an instant. I went blind in one of my eyes in a matter of two hours where I went from perfect vision to complete dark while waiting for a flight at an airport. Since then, and many surgeries later, I still remain officially blind in the eye. To be sure, such events to the body impact the narrative of the analog body. Change is natural with respect to the physical analog self, and the data from the changes becomes a part of the narrative.

The situation with Big Data, which primarily deals with the digital representation of the analog body, is similar. It must be noted that the notion of Big Data is intimately tied to the existence of digital data. It can be argued that there was data about individuals that was available in pre-digital era. Much of the information was distributed in different places, such as a hospital where the person might have received treatment, or a school where a person received education, or a bank where a person has an account. Further, the information was stored on paper or some other media such as micro-film and was sequestered in a place, often a file cabinet in an office somewhere. Searching for a specific piece of information through the paper records was a labor-intensive process and often inefficient. Such data was also susceptible to damage and loss and could erode with time where the paper used to store that data might crumble or the ink would fade. All of these changed with the process of digitizing the data. Now the data was permanent, portable, and easily searchable. It is the digital data that makes up what we call Big Data and there are three major characteristics that are unique to Big Data.

The first aspect of Big Data that needs to be considered is the fact that the volume of the data is unlike anything we have encountered in human history. The numbers are simply astronomical because digital data now exists for a large portion of the human population. Governments of countries such as China and India, with their large populations, have amassed data about nearly every individual in the countries. In other cases, private corporations such as Google. Amazon, Facebook, and other digital platforms have collected data about individuals who have chosen to use the services. The number of users is nearly as large as the populations of India and China. In a similar way, multi-national corporations that offer services at the global level collect data about the people who choose to use their services. Consider, for instance, the number of people who use the Visa labelled credit card. It is no longer the case that the wealthy people of developed countries are the only users of Credit Card or online financial systems. In an increasing global effort to move to a "cash less" society there is increasing penetration of financial systems that rely on digital transactions, where each transaction becomes a part of the large volume of digital data. Other vital institutions such as health care providers are also generating digital data as health records are increasingly being digitized as a record of the overall health information about an individual. The list of places where data about an individual exists can be enlarged to demonstrate that the amount of data is vast. It only takes a moment of introspection to mentally enumerate the numerous places from the departmental store to the educational institution where there is data about people. The pervasiveness of the digital initiative makes it nearly impossible to operate in contemporary societies of the developed and the developing nations without adding to the volume of data that makes up Big Data.

The second notable characteristic of Big Data is the pace at which data is being generated and added to already huge volume of information. This aspect is sometimes called the velocity of Big Data to acknowledge the fact that data is constantly being generated and added to make the volume grow at great velocity. Some of the data addition happens as a result of the changes that the analog being may encounter, as I had mentioned earlier. My digital medical records have been updated to note the issues with vision. Similar changes are done to the volume of data as an individual travels through the various phases of life. Some of the data is also updated synchronously as an individual exhibits normal every-day behavior. Consider the case of using a popular mapping software on a mobile device that has a connection the Internet. Such devices constantly record the position of the device as the device (and its owner) move from place to place – as simple as going to work, or to the grocery store, or to a friend's place. The data comes in at great speed and permanently records the location information. Later, that data can be searched with ease to discover the speed at which the data was collected.

The velocity of the data accumulation that creates the large volume also offers the third characteristic of Big Data – the variety of information that exists about an individual. It is not only the case that the data is about a large number of entities, from an individual to institutions, that is generated constantly, but that data expectedly also contains a large amount of details about the entity. Whatever that can be digitized and stored in permanent records is fair game as pointed out earlier. This is the data variety that makes up the third component of Big Data. Numerous characteristics of each entity is being recorded. For instance, for an individual at any moment in time, not considering the aspect of velocity, there is information about the person's demographic characteristics which could include information that could be typically included in any national Census records; financial information in terms of the amount of money a person earns and the amount the person spends; consumer behavior information in terms of how the person spends money – on that purchases, where the purchases are made and what different forms of payments are used for the purchase; legal information in terms of dealings with law enforcement as in the case of travel documentation, history of legal actions; health information in great detail that could include digitized test results such as X-ray pictures, body scans and eventually information about what opinions a person may hold on a variety of issues that could include political attitudes, social attitudes, opinions about current affairs, religious beliefs to name a few. This myriad of information makes up the large variety that is contained in Big Data.

One way to visualize the three "Vs" is to think of Big Data beings made up of a cluster of bubbles where each bubble is attached to each other and each bubble, representing the elements of variety, are constantly growing at a great velocity, with the number of bubble clusters constantly as the volume of entities are increasing as digital data of new entities are created. In its logical extension, there will be a bubble cluster for every individual and institution. Indeed, an individual or institution may not even be considered to exist if there a bubble cluster did not exist for the entity. It is as if the analog entity – made of up flesh and bones or bricks and mortars – loses legitimacy until the digital bubble cluster has been produced.

This discussion of narratives, narbs, and Big data offer the argument to claim that the objective of surveillance is increasingly this corpus of information that exists about an entity. This information is elaborate and is constantly being updated. There are many challenges to the process of watching the data. There are also many different entities, with varying interests and motives, who want to watch the data. In the next chapter I focus on the different categories of watchers who would be interested in watching this data.

REFERENCES

Andrews, J. D. (1982). The structuralist study of narrative: its history, use and limits. In P. Hernadi (Ed.), *The horizon of literature* (pp. 99–124). The University of Nebraska Press.

Barthes, R. (1975). *S/Z* (R. Miller, Trans.). McMillan.

Fisher, W. R. (1984). Narration as Human Communication Paradigm: The Case of Public Moral Argument. *Communication Monographs, 51*(1), 1–22. doi:10.1080/03637758409390180

Fisher, W. R. (1985a). The Narrative Paradigm: An Elaboration. *Communication Monographs, 52*(4), 347–367. doi:10.1080/03637758509376117

Fisher, W. R. (1985b). The Narrative Paradigm: In the Beginning. *Journal of Communication, 35*(4), 74–89. doi:10.1111/j.1460-2466.1985.tb02974.x

Fisher, W. R. (1987). *Human Communication as Narration: Toward a Philosophy of Reason, Value, and Action*. University of South Carolina Press.

Gadamer, H. G. (1982). *Truth and method*. Crossword Publishing.

Kelly, H. (2012). Police embrace social media as crime-fighting tool. *CNN*. Available at: https://www.cnn.com/2012/08/30/tech/social-media/fighting-crime-social-media

MacIntyre, A. (1981). *After virtue: A study in moral theory* (2nd ed.). The University of Notre Dame Press.

Propp, V. (1968). *Morphology of the Folktale* (2nd ed.). University of Texas Press.

Ricouer, P. (1977). The model of the text: Meningful action considered as text. In F. R. Dallmayr & T. A. McCarthy (Eds.), *Understanding and social inquiry* (pp. 316–334). The University of Notre Dame Press.

Ricouer, P. (1983). The narrative function. In J. B. Thompson (Ed.), *Paul Ricouer, hermeneutics and the human sciences: Essays on language, action, and interpretation* (pp. 274–296). Cambridge University Press.

Ricouer, P. (1984). Time and narrative (vol. 1; K. McLaughlin & D. Pellaur, Trans.). The University of Chicago Press.

Todorov, T. (1977). *The Poetics of Prose*. Cornell University Press.

White, H. (1984). The question of narrative in contemporary historical theory. *History and Theory*, *23*(1), 1–33. doi:10.2307/2504969

Chapter 3
Who Watches?

ABSTRACT

The watching entities can be broadly classified into two groups, institutions (I) and people (P). The I watchers are made up of different elements amongst which the state is the most prominent one. The I watchers also include corporations, educational institutions, and corporations that offer digital services. The P watchers include parents, siblings, spouses, and children. All these watchers make up the spectrum of entities engaged in surveilling each other.

INTRODUCTION

The first two chapters have offered the ways in which surveillance has worked through history leading up to what is often being called the "surveillance state" in the World of the 2020s. It is important to dwell on the idea of the surveillance state briefly to appreciate the shortfall of connecting the notion of surveillance to state alone. To begin with, there is a lack of specific agreement about the term, but it generally refers to the way in which a government can become the one watching its people in an insidious manner to constantly keep the country secure. Many countries can be called a surveillance state given the variety of ways in which the government watches its people. However, as I have indicated earlier, the question of watching has to be far broadened beyond what is captured by terms such as the surveillance state. There are other similar terms that seems to privilege some watchers over others, such as "mass surveillance" and "electronic police state" but each of these terms place specific emphasis on one kind of a watcher.

Such confusion about who the watcher is addressed in this chapter. Here, I lay out a comprehensive representation of the different entities that have gained the capability and interest in watching. In this chapter, using exemplars, I offer a listing of the different watchers. The catalog offered here is built around the fundamental duality of the watchers – as persons (Ps) and as institutions (Is). The P/I nomenclature offers the opportunity to discover the different kinds of Ps and Is that operate and offer some descriptors and names to the watchers so that it is possible to explore the different technologies of watching employed and the implications of the different watchers and the tools they use. This cataloging of the watchers is the starting point of the understanding the practice of surveillance as the practice is placed within the theory of surveillance as described earlier. Given the abundance of watchers in the "I" category, it offers a starting point for this chapter.

The "I" Watchers

It is important to understand the notion of an institution in the context of surveillance. The conventional meaning of the term stems from the Latin term *institutus* which dealt more with the aspect of "institute" as an act of setting up something. The word institution is derived from that origin and has gone on to mean a set of spaces where there is an adherence to a set of conventions and rules that define the way things are done within the sphere. The idea of rules is vital to the description of an institution because those rules structure the relationships within an institution. In most cases the institution itself has a structure that is often well-defined with specific functions and people who do the tasks. It is possible to visualize any institution and be possible to identify its key tasks and functions and how the institution is structured to meet its goals to perform its job (Suman, 2015). It is especially possible to visualize the relationship between structure and goal by considering an institution that has become universal in the Twenty-First Century – the nation state. Governments function as institutions because they offer a certain set of rules and directions for the citizens in a country and there is an expectation that the rules would be followed for the overall good of the country and its people. In the early part of the Century the purpose of the government as an institution was best tested with the appearance of the Global pandemic in the winter of 2020 which affected over one hundred countries and the governmental institution had the goal of saving its population from perishing by imposing a set of rules that the people in the instruction – the citizens – were expected to follow. Similar moments can be witnessed in the Twentieth Century which witnessed two World Wars with governments as institution having to manage critical conditions while in competition with other institutions.

The institution is thus an element of everyday life that originated far in the past with the goal of organizing society in a way that is expected to be beneficial to society and the institution. It needs to be recognized that institutions exist not only for offering greater good to the people served by the institution but for the benefit of the institution itself. Private corporations often exist for the purpose of making profit which often has to be made in a competitive environment where other institutions are also wanting to make a profit by offering similar services or products in the marketplace. The need to remain profitable is essential for an institution to be successful, which in turn means that the people who make up the institution are also benefited from the overall success of the institution. Thus Americans are better off than people in poorer nations because America, as an institution, has remained a successful enterprise benefitting the people who belong to that institution.

The people in the institution are another major aspect of any institution. There are two categories of people that matter to any institution – those who are within the institution attempting to meet the goals of the institution and the those who are outside the institution that are served by the institution and become "customers" of the institution. This differential is very broad, but for the purpose of surveillance by institutions it is important to draw this distinction because it is the people who become the "P" within the model of surveillance suggested earlier.

With this general idea of what institutions are, I offer a list of institutions that act as watchers where the object to of surveillance could be other institutions or people or both.

Governments

Perhaps the best known among the watchers is the government or the state. Generally, the state can be defined as the institution that has emerged as the group that takes on the task of governing the people who live within a certain geographic space. After the end of World War 2 many of the traditional monarchies have been replaced by different state apparatuses which have taken over some of the key aspects of providing the services and protections to the people in a country. Different kinds of states have appeared that have varied from the totalitarian regimes where the state held control over all aspects of life under the rule of a single person who ruled by fear, to systems where the state was supposed to represent the will of the people because the people selected their representatives through an electoral process. There have been many variations to these extreme positions and countries have gone through transformations as the governments have changed and different shades of ruling systems have emerged. The Cold War between ideologically different nations with the threat of nuclear conflict gave way to threats of terrorism where "non-state" actors became a greater threat than conventional conflict. In all its different forms, the government has been in the business of watching.

Nearly every government in the first quarter of the 2000s has some mechanism of watching over its people. The type of government may have an influence on the methods and extent of the watching, but all governments could be found to be watching over other governments through mechanisms of spying and watching its own citizens through many different means. Different governments have different levels of power on the watching process. In some places the government can set up ubiquitous watching systems where the citizens may have little knowledge about the extent to which they are being watched and other governments may have to offer extensive disclosures to the watching that is being done by them. In any case, the government is involved in the process of watching.

It is also useful to categorize the different segments of the state that is involved in the watching process. Almost every branch of the government has a role in watching. For instance, in the United States there is evidence to suggest that the National Security Agency (NSA) has been watching for a long period of time. An agency such as the NSA in the USA, and its counterparts in other parts of the World are involved in watching the people and institutions in the country as well as people and institutions in other countries. Similarly, the local law enforcement in the United States, from local police departments to bureaus of investigation are in the process of watching. The role of law enforcement in watching extends to other organizations that secure the borders of countries such as the Department of Homeland Security and the Department of State in the USA. Similar government units in other parts of the World are involved in watching as well. The government branches that deal with the financial health of the state – from tax collection to enforcing regulations – are also in the act of watching just as branches of government that deliver any kind of service from transportation to public health are in the act of watching. Eventually it is possible to find that nearly every branch of the government has instituted some form of surveillance that keeps an eye on the population of the country and in some cases the population of other countries. There is perhaps no other institutional watcher that is as vast and intricate as the government. The governments in different parts of the World have established different ways of watching but most governments are in the act of watching. Closely following the government are numerous local and global corporations that are also in the act of watching.

Corporations with Physical Presence

There are millions of private corporations that people visit to obtain products and services. These corporations could vary from large warehouse stores to the neighborhood shop selling groceries, as well private corporate spaces such as a bank or a doctor's office. These are places a person must visit to obtain a product or service. In such cases the physical analog body of a person must be placed in the physical space of an institution in order to complete a task that the person must do. In most cases, these are private spaces where an individual is permitted to visit but the space does not belong to the individual. The space is controlled by an institution. There are numerous examples of such spaces. These could be places where products are sold. Consider any shop that one needs to visit. The shop could be a small store where the person might not even be entering the store but walk up to a counter where the storekeeper would sell the products. The customer does not actually access the product, but it is handed to the person. On the other hand, a customer could be in a large store, such as a departmental store where the customer has the freedom to walk through the store and pick out products and then pay for the products at a specific place before leaving the store. In many such places it is possible to leave the space without either buying a product or in some cases without paying for the product (shop lifting). People may also do commercial transactions in enclosed spaces that offer a multitude of retailers as in the case of a shopping mall which is often a large space where a person must go to do the transactions.

A person may also have to enter a physical space for a specific service which does not involve the exchange of goods. In such cases the person is not actually walking away with a product but just getting something done but doing that requires the visit to a physical place. Consider for instance the simple act of getting a haircut. Typically, the person must visit a place to get that service. In a more elaborate way, the process of flying or taking a train involves the purchase of a service – travel. Thus, being on a commercial airplane is the purchase of a service – travel - the person is provided the service because the person has paid for the service. There are other such services where the person is in a space as in the case of a private hospital or medical establishment. Unless the medical establishment is owned by the government, any time a person walks into a hospital, the person has entered the spaces owned and controlled by a private corporation. The same principle applies to a financial institution such as a bank where the person is allowed in because the person needs to obtain a service.

Yet another other commercial place of service which has traditionally required the person to visit a place to obtain what the person wants – such as a restaurant or a place of entertainment. The World is peppered with restaurants of numerous kinds from a street-food seller on the streets of Bangkok to the luxurious restaurants of Paris. In all cases there is a place to visit or a person to interact with to obtain the food and the accompanying "experience" of being in an establishment. The same could be said about a private club or a movies theater where a person must actually go to obtain what the person desires.

There are indeed numerous places that are owned by corporations that vary in size and function where a transaction requires a person to visit the place. The importance of such visits has become painfully clear when there are conditions that cause the places to close, and it is not possible to obtain the services and products. Such situations arise at the time of global and national crisis – from a war to a pandemic – when people are unable to move about freely and are unable to visit the spaces described here. All these places watch the persons who come to their spaces. There is scarcely any corporate space in the developed and developing World that does not include some form of surveillance of the space and the people who visit the place. Much like the government institutions, the corporate spaces are also the sites of surveillance – especially of the physical space and the persons who populate the space.

While physical spaces are a part of the lived experience in the early Twenty-First Century, the increasing digitization of the lived experience also brings a person in contact with institutions that exist both in the physical analog world as well as in the digital space or might only exist in the digital space. Such institutions also have a reason to engage in watching.

Corporations in the Digital Space

There has been a tradition, particularly in the United States, for purchasing products without having to actually go to a shop. In the late 1800s, a pioneer in selling products without the customer having to leave the home was started in the United States by Sears Roebuck. The process developed by Sears was simple – the changes in the postal laws and access in the late 1800s allowed a mailer to be sent to homes in the USA. The customer could choose the product and send out the order and the products would be delivered by the US Mail. Indeed, in an advertisement in the 1930s, Sears made the claim: "Shop the MODERN way – from your easy chair," with the picture of a lady and her young daughter sitting on a chair and looking through the catalog. Indeed, Sears started to offer prefabricated kits that the buyer could assemble into a house; within a thirty-year period starting in 1908 the company sold nearly 75,000 homes (Pruitt, 2018). This history is important to note because some consumers, such as those in the USA, were already used to doing business with corporations without ever going to a "real" store. To be sure, Sears opened its first set of shops several years after launching the catalog. Many other companies all over the World followed the process set up by Sears and the individual consumer was accustomed to picking out a product without actually touching or seeing it and then getting it delivered to the home.

This tendency received a boost with rapid digitization. A company like Amazon nearly took a page out of the Sears catalog and offered a service similar to what Sears did. When Amazon started in July 1994 its objective was to sell books where the consumer would be able to go to a Website and go through a catalog of books and then order and pay for the book online and have it delivered to a real address. Soon after, in 1995, eBay was started which too relied on the network and digitization to match sellers and buyers with postal delivery of the actual product. Increasing digitization continued to lead to numerous such corporations that did not have an analog existence but remained entirely in the digital space, with occasional human-driven customer service, and the transactions – from buying an air ticket through a travel aggregator like Travelocity to purchasing a car through Carvana that delivers cars to the home – these transactions would happen using a digital device. Such transactions included other associated industries such as financial institutions that would handle the financial transaction and delivery industries that would manage the delivery process. All these institutions are also interested in watching over the process from the point a customer orders a product to the point when the product is delivered to the customer.

The watching process involves numerous corporations that may not have any physical existence but has the tools to watch people. Consider the flow in the case of a simple order of a hardcover book from a company such as Amazon. The company is watching the person who is using the digital device to look through the virtual catalog of the "store" to pick out a book or is typing in a name of a book to search for the book. This is information that the person must divulge to be able to obtain the book. Once the book has been found the person will need to offer the location information if the person wants to have a physical book delivered to the address. This requires that Amazon be offered information on location and a physical address. Therefore, Amazon is able to and needs to watch for the product information and the delivery information. This is digital data that the consumer divulges. The next major corporation, also without a physical presence, that gets involved in the watching process is often called a payment processing agency. There are numerous such corporations which offer the support to complete the financial part of the digital transaction where the person can offer financial information to complete the transaction with a company such as Amazon. These institutions such as Authorize.net or Firstdata are also watching the person and collecting financial information that is needed for the transaction to be completed. In some cases, in some countries, the transaction can be completed by a "cash on delivery" terms where the product will actually arrive at the doorstep of the customer and will only be given to the customer if the customer pays for the product at that time. There is no financial institution involved in watching at that point because the customer is expected to pay in cash. However, if the payment is completed at the time of the online purchase, then the financial institutions – such as the credit card processor, the company that brands the credit card such as Visa, the financial institution that issues the credit card such as the customers bank – could all be involved in the digital transaction with the opportunity to watch all the data that is produced in the transaction process. Finally, another institution is watching over the process – the corporation which will ensure that the physical product will actually reach the person who ordered it. The book would thus be delivered by a corporation – including possibly an institution owned by the state or government such as a national postal service. Alternatively, corporations such as DHL, FedEx, etc. could be watching the data as the transaction is completed.

Other than the bank and the delivery service all the other institutions exist in the virtual space. Even with Amazon, the majority of their operations are in the virtual and there is a small slither of "real" Amazon shops (Cheng, 2019). The tendency for an institution that begins as a digital entity and then takes on some analog existence is a trend that can be expected. There are many kinds of institutions that exist simultaneously in the analog and the digital spaces and are interested in watching over the people who come in contact with such institutions. The next section points towards some such institutions which offer important products and services to people.

Multi-Space Institutions

In this category the focus is on three kinds of institutions that can be considered to be foundational to the way people operate in societies. The first set is the financial institutions. The use of currency and the development of an economic system that goes beyond a barter system is tied to the history of civilization and as soon as humans began to use currency it was necessary to have a mechanism to account for how currency was being used. The move from a system of barter and exchange of cattle to the use of the Gold Standard of 1900s and the eventual abandoning of the Gold Standard represents a period of nearly 3,000 years and all through this period there was a need to keep an eye on how the economic system would work, especially in terms of maintaining a standard of ethics in the system where people traded in an honest way.

There was a need to look over transactions was also tied to the development of the bank. Although there are records of bank-like systems as early as 8,000 BC, it is only after World War 2 that the idea of retail banking where people and the financial institution began to have frequent interaction. The bank rapidly transformed to other forms of financial institutions as is known in the first quarter of the Twenty-First Century and there was a keen interest to keep an eye on the way in which the individual was interacting with the financial system. Consider for instance the numerous financial institutions that are involved in relatively simple transactions. A person making a purchase at a real grocery store using a credit card of a particular brand such as Visa or MasterCard, and issued by a particular bank invokes several financial artefacts and institutions – the credit card itself which is equipped with a computer chip for security (Rashid, 2015), the machine used in the store to read the credit card, the virtual credit card processor, the dual-existence bank of the person making the purchase and the bank used by the store to do its financial work, and other virtual financial systems that may become involved in the transaction. Each one of the systems are interested in keeping an eye on the transaction using both real and virtual systems. In some cases, the process is completely in the analog as in the case of a store owner asking to see the back of the credit card to verify a signature as was often the case before the card with the embedded chip became popular, whereas the other surveillance of the transaction would be an instantaneous check of the available credit for the person making the transaction. Given the centrality and the inevitability of financial transactions, these institutions have a great interest in watching the people who interact with them because the people are important for the existence of the institutions and the people often place a lot of trust in the financial institutions. The second set of institutions which can be considered as important as the financial institutions are those that offer health services to people.

Much like every other aspect of everyday life, the healthcare institutions have transformed with the arrival of digital technologies along with increasing concern over offering the best treatment to the people they serve. The delivery of health care is a complex process that includes numerous entities, but it is still the case that most of the services are provided at a physical place. Although there has been a move towards tele-medicine, the fact remains that a person has to usually be at the location where the service would be available. This could be a vaccination location in a developing country or the office of a plastic surgeon offering services that a person chooses to purchase. The space where the services are offered are watched over by the institution constantly through a variety of tools that keep an eye on the people populating the space.

The health care industry also watches the persons the industry serves even outside the spaces controlled by the institution. The increasing digitization of medical information of individuals open up the space for the health care industry to monitor that data as a person goes though different stages of health-related changes with age or a progressive illness. The data is constantly digitized, from the findings of diagnostic tests to the words spoken by the health care personnel when examining the person who is unwell. Much like institutions that operate primarily in the digital space, the health industry and the associated institutions are able to watch the digital data about the patients and this data is available to many components of the health institutions – from the people who are treating the patient to the people who are computing the cost of treatment. In the case of the latter, there is a cross-over to financial institutions that become involved in paying for the sustenance of the health of a society.

Similar to the essential service offered by the health care industry, there is another service that is increasingly considered to be essential – educating the population. There is a growing recognition of the need for education starting at the Kindergarten level and progressing through 16 years of education ending with a college degree. The education institution operates as a multi-space institution as well. In this case, the institution includes the long range of different real and virtual spaces that offer the service of providing education. This particular institution has a characteristic that sets it aside from some of the other institutions discussed earlier in the fact that there is a clear categorization in the type of institution in terms of its ownership. Somewhat similar to the health care institutions which could operate as a private corporation or a state-controlled institution, education, in most of the World is provided either by private groups or by the state. This distinction is important because the structure of the institution brings different amounts of funds available to the institutions to set up systems of watching, but in all cases, there is an interest in watching the people who populate the spaces.

There are two primary spaces that are watched by the educational institutions. First, is the surveillance of the physical space of the institution. In this case the institution is interested in ensuring that there are sufficient oversight of a school or college campus. In some cases, particularly in the United States, a campus could be a vast place and there is a need to watch all parts of the physical space of the campus. This watching is directed towards all the people who may populate the space which includes the students, teachers, staff, and visitors. All these people are subject of observation once they enter the space. The nature of the institution – public or private – would make a difference in the capability to watch often based on legal and financial restrictions.

The educational institution also operates in the digital space as the records of all the people connected with the institution are digitized and available to the institution. These records not only include the performance status of the students who are the service recipients but also all the other people who are parts of the institution. For instance, there is a long-standing tradition in some institutions to gather data about the performance of its teachers. This data is a form of surveillance of the people who teach, just as there is the ongoing tracking of the performance of the students. All of this information is now digitized and available to the institution.

In this discussion, the focus has been on some institutions that could be considered vital to everyday life in much of the World at the time of writing this book, in the spring of 2020. It can be argued that the state, certain corporations, financial institutions, health care and education providers offer products and services which could be considered "essential" for most people. As indicated here, these institutions may be in the real or virtual space or a combination of the two. There are, however, other institutions which could be considered non-essential but have, over time, become a significant part of everyday life.

Other Digital only Institutions

There are some services that have emerged starting in the late 1990s that were purely the product of the widespread adoption of digital technologies. These services did not exist in the analog world in the form that they were available in the digital space. I focus on two broad categories of services that are interconnected – research and entertainment. Consider two activities that were commonplace in the analog World, and still remains popular – searching for information at a library and watching a movie in a theater. In both cases a person would have to go to a specific place to do the research or enjoy the movie and these spaces are usually under surveillance where the library and the movie theater as institutional space would have ways to look at the people who are coming into the space. Both these activities are also available in the digital space where the person does not need to go to a place to obtain the services.

Starting with the availability of the Internet and the constantly growing depository of information in millions of data bases across the World it is now possible to seek and find information about nearly any topic using tools that search through these databases. These include tools such as Yahoo and Google which represents institutions that offer people the research service. These institutions are constantly watching the specific ways in which the services are used by people. The information is offered by the people who chose to use the tools and the people often offer explicit consent to the institutions to watch over the activities of the people who are using the services. The institutions are capable of keeping track of everything a person does and the way the person does the activities. Depending on the level of permission offered by the person, the institutions can watch when a person uses a service, what kind of equipment is used to access the service, where the person was when the service was accessed, and exactly why the service was accessed. Thus, an institution such as Google has the capability to capture every key stroke used by a person when doing a search for information using the Google search engine. This form of information is collected by any institution that operates in the digital realm and offers services to the people.

A second such category of service deals with entertainment and media. The analog forms of entertainment had involved the entertainer and the audience to be at the same location for live entertainment as in the case of the village play or a Broadway show in New York. These entertainment spaces still continue, and the institutions surveil those spaces carefully as in the case of any commercial space discussed earlier. The film technology transformed entertainment where the people who are being entertained were no longer close to the entertainer, but the movie theater remained a space to be watched over by the institution just as in the case of any other institution that would offer a space for the people to visit. The process of surveillance changed with the rapid adoption of radio and television when entertainment moved into the home of the people consuming entertainment. The "one way" nature of the analog technology did not allow for sophisticated modes of watching the audience. The systems offered by the rating corporations such as Nielsen offered broad generalizations about the audience but did not offer any great personalized surveillance opportunities.

The digitization of entertainment changed the scenario when the people consuming entertainment were able to access entertainment products, ranging from full-length movies to news segments, using a set of tools that delivered the products on demand. The person consuming the entertainment products could now "order" exactly what the person wanted to consume without having to wait for the specific entertainment to show up within the television broadcast schedule or having to go down to the movie theater when the movie would be screened based on the theater's screening schedule. The rapid availability of the Internet and variety of tools starting with the smartphone allowed for a certain level of personalization to the experience of consuming entertainment. This was facilitated by the emergence of corporations such as Netflix, Amazon, YouTube to name a few that allowed a person to search through copious amounts of entertainment content and chose what to consume. The capability of searching for specific things to consume required a "two way" connection between the institution such as Netflix and the person at home.

This search capability also opened up the space for the entertainment industry to watch the people consuming the products offered. At a very simple level the institutions are able to continuously see what a person is searching for within the digital space of any of the institutions. Similar to the way in which the search engines are able to track what a person is searching for, institutions such as YouTube are able to keep track of everything a person has put into the search box. Additionally, the institutions are able to tell what kind of tool was used for the search – a cellphone, a tablet, or a smart TV. Such information can be coupled with the place where the search was conducted and where the program was viewed. In some cases, with the use of smart TVs and associated tools such as smart speakers like the Echo product from Amazon, the institutions could also keep a watch on what the viewer was doing when a program was being viewed by the person who searched for it.

The digital revolution has added a "two way" capacity where institutions can interact with the people who come in contact with the institution. This interactive capacity has opened up a space for surveillance that did not exist prior to the rapid digitization of a large segment of our lived experience. This technological development has opened up possibilities where a person can use digital systems to do things that could not have been possible prior to the digital experience and without the assistance of institutions that leveraged the changes to offer completely unique services to people. These are services that were only possible because the vast penetration of digital tools such as the smartphone and the pervasive connection to a global network. Other than the entertainment services there existed a service sector that remained at the interaction of entertainment and interpersonal connectivity – the digital social networks – that became the site where institutions could watch people.

The notion of the digital social network utilizes the strength of the Internet with simple computer applications that allow a person to seek out other people and create a social network that is expected to work in the digital space without any need for a real analog connection between the people. The process requires an intermediary tool that would allow people to connect to each other. This tool remains in the control of an institution. The process started with the release of a platform called Myspace where a person could use the digital platform offered by the company to create a personal narrative and wait for other people to notice the narrative. This approach was then tried out by many other companies all of which were eventually replaced by the industry leader called Facebook. Part of the success of Facebook can be attributed to the fact that the company offered the digital platform to people who already knew each other and the digital connection was yet another way of staying in touch with each other that supplemented other methods such as real life gatherings, phone calls and other digital methods such as sending group messages. However, in the case of Facebook and other such platforms like Instagram the institution only offered the tools to keep people connected. However, these institutions were able to watch everything a person was doing because all of it was in the digital space offered by the company.

The institutions that offer the opportunity for people to congregate in the digital space are able to track everything a person does in the space that is "leased" to the person by the institution. Even if it may appear that the space is owned by the person, it is indeed owned by the institution and the institution can see everything that the person discloses in that space. There is no exact similar aspect in the analog World other than imagining a rented place where the renter can indiscriminately place a camera to watch the person who is residing in the rented space. The platforms that offer the opportunity for people to remain digitally connected are able to achieve a level of institutional surveillance of the person that has not ever been possible in other regimes of everyday life.

As discussed in Chapter 2, surveillance by the institutions occurs both the at I2I and I2P levels. Much of the description so far has been at the I2P level where the institution is in the act of watching the people who come in contact with the institution. The concern over the I2I surveillance moves into the realm of spying as pointed out earlier and we will return to that aspect of surveillance later in the discussion. It is now important to consider the reverse of the surveillance that is initiated by the institution and consider the way in surveillance is conducted by the person.

The "P" Watchers

The history of surveillance has usually not offered a great deal of opportunity where an individual could systematically watch others without some support. As I pointed out earlier, a spy is not an individual doing surveillance because the spy is often backed up with a significant amount of support from some institution. Even if the spies of fiction appear to be unbeatable heroes, the fact remains that the entire might of the spy agency supports the spy. The surveillance by a person is described as a systematic and persistent watching by a person where the person has adopted technologies and strategies to set up a complete surveillance system that has a specific target of surveillance and the watching continues over significant period of time. Personal surveillance has been common where a person may set up a temporary system to watch over someone else, sometimes with the support of an institution such as private investigator, but my focus here is on the people who set up a more continuous form of surveillance.

Parents and Guardians

The first such people are parents and guardians who have taken on the responsibility of raising children. This group of people watch both the analog and digital existence of the wards. The body of the child is under surveillance almost from the time they are born where the parents may set up systems to monitor the child even when the child is in the home. Many people who can afford the tools in developed and developing nations would use simple tools such as a baby monitor to watch a sleeping child in the nursery. As the child grows, parents can begin to watch the emergence of the digital life of a child by monitoring many different aspects of the digital life such as the media that a child consumes, the people that the child makes friends with, the places a child visits, and the things a child purchases among many other details of the digital life of the person. Some of the surveillance can actually be conducted without the knowledge of the person being watched as is often the case with institutions or the parental surveillance is conducted in such a manner where the tools of surveillance and the process disappears from sight – becomes ubiquitous by its prevalence – and the one being watched forgets that the person is under surveillance.

The parent as the person doing surveillance can also extend beyond the child or the ward. Existing technologies can allow for a person to surveil the spaces that a child may occupy and the rhizomatic surveillance with many tentacles available to the parent can get connected with the surveillance system of a school or the monitoring of other people that the child comes in contact with. The parent as a person is not restricted to surveilling the child alone but has the increasing capacity to look at the larger spaces that a child populates both in real life and in the digital. Thus parents can utilize digital devices to surveil the space the device is located in, and assuming the device is with the "watched," the watcher can surveil the spaces surrounding the surveilled person.

Spouses

Another category of people who get actively involved in the act of surveilling are spouses and significant others. The objective of surveillance in this case are the behaviors of the partner. In the traditional form of this surveillance, it has not been uncommon for spouses to engage a private investigator to keep track of behavior. The same process can now be expanded in a way where different tools are employed to do the surveillance. This process involves several different aspects of the spouse that is looked at.

One aspect of this surveillance is watching the spaces occupied by the spouse. Typically, in families, there is a rhythm to life where there is an expectation that a person would be at a certain place at a certain time engaged in a specific activity. For instance, there could be the expectation that a working partner is at a place of employment at certain times. Similarly, if a person states that the person is going to a specific place, then there is an expectation that the person is indeed at that place. The spousal surveillance frequently traces the movement and spaces occupied by the partner. This can be obtained as a digital data that shows the location of a person at any time. This data can be compiled to create a narrative of what a person was doing at any time because the place can become a good indicator of the activity that the person might have been doing. The activity tracking is also strengthened by examining other data of which one common data used by spouses is financial data. In many cases, partners share financial instruments such as bank count, a credit card, or other such financial tools. The data indicating the patterns of financial behavior is often somethings that is looked at by spouses to keep track of the behavior of the partner.

The behavior tracking also utilizes another form of data that examines the communication network of a spouse. The details of the information retained by corporations that offer communication services such as cell phone, internet services, GPS services, etc. all offer information about the people a person could be communicating with. This information offers a way of tracing the different people a person has relations with. This information is relatively simple to gather, especially if there are shared accounts and service providers. This is also a process that is frequently used by parents as a way of keeping an eye on children.

There is another group of people who are accessing surveillance tools to look "after," as opposed to looking over other people. With the dissolution of family systems where the elderly would be cared for by younger members of the family, there is an increasing incidence of the elderly having to cope with old age on their own. The concerned member of the family is now accessing different surveillance tools to guard the elderly family members. In this case two kinds of data become of interest. On one hand, there is an interest in observing the body of the person where it may be possible to keep an eye on the movements of a person within a home. The person being looked at is kept under some form of observation where another person can look at the target of surveillance at will. Simultaneously, there is a growing interest in the observer looking at the data about the target where specific aspects, such as health monitoring information can be called up to note the health of the target. The surveillance utilizes the combination of the real body and information about the body to create a holistic narrative of the condition of the target. It is important to note that although the process here is intended to observe a person, and the observer is an interested person, sometimes it is necessary to engage an institution to be a mediator and facilitator for the process of observation. For instance, the observer may not have immediate access to the health data, but an institution that can offer the health data may have to be engaged for this P2P surveillance.

Overall, the tools available within a family offers access to different kinds of data about the people in the family that focus primarily on location and relationships. People are now increasingly also surveilling outside of their immediate family.

People in General

The access to the smartphone has offered an opportunity of surveillance that can be exercised by any person who chooses to look at a situation and keep a record of the situation. The notion of surveillance as discussed here has been tied to "looking over" and in the case of the institutions there are specific elements that an institution can decide to surveil. Thus, there are elaborate systems to target the object of surveillance and then have a plan and goal for the surveillance. In a similar fashion, people such as parents and spouses may have specific people they are watching, and the surveillance is limited to the targets of interest and some surrounding targets that are relevant for the target of interest.

The situation is different when a person decides to watch over a situation simply because there is an opportunity without any specific goal or specific target that is the object of regular surveillance. The first such category of people are by standers. These are people who were at a specific place at a specific time by coincidence and became witness to an event that might have appeared worthy of preserving. The current tools, which will be elaborated later in the book, make it possible for the by standing stranger to capture the moment. The object being surveilled could be complete strangers in an unfamiliar setting and they are surveilled by a stranger. The people may not know each other at all and there may not even be a future promise of seeing each other, but the captured data can serve as surveillance data. There are increasing incidences of such data capture where the object of surveillance may not even know that an event they were involved in was surveilled, and the watcher may not even recognize the utility or value of the data at the time of surveillance. This is an opportunistic surveillance where the bystander has usually not planned the surveillance as in the case of institutions and other people who usually set out a surveillance plan before engaging in the task.

Similar to the stranger/bystander there is another category of people who are involved in collecting data about specific targets. These are the consumers of products and services. This is a condition where a person collects data when involved in a transaction with another person or institution. This is a process similar to a statement of customer satisfaction assessment, with the vital difference being that the assessment could be done without the knowledge of the service or product provider. In this situation the data collection is done by the consumer of without the knowledge of the seller and the data can become available to other potential customers. This process has become increasingly sophisticated as different institutions have emerged that offer a person a platform where the data can be stored and accessed. In such cases, the institution is not involved in the process of surveillance but only offers the customer a digital space to share the surveillance data. The target of surveillance in this case could be very broad stretching from another person to an institution.

There are thus many different institutions and people constantly engaged in the process of surveillance. The number of observers is increasing as institutions and people can gain access to increasingly sophisticated tools of observation. It is the combination of the tools that are important to examine to see the extent of the surveillance opportunities and the different ways in which the real body and its data-based representation can be observed.

REFERENCES

Cheng, A. (2019, November 21). Amazon Go Looks To Expand As Checkout-Free Shopping Starts To Catch On Across The Retail Landscape. *Forbes*. https://www.forbes.com/sites/andriacheng/2019/11/21/thanks-to-amazon-go-checkout-free-shopping-may-become-a-real-trend/#5dc1b9c5792b

Pruitt, S. (2018, October 16). An Ode to the Massive Sears Catalog, Which Even Delivered Houses by Mail. *History.com*. https://www.history.com/news/sears-catalog-houses-hubcaps

Rashid, F. Y. (2015, October 2). EMV sets the stage for a better payment future. *CSO Online*. https://www.infoworld.com/article/2988549/emv-deadline-fraud-time-bomb-is-ticking.html

Suman, S. (2015, October 26). Institutions: Meaning, Characteristics, Role and Other Details. *Economics Discussion*. https://www.economicsdiscussion.net/articles/institutions-meaning-characteristics-role-and-other-details/13121

Chapter 4
How Is Watching Done?

ABSTRACT

The process of surveillance has changed over time, as the object of surveillance—the narratives—have evolved. The primary mechanism of surveillance involved studying the analog body by watching the activities that the body performed. As such, the visual process, using cameras of different capabilities, has been a key way for watching. With the increasing digitization, the watching has relied on methods that capture the data about institutions and people.

INTRODUCTION

In the last chapter I pointed towards the different categories of watchers that make up the people and institution who are engaged in the process of watching. The initial categorization offers a point of departure, but more details would be added as I look at the different ways in which the watching is cone. To be sure the methods of watching have developed with time. The early days of the Panopticon and watching from the watch tower has certainly been improved upon. Similarly, eavesdropping on people talking in a café in the old East Germany, or intercepting personal correspondence in many totalitarian governments has now been improved upon. The technologies have certainly become more sophisticated than ever before, and the developments are unstoppable.

In this chapter I begin by examining the object of surveillance focusing on the body and its representation. I propose that there is simultaneously an analog object that is being watched along with the digital representation of the analog object. As such, the act of watching involves a tool that can watch the body – the camera and there is a tool that can watch the representation – systems to track data. This chapter elaborates on the camera and data watching to eventually set the stage for exploring the primary motivation for surveillance.

The Body and Its Representation

When a person arrived at Ellis Island on a boat from Europe when America was still true to its founding principle of accepting the weary from all over the World the focus was on the body that arrived on the ship. In a famous moment in the film *Godfather 2,* when the young Michael arrives into America, his body is inspected for disease first and then he is given a name based on the village he could name. At that moment, the body of the boy was represented in a name. This repeats itself in many different ways for individuals. The most fundamental representation of a human body in society is the name. Even before the body is seen there might be a representation of the body that becomes central to judging the body. My name, "Ananda" which means "joy" in the Bengali language is dangerously close to a common Western name, "Amanda." My representation in the West is one letter away from changing my gender. In my 35 years of living in the West, I have frequently been referred to as a woman because the name was "corrected" by an editor.

We all are made up of two parts. On one hand is the flesh and bones self that lives the "real" life from birth to death. This is the object that changes over time. This is the self that moves through space. As people live their lives the body might move from place to place over time. It is said that the millennial generation will move once every two years as they change careers and relationships. The body also changes with time by the sheer unalterable force of biology and aging. There might be many things that the body can do to slow the changes with time but there is a certain inevitability about the fact that the body will change with time. The body also acts in different ways. At any moment in time the body could be doing something observable such as going from one place to another, participating in a commercial act such as going to a shop, going to a doctor, or sitting and watching TV at home. Each of these moments represent a particular behavior and tells something about the body. All of this is worthy of watching in the contemporary surveillance arena.

While the body has been the focus of surveillance from the early days of watching, the body has been constantly supplemented with information about the body. As discussed in Chapter 2, Big Data is the representation of the body and this is as important as the analog body. The real body leaves its digital trace as it moves through space and time and all of the digital traces are fair game for surveillance. The totality of the person (P) being watched is made up of the sum of the real body and its representation. Neither one is sufficient by itself. Both have to be watched in unison so that it is possible to connect the real body with its digital self and be able to create a composite picture of the person. The same goes for an institution (I), where the brick and mortar presence of an institution needs to be matched with its digital presence. This combination is especially important because it may be possible to find anomalies in the combined image which might have been missed if only one was watched. Some people or institution might look quite appealing in the digital representation but delving into the real body might show things that the digital presence did not. In the extreme cases the real and the digital may actually contradict each other and the contradiction itself might offer useful information.

The key aspect of the body that is of interest is the behavior of the body along with specific elements of non-verbal communication. Within the discipline of communication much attention is paid to the way in which people signal messages through nonverbal means. Consider for instance the act of telling a lie. In most cases people try not to make eye contact with the receiver of the message when lying. In most cultures, there is a great deal of cognitive discomfort when lying, and eye contact amplifies the discomfort. There are numerous behavioral elements that can be indicators of attitude or intent of future behavior. Thus, a person who is attempting to hide something, may behave in a specific way that could "give away" what they are hiding. In a similar way specific behavior may indicate the intent of future action and by observing the behavior future action, especially if it is an action that could be considered to be potentially harmful or criminal, might be discovered and prevented. Therefore, there is a great interest in watching people especially when the person may not realize that they are being watched. As discussed earlier, much of surveillance has relied on making people docile by reminding them that they are being watched as in the case of the Panopticon. However, there are times when people do not notice that they are being watched and let their guard down. At that moment, the body becomes a source of information to the watcher.

The body also moves around in space. Unless there are reasons that the body is restricted in movement due to specific barriers, a person would usually be at different places at different times. A working person may have a specific routine of going to work every day, perhaps using the same public transport system every day or the same driving route. The body would then be at a place for a certain length of time, perhaps in an office, and then return home. These spatial routines are commonplace for millions of people and the location can offer information as well. This is especially true if there are variations from the routine which may indicate a set of behaviors that are different from what is expected about a person. The object of observation in this case is not just the routine, but the pattern in the routine, and eventually the variation from the pattern.

A pattern of behavior based on repeated routines of movement and predictable location also suggests that the body is in contact with other people. Thus, a person going to work every day is expected to be with co-workers. This information is vitally important in certain kinds of surveillance as was exposed in the COVID-19 pandemic of 2020. It was important to not only watch some specific indicators of the body such as body temperature, but it was also important to learn about the different locations of the body and the people the body came in contact with because all of these factors would be indicators of the body's exposure to infection and the potential of the body exposing others. Thus, when surveilling the body, it is essential to watch the interactions of the body with other bodies. Here too the key is watching the patterns. For most people, the interactions are predictable and the variation from the routine is usually a "flag" that suggests that the body may be involved in activities that is worthy of closer attention.

While the body has traditionally been the object of surveillance there is now the representation of the body that has become equally critical. The importance of data as the object of surveillance becomes especially important with the rapid digitization of information, where critical personal and institutional information is converted to standardized binary data that does not have a "physical" existence as a piece of paper, a photograph or a film. This digital data is the representation of the real body.

The digitization of everyday life has led to the development of a condition that I have described as the cybernetic life. In the first two decades of the Twenty First Century a large portion of the global population has developed a digital persona that resides in the virtual space created within the Internet network. Billions of people now live simultaneously in the real world and the virtual world effectively creating an existence in the combination of the two worlds – the cybernetic world – where the person and the machine intersect. The traditional life story of a person built around the place of birth, significant life events and other things that happen in the "real" is supplemented by an interconnected story that addresses the digital existence of the person. Given that surveillance is about unraveling the narrative of a person or an institution, a complete understanding of the narrative requires watching the digital presence of an entity.

This presence is made up of data. There are many tools that offer easy access to the data in the form of portals that allows the analog entity to interact with the digital information but behind the portal is a vast amount of data. Consider the case of a digital network like Facebook. The user experience of the digital network is built around an application that offers an easy way to create data as in posts and pictures, and access data when looking at the posts and pictures of others. The application program is simply a gateway into the vast amounts of data that is stored in computer memory in the numerous data centers of Facebook. This data is accessed in a user-friendly way when the application is used. This principle is true for every digital facility that is used by any entity. The goal of creating the application is to allow easy access to the database both to add to the database by volunteering data and allow limited access to the database to retrieve information. Even the act of checking on the amount of money available in a bank account is done through the portal (online banking) that offers access to the entire database of information that resides with the bank. It is this data that composes the digital narrative and thus the data is an ideal candidate for surveillance.

Current methods of surveillance have evolved to be able to keep an eye on both the physical body and the corresponding data. The primary tool for observing the physical body is the camera.

Camera

The most popular technology used for surveillance of the analog body is vision. This is where surveillance takes on its literal meaning of being watched. This has been the task of the classical spy – a person who blends into the surroundings of the watched and keeps an eye on the watched. As I have mentioned earlier in Chapter 1, the process of espionage gave rise to the act of watching a body. Ancient civilizations such as those in the Indus Valley, China, Egypt, Greece, and Rome all have records of individuals who would watch and report on other people. In these ancient cases, the process of watching was left to the human spy. There are certainly drawbacks to the use of the human being as the recorder of images because such recordings rely on the skills and memory of the observer. One needs to have the skills to remember the exact things the watched body was doing in order to be able to produce valuable information about the body. The records, unless put down on paper, would also disappear if the spy were caught and killed. However, it is also this personal observation that became the basis of the Panopticon design of Bentham because when Bentham was thinking of the prison, the presumption of observation was that a person will actually be situated in the tower watching over the prisoners. Although such prisons did not become commonplace, to this day, one can see watchtowers in protected places and the towers would have people watching on other people. When the watched can be quartered within a manageable space, the watch tower and other similar forms of observation can be used to surveille the bodies. There were always limitations to such surveillance because it was prone to failure due to human error. The human eye could mistake one body for another or could simply miss an important act of the body because the eye had looked away. Such failings of the human eye as the primary tool for surveilling the body needed to be addressed.

The problems associated with humans watching over bodies was addressed with the invention of the camera. The camera as a part of everyday culture started to become popular in the early 1900s when George Eastman (1854-1932) an American entrepreneur started to make an inexpensive camera available to the consumer market under the tradename of Kodak (Masoner). By the time Word War 2 comes around a small camera was available and photo journalists started to use the camera to capture images of the War and after the end of the War, the camera started to become a part of everyday life in the more affluent countries in the World, and eventually became available globally as many manufacturers started to offer cameras at a variety of prices. All the camera used a standardized film, commonly 35 mm in width, which needed to be treated by a trained professional to produce the image. The images were relatively stable and would last the test of time and created a relatively permanent record of the what the camera observed. Naturally, what was on the image was in the control of the person operating the camera, but once an image was captured it could be duplicated and was considered to be a reliable record of reality.

The camera quickly became a tool for I2I and I2P surveillance as the technology developed in two directions making it an appropriate tool to not only observe bodies and behavior but also places that needed to be surveilled, especially if those places would contain enemy bodies. The first major ongoing development of the camera that made it suitable for the two categories of surveillance was the miniaturization of the camera. With the beginning of the Cold War between former Soviet Russia and the United States after the end of World War 2 there was significant amount of research on both sides to make cameras that were small enough to be hidden away. There were numerous such cameras being used both by the West and the Communists. Most of these cameras had some commonalities that continue today. First, the cameras were small in size making them easy to transport. For instance, the Tesssina 35, invented by an Austrian, was small enough to fit into a cigarette packet. With the miniaturization came the ability to conceal the camera so that it would not be easily noticed as also in the case of the Minox that was widely used by the CIA.

The second major development in camera technology that made it suitable especially for I2I surveillance following World War 2 were lenses that could capture accurate images from a great distance. This allowed a camera to be placed very high up in the sky, over enemy territory, and capture pictures that could offer clues to what the bodies on the ground were doing. This technology was used by the United States with their legendary U2 planes that flew regular reconnaissance missions over Soviet Russia capturing images on the ground while flying about 10,000 meters above. The early flights, in the mid-1950s, used a combination of special film and the A2 camera assembly which had capabilities of picking up tiny objects on the ground. The development of these special lenses was accompanied by the use of the "zoom" lens assembly. These were lenses that had the capability to adjust the focal length (^Black et al.; Elizabeth, 2019) of the lens to be able to capture images at a great distance. This capability allowed cameras to capture a narrow field of view with great degree of accuracy, thus it was possible to "zoom" in on a person far away and capture the face of the person with great detail. Cameras with the appropriate lens assembly could do this with great ease in the case of I2P surveillance. The combined capability made it possible to capture pictures of people from great distance with formidable accuracy. Such pictures would be become incriminating evidence against people who might have been watched by the state.

The miniaturization of the camera did not remain restricted to the specialized cameras and that feature started to become available to consumers as well. The consumer cameras which were usually large with elaborate lens assemblies and different methods of advancing the film gave way to fixed focus cameras which could start to use smaller film size. The small cameras could now be used by people to capture images without having to carry around large equipment. Companies like Kodak started to manufacture the cameras with film cassettes that could easily be carried in a small bag. These cameras opened up the possibility of a person being able to take pictures of another person or an institution and using that picture as a product of surveillance. While this was not the principal use of the camera, it remained a possible use of the tool. One of the key aspects of the camera in P2P or P2I surveillance was the fact that it was based in film, and the size of the film determined the size of the camera. For instance, a camera that used the popular 35 mm size of the film, would need to be able to accommodate that film cassette in the camera. Since these were commercial cameras, and not meant for specialized use, they were mostly manufactured to use the popular 35 mm size limiting how small the cameras could become. Simultaneously, the lens assembly, even with the simplest fixed-focus cameras, had to be sufficiently large to allow for sufficient light to enter the camera to capture an image. This was also in the realm of analog cameras where the primary mode of capturing the image was a chemical process that imprinted the image on plastic and paper.

The usefulness of the camera as a device for P2P and P2I surveillance was advanced with the invention and popularity of the digital camera which no longer needed the physical film to capture and display an image. Instead, the image is captured by a device like a Charge Coupled Device (CCD) which would be able to convert the information about the light falling on the device into binary data which could then be stored like any other data on to a memory device. Later, that data could be interpreted and the information about the original light falling on the CCD converted back to an image to be displayed on a computer monitor. Although there were initial experiments with digital cameras started in the mid-1970s, the commercial camera did not become viable until about the late 1980s (^Trenholm). The trajectory of the digital camera was similar to the development of the overall digital technology where computers were becoming smaller and new devices such as cell phones were becoming available. There was a quick convergence between the cell phone and the digital camera where the two functionalities were packaged into a single device taking the camera to the people at a rapid pace.

The penetration of the smartphone motivated the use of the camera for many different purposes which went beyond the act of taking pictures of friends and family. The converged tool allowed for nearly unlimited capability by a person to capture still and moving images. The convergence – fact that many functions could be done by a single tool – led to the usefulness of the smartphone. This tool had a built-in powerful camera, ubiquitous connection to the Internet, availability of nearly unlimited storage, and the growth of digital networks as sites to share images all worked together. As a result, a person was empowered to not only create content but distribute the content through a myriad of networks. It is the confluence of these different factors that created the ability to use the smartphone as a tool for P2P and P2I surveillance where the "watcher" was no longer restricted to the institutions (I) but expanded to the person (P).

In the case of P2I surveillance this meant that a person was able to watch an institution and circulate what the person was observing. One of the key ways in which this was utilized when a person with a smartphone would be able to capture actions taken by an institution. In the absence of the smartphone the action of the institution would have remained unnoticed and thus unknown to the World. Two examples help to illustrate the process. In a passenger captured the video of another passenger being dragged off the plane on a United Airlines flight (Zdanowicz & Grinberg, 2018). The video was distributed using the digital networks leading to widespread concern about the way in which the airlines, an institution (I), would treat some passengers. This P2I phenomenon was possible because it was possible to observe the actions of the institution which would have remained hidden in the absence of the surveillance. Another landmark example of P2I happened in 2020 when a bystander captured the image of a police officer killing a suspect. This video led to the eruption of nationwide protests across the World. Here too, the institution was surveilled by a person leading to the release of information that might otherwise have remained hidden.

An important point to note about this form of P2I surveillance is the fact that the process may not remain "hidden." In earlier discussions about surveillance, I have suggested that I2I and I2P surveillance is sometimes done surreptitiously where the watched may not be aware that they are being watched and the product of the surveillance, perhaps a set of pictures and videos, may also never enter the public sphere. Such surveillance can remain hidden until they become useful for specific action such as use by law enforcement. Thus, the footage from a Closed-Circuit TV (CCTV) camera can be valuable for investigation of crimes. On the other hand, P2I surveillance often enters the public sphere and becomes powerful because of its visibility. The product of the surveillance becomes an empowering tool that can be mobilized to demand accountability from the institution that has been surveilled. The nature and motivation of P2I surveillance is different from all the other forms of surveillance because this is a relatively new and unique phenomenon unlike all the other mechanisms of surveillance. It is only the availability of the tools that has made this process possible adding a layer to surveillance that did not exist before.

In surveilling the body, the key purpose is to watch what the people are doing. In summary, the primary tool used to capture this information is visual data captured with different kinds of cameras. The capture devices can be controlled by institutions or people empowering the watcher by access to the device. The tools could vary from elaborate satellite-based cameras to smartphones in the hands of youngsters. The cameras could be completely hidden away where the watched would have no idea that there is a camera, or the watcher could be completely aware that they are being watched. The videos could remain private or can become easily available on digital networks where the actions of a surveilled body can become visible to the World. Finally, the image, which is considered the primary data, can be connected with other information about the image – the meta data – to offer insights about the surveillance process. For instance, the meta-data could describe the place where the video was captured, the time, the kind of equipment used to capture the image and other such information that embellishes the information available in the image. This leads to an examination of the way in which data itself becomes the object of surveillance.

Data as Object of Surveillance

Just as in the case of surveilling the body with many different kinds of cameras to discover and record different aspects of the different bodies – the person or the institution – there are different kinds of data that can be watched. As in the case of the camera with differential access between the person (P) and the institution (I) there are differences in access to data based on who the watcher is and who is being watched. To begin with, it is useful to categorize the data into a set of broad groups which can be applied to both persons and institutions.

One of the keys to surveillance is the construction of a narrative. For instance, in the case of I2P or P2P situations the process of surveillance creates a narrative of the person, whereas in the cases where the target of surveillance is an institution (I) the process of surveillance creates a profile of an institution where numerous data points can be connected together to create the narrative. A narrative requires a protagonist and people and institutions that surround the key actors. A first data category is thus descriptive that attempts to offer an enumeration of the characteristics of the institution and its key patterns of behavior. This is a vast category that has numerous elements. First, the narrative is made up of answering the "what" question about the object of surveillance.

A common starting point for answering the "what" question is the descriptive data. This can be considered to be demographic information in the case of a person (P). Such information helps to describe the person around relatively stable biological attributes. For instance, a person could be born with a specific biological gender, with a set of specific racial indicators and perhaps even some specific individual characteristics such a relatively permanent physical marker such as a "birth mark." These characteristics can be enumerated as data and can be updated with time and the changes recorded as data. Additional markers develop with time such as levels of education, wealth, affiliations with groups that also offer deeper descriptions of the person. A similar strategy can be applied to institutions (I) where financial, location, size, and function information help to describe an institution. There are specific numeric markers for such information as well and institutions can be classified within specific categories, just like a person, and that information is digitized and available. Consider for instance, the elaborate Standard Industrial Classification (SIC) system in the USA that offers code numbers and institutions can select the codes that offer the best descriptors. Financial records, employee listing, location and other such information all become answers to the "what" question. For both people (P) and institutions (I) this answer becomes a key aspect of the narrative that can be produced by surveilling the data. When this data is collected periodically it is possible to trace the changes in the narrative allowing a historical look at the entity under surveillance.

Tracing the data over time begins to answer the "when" question about the person or the institution. The question related to time becomes especially important when it is important to look for patterns in the narrative. In the case of a person this could offer a narrative that is based on digital data that is collected even before a person may be born. Companies in 2020 in the USA would offer digital images of ultrasound tests for pregnant women to help monitor the health of a fetus. Such data collection continues through the entire lifetime of a person, and it is possible to identify patterns in the data when examined over time. Every element of the data that answers the "what" question can be mapped over a timeline to show how the descriptors of an entity has changed over time. Sophisticated computational tools can sift through large volumes of data to expose the way in which the narrative of an entity changes over time.

This longitudinal data is also important for institutions. Just as in the case of the person, it is possible to take snapshots of the descriptors of an institution and trace how the narrative changes. Much of I2I surveillance has relied on the temporal aspect of information. Constant surveillance of the data generated by a nation offers competing nations a strategic advantage. For example, during the pandemic of 2020 there were several accusations that different countries were spying on each other to gather data about the progression of vaccine research to remain ahead (Kelion, 2020). That kind of data is time-sensitive and requires constant surveillance to note the changes that are happening over time. The answer to the "when" question is coupled with the answer to the "where" question that examines how the data is connected to specific places at different points in time.

A good illustration of the where question comes from popular applications that rely on the Global Positioning System (GPS) that became ubiquitous in smartphones. The GPS system appeared as a consumer option starting in the early 2000s and very soon became a part of smartphones because of developments in the technology of locating a cell phone. Early reliance on a satellite-based system gave way to hybrid systems where a cell phone could be located based on satellite signals as well as the cell tower that the phone would be connected to. The increasing affordability of including the GPS technology in the phone and the increasing penetration of the smartphone within large segments of the global population offered the opportunity to gather data about the location of a smartphone. The process would also require the intervention of groups that would make the GPS information usable. For instance, a GPS locator can offer the exact latitude and longitude of the location of the receiver. This information is relatively useless unless the information can be connected to a map showing what the numbers represent. Further, the map could be used to calculate optimal routes between different points on the map and the GPS information could be used to track the movement of the receiver as it travels from one point to another. The GPS data was thus connected with mapping data for the convenience of the user. From that point, the corporation that would offer the mapping software also started to gather the location data of the smartphone.

Assuming that the smartphone is nearly "glued" to the person, it is now possible to find the answer to the "where" question by gaining access to the location data that is being collected by institutions(I) such as Google and Apple as a person(P) uses the mapping software to find routes. In some cases, the process happens in the background and a person may not even notice that location data was being gathered and stored continuously by the companies that offer maps. Most such institution offer legal disclaimers about the data, and even allow users to disable the data collection process, but it is becomes the responsibility of the person to be mindful of the process and remember the way in which the data is being gathered. The location data is most relevant for entities that tend to move frequently. This form of data may not be very crucial for institutions that are geographically stable and have brick and mortar fixed offices that do not tend to change. The data is generally much more vital for the person who is on the move more frequently. It is possible to watch the movement carefully when the location data is connected with other data about a person such as the answers to the "what "and "when" questions. However, what is of importance too in surveillance is to understand "how" an entity performs a behavior in order to gather a usable narrative about the entity.

Both people and institutions have specific ways in which they do things. For instance, a person (P) may periodically purchase a set of food items from a store that the person frequents. A company (I) may periodically purchase a set of raw material from different vendors. These are simple examples of how entities perform everyday activities. The list could become quite large when looking at the details of each of the activity and how it is performed. This is especially true in the case of people where individuals would often repeat a set of activities building a pattern, as explored in answering the "when" question as similar activities are done in repetitive ways. These activities, and how they are done, generate a large amount of data which can be surveilled. This data may not be the principal data under surveillance but offer information in the way of meta-data about the activities. For example, a purchase by a person at a grocery store may demonstrate that the person uses a specific form of payment, a specific form of transportation to go to the grocery store and always goes through the self-service payment point as is offered in many stores in different parts of the World. This information creates a profile of behavior that not only shows "what" the person is doing but the exact steps that the person follows to do the task. Over time, this data accumulates to look for moments when the pattern is disrupted, which in turn could indicate that there is something special going on with the person. Such patterns are also crucial for institutions when circumstances disrupt the rhythm of activities. The pandemic of 2020 demonstrated the importance of the answer to the how question. For example, the pandemic led to the closure of hair cutting salons across the World. But as things improved the businesses began to reopen with new ways of doing things with limited number of customers or service in an open area. Such changes to the question about "how" the institution does "what" it is meant to do offer the opportunity to watch for disruptions that could be a symptom of a larger issue.

The objective of surveilling data is to answer the different questions discussed here. The combination of the information gathered through the surveillance of the analog existence of an entity and the compilation of the digital information about the entity, in combination, produce a narrative about the entity. This narrative offers an insight into the entity that goes far beyond the Panopticon or the traditional means of watching over people and institutions. The level of detail has increased with advances in technology and changes in regulations where different aspects of the life story can now be observed and permanently recorded. The level of detail in the story continues to grow as tools of observation become increasingly sophisticated and capture the information of larger number of subjects. In 2021 it was expected that the number of video surveillance cameras would grow to about 1 billion cameras with the fastest growth being in countries such as China, India, and Brazil (Lin & Purnell, 2019). At the same time, increasing number of people are connected to digital platforms such as Facebook and Instagram where they are constantly generating information about themselves. Institutions too are having to find digital pathways for themselves to survive in a World that saw some significant transformations after the historical pandemic of 2020. All such digital information is appended into the narrative that results from the practices of surveillance.

The next question is to begin to understand the motivation for creating these narratives. As demonstrated here, surveillance is not only about I2I or I2P where an institution initiates the process as was the case in the past, and much of the surveillance research focused on understanding why institutions want to watch over other institutions and people. In 2020, surveillance is far more widespread and in the next several chapters I examine some of the key motivators for surveillance. It should be noted that the motivators are separated for the sake of analytic simplicity, but it is often the case that the motives intermingle. I look at the key motives of offering security and commodification of the surveilled as the primary motivators for the different forms of surveillance.

REFERENCES

Black, D., Berkenfeld, D., Silverman, L., & Corrado, M. (n.d.). Focal Length: Understanding Camera Zoom & Lens Focal Length: Nikon. *Nikon*. https://www.nikonusa.com/en/learn-and-explore/a/tips-and-techniques/understanding-focal-length.html

Elizabeth. (2019, April 29). What Is Focal Length in Photography? *Photography Life*. https://photographylife.com/what-is-focal-length-in-photography

Kelion, C. F. L. (2020, July 16). Coronavirus: Russian spies target Covid-19 vaccine research. *BBC News*. https://www.bbc.com/news/technology-53429506

Lin, L., & Purnell, N. (2019, December 6). A World With a Billion Cameras Watching You Is Just Around the Corner. *The Wall Street Journal*. https://www.wsj.com/articles/a-billion-surveillance-cameras-forecast-to-be-watching-within-two-years-11575565402#:~:text=The%20report%2C%20from%20industry%20researcher,little%20over%20half%20the%20total

Masoner, L. (n.d.). Explore the Major Advances in the History of Photography. *The Spruce Crafts*. https://www.thesprucecrafts.com/brief-history-of-photography-2688527

Trenholm, R. (n.d.). History of digital cameras: From '70s prototypes to iPhone and Galaxy's everyday wonders. *CNET*. https://www.cnet.com/news/photos-the-history-of-the-digital-camera/

Zdanowicz, C., & Grinberg, E. (2018, April 10). Passenger dragged off overbooked United flight. *CNN*. https://www.cnn.com/2017/04/10/travel/passenger-removed-united-flight-trnd/index.html

Chapter 5
Why Watch?
Security

ABSTRACT

The most popular justification for surveillance has been providing security to the ones being watched. Most institutions and people who are involved in the process of surveillance have argued that having the information about the narratives allows the watcher to create a more secure environment. This argument allows the watcher to institute different methods of watching for the different contexts of surveillance showing that all the watching eventually makes the ecosystem more secure.

INTRODUCTION

In this chapter I look at the most common rationale for surveillance – security. First, I offer an overview of the notion of security in general terms to understand why security is a fundamental need. Next I offer the way in which security is used as the reason to watch within the four contexts of surveillance explained earlier. I conclude with the notion that security is connected with the other reasons for surveillance.

The outcome of surveillance is the construction of a narrative. In every instance of surveillance the outcome is to gather a better understanding of the entity under observation. This narrative is made up of a set of data points which are usually collected using tools that can be deployed at various levels of sophistication based on who is watching. However, the primary difference between different forms of surveillance is based on the sophistication of the technology deployed to watch. In some ways, the technology that is used to do the watching is inconsequential other than the details of the story that can be constructed from the data. Those with better technology can construct a more detailed and elaborate narrative. For instance, the narrative about an incident produced by the person (P) capturing the acts of the law enforcement institution (I) in a P2I situation might be made up of unsophisticated smartphone cameras videos but it could tell as compelling a story as one constructed with the use of spy cameras that capture images in great detail. The level of details of the story could have an impact on the effectiveness of the story but the act of constructing the story begs the question: Why even construct the story? More elaborately, it is important to understand the motivation behind constructing the numerous stories that result from the rapid growth of surveillance technologies as discussed earlier.

The next few chapters offer some of the key rationale that are utilized to justify the construction of the narratives through the various processes of surveillance. I use examples from past notable cases of surveillance and the way in which those instances have been supported by the "watcher" to suggest that there are certainly powerful reasons to engage in the process of surveillance to gather the data to collect the stories. The most common rationale for surveillance revolves around the notion of "security." The use of security as a rationale for surveillance is an especially meaningful because surveillance is meant to be covert. Much of what has been discussed thus far deals with the situation where the act of surveillance, be it gathering data about individuals or the process of photographing land masses from the sky is meant to be done without the knowledge of the watched. Thus a public rationale for the acts of surveillance are only needed when the watching process has been discovered by either the watched or another independent group who is monitoring the watcher or the act of surveillance is discovered by the watched. It is at those moments when the surveillance process becomes visible that there is an urgent need to offer an explanation for the act of surveillance and security is frequently invoked as the rationale.

The Notion of Security

The idea of security can be considered to be one of the most fundamental of animal instincts. Every animal needs to feel secure and protected from predators. The very existence of a species can be threatened if it cannot identify threats, communicate it to others in the species and eventually develop a mechanism to challenge the threat. In the case of animals there is a process of constant watchfulness to examine the surroundings and be aware of the presence of others in the space. Biologists have spent time studying the ways in which many birds and primates are able to keep an eye on their habitat and when a threat is observed the animals use special kind of signals to communicate information about the danger to other animals in the space. This process has received scientific attention because it signals a level of cognition that can offer ways of understanding how animals communicate with each other (Magrath et al., 2009). The key issue is that gaining a sense of security is an instinct that could be essential for the continued existence of a species.

This fundamental importance of security is also reflected in the observation of the human system. Consider, for instance, the way in which a topography of human needs have been developed by Robert Maslow in 1943 which suggested that human activity can be progressively be categorized as a mechanism to fulfill a set of increasing specialized needs that culminate in the fulfilment of the need for self-actualization where the a person attains "full potential" in one's life including the fulfilment of the needs of creative activities. The progression of needs is presented as an equilateral triangle where the apex of the triangle represents the issues of self-actualization and the broad base of the triangle represents the basic needs that must be fulfilled as humans. Maslow suggests that there is a progression of the fulfilment of the needs moving upwards from the broad base of the triangle to the narrow apex of the triangle. Starting with the basic need for sustenance and shelter, the model suggests that the second layer of needs is for "security and safety." These needs must be fulfilled before a person can consider moving up the hierarchy of needs and fulfilling psychological needs and the needs for self-fulfillment. The vital nature of the need for security is emphasized in this widely accepted model to understand human behavior. In one interpretation of the basic needs for security, it is stated:

Once an individual's physiological needs are satisfied, the needs for security and safety become salient. People want to experience order, predictability and control in their lives. These needs can be fulfilled by the family and society (e.g. police, schools, business and medical care) (Mcleod, 2020).

This model emphasizes the role of society in fulfilling this need for security and that becomes clear in the progression of human civilization when there are specific ways in which the need for security is globally codified.

World War 2 demonstrated that there was an acute need to ensure a systematic description of human security and find ways to offer the security. The division of the World into two political camps and the onset of the Cold War also indicated that there were ongoing tangible threats to human security and many nations took on the task of protecting the security of its people in an organized way that went beyond the earlier forms of securing a nation and its people. This need for human security and the imperative to provide the security was placed on nations and global organizations. Consequently, the United Nations – a product of World War 2 – took on the task of elaborating on the notion of human security to offer a standardized description that all participating nations would find agreeable. This initiative took shape nearly fifty years after the end of WW2 with the publication of the UN Development Program Human Development Report New Dimensions of Human Security. Here the term "human security" was introduced focusing on: "universal, people-centered, interdependent, and early prevention (Gazizullin, 2016; Johns, 2014)." This initiative came much after the preliminary initiative to establish a sense of national security after the devastation of World War 2.

It is important to distinguish between the notion of national security and human security to understand how the different aspects of security relate to the process of surveillance. The idea of national security is a cornerstone for the definition of a nation. For instance, the oath of office of the American President makes it explicitly clear that the job of the President is to "protect and defend" the Constitution of the United States – which signifies the nation. Similar language can be found in the vital documents of all nations and every nation retains its right to secure itself from aggression. Indeed the post-War establishment of the United Nations and especially the UN Security Council established in 1945 is geared towards the protection of the security of nation states through debate and dialog as opposed to armed conflict. This notion of security – to protect the borders has been a part of human civilization and ancient conflicts can be traced to disputes over borders and the need to question the borders and sometimes aggressively defend the borders.

There are thus two forms of security that are of interest in modern history and the UN offers a global perspective on a matter that is of interest to most nations. Every country, on its own, also has its own focus on security which have changed with time. These two ideas of security, however, become wrapped with each other when the idea of security is examined from a narrative perspective aimed towards understanding the way in which the idea of security is articulated and circulated. While the act of securing a nation and its people has some specific practical aspects such as the existence of the military and the surveillance apparatus discussed earlier, the notion of security must also be narrated for institutions and people to accept the systems that ensure the security. This presentation of the need for security is as vital as the specific mechanisms that are used to maintain security. The motivation and the justification of the machinery of maintaining security lies in the way in which security is imagined in the public sphere. In the 2015 book *Narrative and the Making of US National Security* Ronald Kerbs demonstrates how competing security narratives have been constructed and deployed through the history of the United States that includes the discussion of President Reagan's attempt to construct a story about the Contras in Nicaragua to create a narrative about America's tough stance against Communism. This, and the other examples in the book, remind us that while the act of securing a place is crucial it is almost equally important to be able to justify the acts of security by presenting a convincing narrative to back up the acts. This is true for most nations and institutions as seen in the work of Felix Ciută who writes about the way in which narratives and identity play a role in describing security in the European context (2007). These arguments can be extended to other parts of the World as well.

The process of surveillance is thus justified by suggesting that gaining security is an important aspect of life and this need is constructed through specific narratives at different moments in time. It is therefore important to note how the idea of narrative is deployed in the four distinct contexts of surveillance described earlier.

The best-known instance of security can be found in the context of I2I surveillance where one institution, usually a state, would be surveilling another as a way of securing the watcher's country. As discussed earlier, this is the process of spying and most instances of spying has been framed within the narrative of security where all such activities have been motivated by the patriotic need to ensure that one's homeland is safe from aggression. This narrative has been recognized by nations and has been articulated as the motivation behind the way in which nations conduct their espionage operations. Consider for instance the way in which the Director of the Center for Security and Intelligence Studies at the University of Buckingham in UK described the incident related to Sergei Skripal, a Russian spy who was poisoned in UK in 2018. The Director said, "Russia has abandoned communism, but it has not abandoned the concept of an intelligence and security community that will stop at nothing to safeguard the Russian state." This is the primary motivation for the act of I2I surveillance which can sometimes transform into situations that go beyond the mere "watching" and takes turns where the institution could utilize methods called into question on moral and ethical grounds.

Given that the security narrative drives the I2I surveillance, the eventual goal of the process is gaining an advantage on the adversary by gathering information about the opponent. The flying of U2 planes over USSR and the use of satellites to monitor electronic messages all fall into the general category of surveillance where the focus is of information. However, at times, the gathering of information as a part of I2I surveillance can be called into question. This became clear when it was found that United States was operating "enhanced interrogation" techniques to extract information from the people captured in the war of terror that started after the attack of September 11, 2001 when the World Trade Center towers in New York were destroyed along with the death of thousands of civilians. This horrific attack led to the need for retaliation against the Al Qaeda that claimed responsibility for the attack and an urgency to ensure that the country was safe from other attacks. One of the key ways to ensure the security of the nation was to extract timely information from Al Qaeda operatives who were captured by the US. However, the obtaining the information eventually involved methods of interrogation that were disallowed by international treaties leading to significant embarrassment of the US. However, the whole process is a part of the security narrative that claimed that everything was done to ensure national security. Consider the quote from John Rizzo a CIA attorney:

The reason the enhanced interrogation program came to be in concept was a few months after 9/11, when the CIA first began capturing and holding very high-level Al Qaeda officials, beginning with a man named Abu Zubaydah. Abu Zubaydah made it clear shortly after his detention and confinement, after days of regular sorts of questioning, that he simply was not going to say anything else, and that he made it clear in his own smug and arrogant way that there were certain things he knew that were going to happen, but he wasn't going to tell his inquisitors, and they couldn't make him. That gave the impetus to coming up with, if legally possible, a set of techniques that would work on someone like that, who was thought to likely have information about a possible next imminent attack on the homeland (PBS).

The key to the process was the possible future attack on the interests of the United States. In such situations, the I2I process is couched within the narrative of national security and thus appears justified as a surveillance process when one nation would covertly watch another nation. If the covert process becomes compromised, the issue of security is invoked to justify the act.

While the nation state invokes the notion of security of the country as the primary motivation for I2I surveillance, the situation shifts slightly when the institutions are private entities, such as corporation that are surveilling their competition. The motivation is still ensuring security of the corporation, except now in terms of financial security and the protection of proprietary business processes. The surveillance of another company is to ensure that that other corporations do not gain access to private corporate information. Thus, one company may be watching another just to ensure that the watched institution is not itself engaged in watching the watcher.

The I2I condition can almost be considered to be a constant battle over security as the watcher and the watched are perpetually in the process of outwitting each other to ensure that the security of the institution, and the people it represents, is constantly protected. The presumption in the I2I situation is that the institution as an entity is the threat and institution is the focus of attention. However, a similar rationale is utilized in the case of the I2P condition as well.

I2P

The I2P condition has grown rapidly with the availability of tools that allows an institution to pinpoint a person for surveillance as discussed earlier. There are two primary arguments offered in justifying this process where both the arguments offer the common theme that some individuals pose a threat. The difference in the arguments stems from the answer to the question: Who do the people threaten?

The first response to the threat assessment is that a person could threaten the people around them. This is typically the motivation to surveil people who could have the potential of causing large scale harm to others and thus the institution has the responsibility to protect the other people and thus surveil the "people of interest." The I2P process has been around for a long period of time but has come to focus on the post-World War 2 period when the World was clearly defined into two estates led by the United States and USSR. This is the period of I2I surveillance when it was also becoming clear that there were specific people in, for instance America who worked for Russia to bring harm to the people of America. This suspicion offered the opening for a country such as America to keep an eye on a specific person who may be planning harm to the people of America. This historical context changed in the late 1980s with the slow demise of the Russian superpower and a thawing of the Cold War. However, the I2P situation came into greater focus in the latter part of the Twentieth Century with new conflicts that emerged between Islam and the Western World, particularly America. These conflicts, some of which involved another country, as in the case of the war with Iraq in August 1990, involved institutions, but with the changing global landscape it was becoming clear that conflict might not always be between countries but a country could face a threat from a person, or a small group of people who could not be characterized as another institution. Consequently, there was the recognition that there were collections of people who posed a threat and needed to be surveilled for the security of the threatened country and its own people. This justified the notion of I2P where the vast strength of the institution could be brought to bear upon the "person of interest." The combination of terrorism as a tool of conflict where the object of the attack was not an institutional military or security apparatus, but the civilians of a country offered the justification for countries to adopt surveillance of people who the institution suspected to be a threat to the people.

The idea of the person of interest also emerges within this historical backdrop where the idea is used to refer in a specific way to offer the institution to focus on the person. Thus, "it may be used, rather than calling the person a suspect, when they don't want their prime suspect to know they're watching him closely (US Legal)." It is important to note that the aspect of watching is crucial in the description and this fundamental justification leads to the establishment of numerous programs of I2P which are codified within the legal framework of countries. Consider for instance the way in which laws were enacted and then repealed that addressed how an institution could treat a person who posed a threat to the country as in the case of India which brought in the Terrorism and Disruptive Activities Prevention Act (TADA) following the assassination of the Indian Prime Minister Mrs. Indira

Gandhi in 1984. This law allowed the state institution to observe the activities of individuals who were considered a threat as a terrorist who had the goal of inciting fear among the people of the nation. Although TADA was repealed in 1995 there were other similar laws that followed in India and elsewhere with the emergence of yet another threat from "stateless actors" who were usually a loose collection of people with the single motive of bringing harm to their adversaries.

The idea of the non-state or stateless had exited for a long period of time, with agencies such as the Red Cross which acted as a non-governmental organization. However, such organizations did not pose a threat to security like the groups in the late 1990s which were designed with the express purpose of bringing harm to other people. The threat of the stateless actor culminated in the Western World with the September 11 attack on New York in 2001. This attack brought the process of I2P into sharp focus and offered a global justification of the I2P surveillance with the objective of securing the lives of civilians which proved to be the target of the non-state actors such as Al Qaeda. Attacks on people in Madrid, London, New York, Mumbai and Paris all offered the rationale for the rapid expansion of the I2P apparatus and the establishment of the "person" as a subject of state surveillance as proposed by President George W. Bush in 2001 in a call to fight the individual "combatants" and no longer just an axis of enemy nations (O'Connell, 2005). This rationale saw expansion in organizations such as the National Security Agency (NSA) of the United States which represent the "black" programs for the securing the nation. Allegedly, the operation and financial structure of such agencies are held as secrets, but some estimates suggest that NSA budget saw a 50% increase between 2004 and 2013. Although the NSA acts as a relatively secret organization it was becoming clear that one of its activity related to individuals and, "included collecting phone call data and monitoring online activities (Sahadi, 2013)."

While the organizations such as NSA and RAW used securing people for I2P surveillance the second rationale was securing the institution itself. In this case, the emphasis is on the way in which a person could become a threat to an institution. For instance, the 1993 film *The Firm* brought this into sharp focus when the protagonist, an honest young lawyer in a law firm that represented criminals, is the subject of surveillance by the firm so that the person does not pose a challenge to the institution. There are many more references to such I2P in fiction where reality has mimicked fiction with the intent of securing the institution against attacks by rogue persons whose interest is to actually attack the institution itself making it justifiable for the institution to install elaborate processes of surveillance. Incidents such as the attack on the digital presence of the Minneapolis Police Department in America offers an example of a situation where the target of attack is police institution which offers the police to exercise their prerogative of protection by construction elaborate I2P surveillance systems to watch out for other persons that may wish to bring harm to the institution.

This particular aspect of I2P surveillance is also frequently seen in the case of private institutions and corporations who feel the risk of competitors who may use people to gather proprietary information that could be useful for the competition. The justification of protecting "know how" or corporate secrets allows for a transparent I2P where the people working for the institution might be well aware of the specific forms of surveillance that they are subject to and implicitly agree with the process of surveillance by their willingness to work for the institution. Indeed, the process of I2P surveillance might actually be combined with the corporate standard operation procedures where the person working for the company is expected to use a tool or system to make the operations of the company more efficient, while the process also watches over the person working for the company. Consider for example the development of a proprietary tool called "UPSNav" that the multi-national corporation United Parcel Service (UPS) deployed in 2018 and described it as a tool to make the work of its drivers more efficient. The press release from UPS stated:

With the new navigation tool, ORION gives drivers directions to all those stops in precise detail – even to loading docks and receiving areas that are often on opposite sides of a building's main entrance. UPSNav provides UPS drivers with a new level of accuracy and precision, which enables them to operate at top efficiency. It also improves the customer experience and opens the UPS platform to provide new products and services.

The statement from UPS does not make any mention of the fact that the tool also acts as an implicit form of I2P surveillance system that knows where the vehicle, and the driver, is at any time. The drivers are generally willing to accept this form of I2P surveillance because this is considered a part of the expectation to have the privilege of working for the corporation. These processes can get exaggerated when there are external forces that makes an institution vulnerable and the institution can install surveillance processes where the institution must maintain its legal liability and protect its reputation as was the case during the pandemic of 2020. Many institutions, such as colleges and universities installed data collection processes, where the people involved with the institution would have to volunteer information in order to be able to access the institutional properties and spaces. For instance, one university required all the people using the campus to complete a digitally available form every day to gain access to the campus and the requirement was imposed to: "help promote health and safety on our campus (Sneezesafe, 2020)." Of note, is the emphasis on the notion of the institutional campus, albeit it is made up of people who populate the campus.

The process of I2P is generally justified with the intent to protect the institution, and consequently the favored people of the institution – law abiding citizens and loyal corporate workers – from the people whose intent is to bring harm to the institution and its preferred constituents. This justification is reversed in the case of the P2I surveillance where the people feel the need to watch over the institutions.

P2I

A sense of suspicion about the motives of large government and large corporations has been a part of life for a long period of time and significant global political movements have been instigated by people who have risen up against a tyrannical government and led to sea changes in political and social life. In the 2000s such movements have brought forth changes in polities and the way a person could be treated within society. Organizations such as change.org make it a point for people to be able to initiate movements that can secure personal freedom and liberty that is frequently codified in national Constitution and legal documents but are not necessarily followed by the institutions. As stated earlier, people now have the technological ability to watch institutions and with the motive to secure people from institutions that needs to check on frequently.

The rise of P2I surveillance is cast within the arguments of securing personal freedoms by capturing and widely circulating evidence of what a person might consider to be evidence of institutional action that threatens personal liberties. This motive is best understood by observing the ways in which institution attempt to restrict P2I. In the United States the issue of restricting the P2I process is addressed by the Defense Imagery Management Operations Center and this unit deals with issues that relate to American military personnel who are able to use personal cameras to record and circulate images from battlefields and other spaces that are considered to be in the realm of the institution. In the case of the military, the popularity of the personal cameras such as those produced by GoPro allowed individual soldiers to distribute combat footage over the digital networks and eventually to sell them to institutions that would utilize the videos for commercial purposes, part of which could lead to a critique of the way in which a massive institution such as the US military conducts its operations. Such an issue had come to the forefront in the case of the infamous pictures from the Abu Gharib prison that was used to hold and interrogate enemy combatants after the fall of Iraq to the American military. There were soldiers like Sabrian Herman who personally took pictures of the battle fields and the prisons which later became public leading to the controversy over the prison that was eventually reported in 2004 by the mainstream media (CBS Interactive, 2004). Until the matter was reported in shows such as 60 Minutes, the issue remained within the realm of P2I surveillance where the motivation to capture the images was, "just show what was going on, what was allowed to be done (Morris, 2008)."

The statement about Abu Gharib becomes an example for securing a moral and ethical standard that the people wanted to uphold in surveilling institutions. The rapid penetration of the smartphone in the second decade of the Twenty-First Century offered the opportunity for increasing P2I surveillance where the motivation can be traced to the desire to ensure the security of the freedom and voice of the single person in the face of the massive authority of an institution. Several such instances offered demonstrations of the way in which a single person armed with a camera was able to call into question the authority of states and corporations. For instance, in 2017 a video of a passenger being forcibly removed from a flight by United Airlines received significant popular attention as an amateur videographer captured the moment and exposed the act of the institution, in this case the Chicago Department of Aviation security, to the World ensuring the fact that such events are not repeated and the people responsible for the act were disciplined (Neuman, 2017). A much more resounding surveillance occurred in 2020 where a seventeen-year-old woman captured the murder of George Floyd and triggered a World-wide movement against the use of excessive force by law enforcement institutions. The motivation, according to the person who shot the video was to let the World know of what she was seeing that she felt occurs too often, and in her words, "the world needed to see what I was seeing. Stuff like this happens in silence too many times" as reported in the Start Tribune (Jany, 2020). These words echo the sentiments of the soldier who captured images of the Abu Gharib prison in Iraq.

The motivation to secure the voice of the lone person in the face of institutional adversary becomes one of the key arguments of persistent surveillance of institutions by people. As stated earlier, the P2I process involves much more than the use of the camera and moves on to the processes where people can speak about institutions and express their concerns through digital forums ranging from outlets such as TripAdvisor to other watch groups that offer the person the voice to secure the ability of people to watch and report on institutions. This ability to watch is also seen in the case of P2P situations where the motive of securing personal freedom is accompanied with the motivation of securing the safety of another person.

P2P

The P2P surveillance has been the result of increasing access to tools that has empowered people to watch other people. As discussed earlier, the context of the watching can be within families or amongst a small group of people who are affiliated in some way that does not involve an institution. However, in most such groups of people there are specific relationships of power where some of the people might feel both an obligation and the rights to surveil others. The process of surveillance itself can become the basis of the power and watcher argues that the watching is needed to ensure the personal security of the watched who needs the security that the watcher can offer.

A simple analogy of this argument of securing the watched can be found in a technology that has been available since the manufacture of a baby monitor. In 1938 the Zenith Corporation in the United States introduced a product called "Radio Nurse" which was advertised in *Radio Today* as, "the idea of safety and convenience in home where children or invalids need a simple and dependable and portable connection with their keepers." The language of the announcement sets the stage for the utility of the tool as a connection between those who need protection and the "keepers" who can protect them. Moving ahead nearly a century from the time of the Zenith product the tools have become much more sophisticated yet the rationale for baby monitors have not changed too much when a popular product claims, "as a new parent, you always want to keep a close eye on your baby (GP, 2011)," continuing the notion of surveilling a child with the necessary and vital objective of protecting the vulnerable person.

In the first part of the Twenty-First Century the notion of security that begins with watching the vulnerable such as children, elderly and those who need constant support, gets extended to everyone who can be watched and the watcher was able to conjure an argument for security to people who might not have had the need to be watched. The process of watching was now cast in the argument that the watcher was in some ways incapable of protecting the self and thus needed the other person to install the surveillance system to secure the protection of the vulnerable person, even if the person did not necessarily need to be watched. The popular TV series called *Big Bang Theory* makes this point well in the final episode of the seventh season of the comedy series where one of the key protagonist, Shelodon, is missing and one of his friends, Leonard, tracks the cell phone of the missing person. When asked why Leonard is tracking the phone of his adult friend, Sheldon, the rationale is based on a previous incident where the vulnerable Sheldon was lost in a county fair which prompted Leonard to begin to track the phone so that Sheldon would not be lost again.

This fear of losing the loved one supports the fundamental desire to keep an eye on the other person. One of the key aspects about this logic is the level of stealth used in the surveillance process. In the case of the baby monitor it can be argued that the infant being watched may not be aware of the watching process, but when the same process is extended to the youth and adults there needs to be a decision about the level of transparency used in the P2P surveillance process. Most of the babies who were monitored in the crib eventually grow up to be youth and adults. However, the process of monitoring them do not necessarily end because the desire to ensure security for the loved ones remains an essential trait of normal human beings and the technologies are increasingly amenable to the process, where the people are willing participants in the process of surveillance where there is an implicit acceptance of the surveillance process because it promises security. This process happens between people in a community and promotional language from the providers of the tools remind the user of the centrality of the surveillance. Consider for instance the popular function of "family sharing" offered by Apple where members of a close group can share each other's information (Apple Corporation, 2021). Although the term "family" is frequently used, the system can be set up between a group of people who agree to chare their information, which includes the location of each person. This is an important aspect of P2P surveillance where the people generally appear to be willing participants in the process. Perhaps, the matter disappears from sight after setting up the system, and people become unaware of the ways in the system can be used to watch, and it becomes a fabric of the lived experience of the surveillance.

The matter changes when the P2P surveillance becomes covert, and the watched is unaware that the person is being watched. The justification of security alters at that point. Usually the motive is to ensure the security of the watched, but in cases where the surveillance is opaque it is the security of the watcher that becomes more important. Now the objective is to ensure that the watcher is not threatened by the watched. In most cases the threat is on trust, another notion that has to be invoked to understand the way in which security and trust becomes connected in the P2P situation.

The P2P context presents a situation which has some analogy with the I2I situation where there is some similarity between the watcher and the watched since both feel that the other cannot be trusted. Thus, even though there is surveillance of mutually friendly nations, the I2I situation is more pronounced in the cases where the nations might consider each other to be threats. Historically, since World War 2, Russia and USA have surveilled each other with the sense that the other nation cannot be trusted, whereas there is much less evidence of surveillance between nations such as Canada and USA. This notion of trust is connected to security because the threat to security is far less from those who can be trusted. Surveillance is needed to ensure the security of a nation because the other nation cannot be trusted. This process happens with the P2P situation as well, where one person could feel threatened by another person who cannot be trusted. In these cases, it is the lack of trust that creates the threat to security which leads to the need for the P2P surveillance. Consider for instance, the commentary from a marriage counsellor who claimed in a 2017 article, "trust allows the couple to be vulnerable with each other, and know that the other knows their fears and flaws and weaknesses and won't use it against them (Pilossoph, 2019)." It is this aspect of vulnerability that can be the motivation of the P2P surveillance. The fear that one could be harmed by another person leads to the compelling need to surveil the other person as a possible threat. This form of P2P surveillance presumes that knowing the activities and behavior of the surveilled may offer indicators that the watcher can then utilize for security. In such cases, it is not only the security of the body but also the security of the mind where the watcher could be testing the security of the trust placed in another person. This process is, however, not new and unique to the technologies available now, but has been around for some time, albeit, without the person watching another person, but one individual could engage another person to watch someone to gather information. The typical argument is an appeal to security where the investigator would offer proof that would help secure the client if the watching reveals that the suspicions were true. Consider for instance the promotional material that states:

If you find that you are unable to definitely prove or disprove your spouse's cheating, it may be time to consult a private investigator. They have the skills and experience to prove or disprove your suspicions. As a bonus, they can provide evidence that can be used in court if it gets to that point (Darrin, 2020).

New technologies make the process simpler by allowing a person to do the work that private investigators with the eventual goal of establishing a sense of security for the watcher.

The arguments for security all focus on the creation of a narrative that demonstrates that the watched is a threat to security. This narrative offers the rationale to take specific action to ensure security by considering the specific aspects of the narrative that offer speak to the matter of security. However, a narrative based on surveillance has other uses as well, and it is useful to have a narrative which can cast sufficient light on the watched to describe the watched in great detail where the narrative can be used to commodify the watched and "package" the commodity for financial and other advantages. This is examined in the next chapter.

REFERENCES

CBS Interactive. (2004). Abuse At Abu Ghraib. *CBS News*. https://www.cbsnews.com/news/abuse-at-abu-ghraib/

Darrin. (2020, March 3). How To Catch a Cheater: Tips from a Private Investigator. *North American Investigations.* https://pvteyes. com/private-investigator-tips-on-how-to-catch-your-cheating-spouse/#:~:text=If%20you%20find%20that%20you,it%20gets%20 to%20that%20point

Family Sharing. (2021). *Apple.* https://www.apple.com/family-sharing/

Gazizullin, A. (2016, March 5). The Significance of the 'Human Security' Paradigm in International Politics. *E.* https://www.e-ir. info/2016/02/29/the-significance-of-the-human-security-paradigm-in-international-politics/

Goettsche Partners. (2011). GP. *Amazon.* https://www.amazon.com/ gp/product/B07MHCFCBG?tag=p00935-20&ascsubtag=07o0e56a6 zGrXrHH0cJuHfY

Jany, L. (2020, May 27). Minneapolis police, protesters clash almost 24 hours after George Floyd's death in custody. *Star Tribune.* https:// www.startribune.com/minneapolis-police-marchers-clash-over-death-of-george-floyd-in-custody/570763352/

Johns, L. (2014, July 11). A Critical Evaluation of the Concept of Human Security. *E.* https://www.e-ir.info/2014/07/05/a-critical-evaluation-of-the-concept-of-human-security/

Magrath, R. D., Pitcher, B. J., & Gardner, J. L. (2009, February 22). Recognition of other species' aerial alarm calls: speaking the same language or learning another? *Proceedings. Biological sciences.* https:// www.ncbi.nlm.nih.gov/pmc/articles/PMC2660948/

Mcleod, S. (2020, December 29). Maslow's Hierarchy of Needs. *Simply Psychology.* https://www.simplypsychology.org/ maslow.html#:~:text=Maslow's%20hierarchy%20of%20needs%20 is,hierarchical%20levels%20within%20a%20pyramid.&text=From%20 the%20bottom%20of%20the,esteem%2C%20and%20 self%2Dactualization

Morris, P. G. (2008). Exposure. *The New Yorker.* https://www.newyorker. com/magazine/2008/03/24/exposure-5

Neuman, S. (2017, October 18). Officers Fired After Forcible Removal Of United Airlines Passenger. *NPR*. https://www.npr.org/sections/thetwo-way/2017/10/18/558469185/officers-fired-after-forcible-removal-of-united-airlines-passenger

Newsroom: About UPS. (n.d.). *About UPS-US*. https://www.pressroom.ups.com/pressroom/ContentDetailsViewer.page?ConceptType=PressReleases&id=1543925402585-887#:~:text=%E2%80%9CUPS%20drivers%20make%20an%20average%20of%20125%20stops%20each%20day.&text=It%20uses%20the%20UPS%20data,delivery%20or%20pickup%20point%20changes

O'Connell, M. E. (2005). Enhancing the Status of Non-State Actors Through a Global War on Terror? *NDLScholarship*. https://scholarship.law.nd.edu/law_faculty_scholarship/94

Pilossoph, J. (2019, May 23). Column: Tracking your spouse's phone – peace of mind or lack of trust? *chicagotribune.com*. https://www.chicagotribune.com/suburbs/lake-zurich/ct-ppn-column-love-essentially-tl-0629-20170622-story.html

Public Broadcasting Service. (n.d.). Voices from the "Dark Side": The CIA Torture Debate. *PBS*. https://www.pbs.org/wgbh/frontline/article/voices-from-the-dark-side-the-cia-torture-debate/

Sahadi, J. (2013). What the NSA costs taxpayers. *CNNMoney*. https://money.cnn.com/2013/06/07/news/economy/nsa-surveillance-cost/index.html

SneezSafe. (2021, May 18). *Our Way Forward*. https://ourwayforward.wfu.edu/students/sneezsafe/

US Legal. (n.d.). Find a legal form in minutes. Person of Interest Law and Legal Definition. *USLegal, Inc*. https://definitions.uslegal.com/p/person-of-interest/

Chapter 6
Why Watch?
Assessment

ABSTRACT

The process of surveillance allows the watcher to assess the worth of the life story of the watched. In certain cases, this has significant value. In the case of I2I, one of the outcomes is better understanding of the competition; in some cases, such as I2P, there is a better understanding of the "worth" of a person. For the P watcher, there is an assessment of another person just as the person can now assess institutions.

INTRODUCTION

The notion of security has been a compelling and universal justification for different forms of surveillance because a need for security, as discussed earlier, is a universal need. It is difficult to argue against a process that makes things safer for people. Most social and political systems, from relatively "open" democratic countries to "closed" totalitarian systems can make the argument that surveillance is needed to ensure the protection of a place and its people. This was demonstrated after the 2001 attacks on the World Trade Center in New York which was followed by significant changes to the security protocols for air travel worldwide. And most passengers accepted the changes and the enhanced scrutiny at airports because it offered a sense of security, knowing that there were no potential terrorists in the airport and on the planes. This argument for security was repeated, again within the travel industry globally in response to the pandemic of 2020 and people traveling readily accepted the new travel protocols such as reporting tests for virus in the body to frequent recording of body temperature and contact information as a part of the process of securing the World against the spread of a disease.

What is shared in the experiences of surveillance is the creating of a narrative about a person or an institution that results from the persistent watching. This is the principal outcome that is achieved from the processes and in this chapter I would demonstrate how surveillance is justified by arguing for assessing the characteristics of the personal or institutional story. Here, I argue that the logic for watching is no longer only securing the safety of the person or the institution but assessing the "worth" of the person or institution. The pervasive surveillance offers the opportunity to create a relatively elaborate story and then consider what the story says about the person or institution. I call this motivation of surveillance – assessment. This logic is used, along with the justification based on security, in nearly every instance of the different forms of surveillance discussed earlier. This narrative has also been called a profile.

Profile

The term profile has been in use for as long as it has been possible to produce a narrative about a person or institution. As I stated in my earlier writing, "pervasive narb-based profiling can have some significant impacts on how we live our real and digital lives (Mitra, 2014)." In the case of a person the profile is a composite image that includes many different pieces of information about a person which all add up to create a nearly complete life story of the person. The information is gathered using many different forms of surveillance and the process of creating the story is often called profiling. The primary use of the process has been in criminal investigation where people in law enforcement would carefully examine the available evidence to create their best assessment of the possible characteristics of a perpetrator. One way of describing profiling in the context of criminal investigation has been to focus on obtaining a description of a person:

To help investigators examine evidence from crime scenes and victim and witness reports to develop an offender description. The description can include psychological variables such as personality traits, psychopathologies and behavior patterns, as well as demographic variables such as age, race or geographic location. Investigators might use profiling to narrow down a field of suspects or figure out how to interrogate a suspect already in custody (Winerman, 2004).

The last part of the description of profiling is vital when profiling can be expanded beyond the realm of law enforcement because interrogation is a special form of communication, and the profile offers a framework that can be utilized for communicating with a person. Increasing details in the profile would offer increasing information that would allow for greater specificity in messaging with increasing reference to custom information about the person.

The work of surveillance is gathering the information to create the profile which becomes the identity narrative of the person being watched. The goal of the acts of surveillance is to produce as complete a narrative as possible. There are different terms used within different disciplinary contexts, but the eventual goal is to gather and collate information about people. The scope of the process is determined within disciplines by the specific needs within the domain. For instance, in law enforcement profiling is targeted towards people who could be suspects, in the realm of race politics and social justice the process of profiling becomes synonymous with "racial profiling" where a description of a person is derived merely on the basis of the physical features of a person, and in the realm of health services a "lipid profile" offers a description of a person in terms of presence of fat in the bloodstream. Eventually, all these different processes can be summarized into the process of creating a narrative of the watched, and for the purpose of the discussion in this chapter, I will be using the term "narrative" as the overarching descriptor of the outcome of surveillance.

The objective of the processes of surveillance is to create the narratives. It is no longer the case that the narrative is contained within specific domains such as law enforcement and medicine but the pervasive and persistent methods of watching allows for the creation of narratives of anyone who can be watched. It no longer matters if the person or the institution is of any special interest, but a narrative can be produced as long as the entity can be watched. It also does not matter who watches the entity. The narratives are created in all the four contexts of surveillance and the narratives can be used by any of the watchers discussed so far. The process of surveillance is justified by attaching a value to the narrative and it is argued that the watching is necessary to assess the value of the narrative, and the entity, to the watcher.

Assessment of the Narrative

Each context of surveillance offers different kinds of value judgments to the narratives with different types of utility and the watcher knows how to best use the narrative.

I2I

The I2I context of surveillance offers a clear judgment about the relationship between two institutions. The narrative that emerges out of the constant surveillance of another institution helps the watcher to make specific decisions about the other institution and the surveillance is justified by the fact that the narrative is essential in better understanding the motives and nature of the other institution. This is no longer only a matter of security but more to assess whether the narrative of the other entity offers a deeper understanding of the watched institution. This logic is most applicable, for instance, in I2I context when there are no pre-exiting problems between two countries, but they still watch each other. The rationale for surveillance based on security is not supported when there is spying between two apparently "friendly" nations but watching can be justified by claiming that the watching offers greater insight about the other country. To begin with, the narrative that is derived from the I2I surveillance can be assessed to verify what the other institution publicly says about itself. As stated in a 2013 article, one key reason to do I2I surveillance between what appears to be allies, is to "to make sure they're still allies (Gewirtz, 2013)." The I2I process creates the narratives that become the focus of assessment that can be crucial to the relationship between institutions.

The need to assess the narrative of watched institutions applies most often to nations and countries where there are clearly defined allies and enemies at any moment in time. The assessment of the narratives is also justified on the basis that these narratives shift with time which is why there is a special emphasis on ensuring that they are "still allies." A justification based on assessing a narrative could quickly move to a justification based on security when the narrative changes. This is especially the case when the watched knows they are under I2I surveillance and does things that create a false narrative. Consider the situation when the CIA was unable to predict the testing of nuclear devices by India in the summer of 1998. Although by the late 1990s, India would be considered an ally by the US, there was I2I surveillance targeted to India, especially in the form of satellite imaging of the landmass. The justification was primarily ensuring the "ally" status of India and Indian military were aware of the surveillance and thus created a false narrative for the watcher that camouflaged the real narrative on the grounds in the test site in Western India. Eventually, the watcher was tricked into believing the alternative narrative. Such situations arise occasionally and is the result of the way in which narratives become the basis for assessing the value of the watched institution. The process of continuous I2I surveillance makes it important to constantly assess the narrative and keep an eye on the watched to see how the watched might be transforming with time and how the narrative needs to be assessed as things change. In the case of the CIA, there was greater caution attached to watching India as the narrative changed after 1998 and there was a need to watch more carefully to be able to construct the authentic narrative about the watched. Eventually the objective is to capture the constantly transforming narrative to assess the value of the entity along a variety of different factors of measurement. This process becomes even more vital and elaborated in the case of I2P surveillance where the notion of assessing the narrative becomes central to the purpose of surveillance.

A similar logic can be applied in the commercial domain where institutions would keep an eye on another institution, in a covert or overt way, to assess what the competition is doing. As discussed earlier, there are many instances of commercial I2I surveillance, and they cannot all be justified on the basis of a threat to security of an institution but a more plausible justification lies in assessing the status of the competition to anticipate their next move. In the case of commercial I2I surveillance the distinction between security and assessment may become blurred but generally the defense for commercial I2I watching has been framed within the logic of assessment.

The situation is a little different when an institution can justify surveillance of a person on the basis of assessing the value of the person to the institution. Here again, the focus is on the profile.

I2P

The idea of the profile has been used in the case of assessing a person for a long period of time and there are specific methods to create and assess the profile. Consider for instance the notion of a passport, first used in ancient civilizations with some records of king Artaxerxes offering papers for the safe passage of a person beyond the Euphrates in 450 BC. Until about the mid-1800s, the passport served as a document for "safe passage," similar to a ticket, where a country or a monarch would offer these documents to people to smoothen the travel of the person across national borders. It was only after World War 1 and the increasing migration of people to the United States that the passport became more of an "identity document" than that of safe passage. As stated below, the passport told the story of the person to whom the document was issued:

The first modern British passport, the product of the British Nationality and Status Aliens Act 1914, consisted of a single page, folded into eight and held together with a cardboard cover. It was valid for two years and, as well as a photograph and signature, featured a personal

*description, including details such as "shape of face", "complexion"
and "features". The entry on this last category might read something
like: "Forehead: broad. Nose: large. Eyes: small (Pines, 2021).*

Since the early 1900s the passport has increasingly become a
narrative document and the information in the passport has become
more elaborate and the combination of the electronic chip in passports
and the pages of the document of the Twenty-First Century carry a
treasure of information about a person. The pages contain information
about age, nationality, places the person has traveled to, the places
a person has been allowed to enter using visas, and biographical
information including biometric information such as fingerprints. In
sum, the passport, along with a visa based on the information in the
passport, offers a profile of a person that allows an institution, such as
a country, to assess if the person represented by the passport is worthy
of admission into a country. This assessment is based on the narrative
offered by the passport starting with the foundational story of which
country a person may belong to. Thus, if a person's profile is offered
by a country like the Japan or Singapore in 2020 then the narrative is
sufficiently strong that the person will be allowed into 190 countries
just based on the strength of the passport, whereas, if the narrative is
offered by Pakistan, in the form of a passport issued by Pakistan, then
the person is only allowed in 31 countries without a visa being issued
by the country. The visa is essentially the permission to enter, based
on the narrative offered by the passport and other details of the person.

The example of the passport is particularly telling because the
passport is the product of institutional surveillance that is accepted by
the person when a person applies for a passport. For instance, in India,
the process of obtaining a passport requires a verification of the identity
of a person by the police from a local police station unless the narrative
of the person is already assessed to be trustworthy as stated here: "In
most cases, of issue of fresh passport, pre-police verification would
be required, exception being Government servants on submission of
'Identity Certificate'." Yet, this process of surveillance is not necessarily
justified by a need to ensure security but to create an official narrative
that has been verified and attested by in institution that has surveilled a

person extensively before issuing a passport. This process of evaluation is seen in other cases of I2P surveillance as profiles and narratives are developed to determine the "worth" of a person within different kinds of assessment domains – such as the permission to enter a country or the ability to obtain credit or admission into an educational institution.

The worth of the narrative, and thus the person, takes on a commercial value as well which justifies the process of I2P surveillance. In the case of documents such as the passport, the objective is to assess if a person should be allowed to travel between countries. Generally, a majority of the people are found to be worthy and the data and narrative may not have much use other than when a person is crossing borders, which for a majority of people in the World is not a very frequent event. On the other hand, I2P surveillance that collects data about a person, as in the case of search engine providers that capture search terms, assess the data to create a profile that could be valuable as a commodity that can be transacted in a market place. The transaction may not involve outright selling or buying of information about a person, but it utilizes the person's story to be able to direct the appropriate message to the person. The rationale for surveillance in such cases is to collect the information to construct the profile which helps to customize the message. This is also not a secret covert form of surveillance, but the process and its details are disclosed by the institutions, even if the people being surveilled may not be necessarily paying attention to the rationale. Consider the following segment from the disclosure offered by Google as reasons why a person may see a specific advertisement:

Your info:
Info in your Google Account, like your age range and gender
Your general location
Your activity:
Your current search query
Previous search activity
Your activity while you were signed in to Google
Your previous interactions with ads
Types of websites you visit
Types of mobile app activity on your device

Your activity on another device
Other info:
The time of day
Info you gave to an advertiser, like if you signed up for a newsletter
    with your email address
Google can personalize ads so they're more useful to you (Google).

The last sentence in the disclosure is particularly important because the process of surveillance is framed within the rationale of creating an institutional profile that make matters more useful to the person being surveilled. Yet, the information is shared with advertisers appropriately based on the assessment of who the person is. Unlike the passport, every person using the search engine provided by Google is worthy of assessing and potentially offers valuable information.

The I2P data surveillance takes on a more powerful assessment value when decisions about a person may hinge on the way the information collected through surveillance. It has become increasingly clear that institutions like to surveil and assess the people connected to the institution. The process is intended to examine the narrative of a person to determine the 'value' of a person for an institution. The widespread nature of I2P assessment and the variety of data sources that are available to institutions make this process a very elaborate mechanism of collecting information of people who may have no reason to be suspected of a security concern, but an institution may merely want to know the 'fit' of a person with the institutional expectations. Consider for instance the manner in which academic institution across the World are interested in gathering information about prospective students to determine if a student should be permitted to attend an institution. It has become increasing evident that academic institutions are attempting to better understand their applicant by attempting to obtain the self-generated information that people in the demographic category of applicants place on digital social networks. Kaplan, a company that has for decades offered courses in preparing for the college admission tests such as SAT and ACT, has also been tracking the information about the way in which college admissions personnel in the USA have been using the information available in digital social networks to learn more about the applicants. The process started very soon after it was clear that the postings on such networks offer an alternative glimpse at the life story of the applicant that is not captured in the traditional artefacts of the application package – the standardized test scores and essays written to accompany the admission application. A series of studies conducted at the University of Dartmouth in Massachusetts, USA have demonstrated that there is active engagement by the college admissions staff in numerous American universities where the staff use digital social network tools such as Facebook and techniques such as blogging to connect with the potential students. Such connections as used as a marketing tool for institutions. However, it is also clear that the institutions use the tools to obtain a better understanding of the applicant, as stated here:

There is also some indication of using these sites for evaluation. Social networking sites provide an insight into the lives of students that cannot be underestimated. As more and more young people spend increased amounts of time on these online networks, those interested in them (employers or schools) will continue to watch and read the publicly available information and include their impressions in their decisions to accept or hire candidates.

The data from the specific study shows that 20% and more of those polled in 2010 claimed that they "researched" potential students using "social media" and search engines. The key to the finding is the notion of "research" where the objective is indeed to construct a narrative of the individual by watching them within a space where they reside. The discursive digital space where the individual is constructed and distributed through narrative bits, narbs, which in compilations offers an identity narrative of the person being watched. As stated by the researchers, those who are watching, such as the colleges, find value in this form of surveillance in better designing who will eventually occupy the real space of the institution as students (Luong, 2012; Singer, 2013). Similar situations can be discovered about the way in which employers would assess the value of a job applicant based on information that would go beyond a review of the traditional resume and the letters of reference.

It stands to reason that institutions who would be making an investment in an individual as a new employee would want to ensure that it is a wise decision. In most transactional situations it is important to know what one is paying for, and often looking at what is shown in a resume and an interview is not enough to evaluate the subject. It thus appears reasonable to delve deeper into the background of a person to learn more about the value of a person. This form of I2P surveillance, may even not qualify for a strict definition of "surveillance" because that may not be done in a covert way, or may not even be seeking out information that is not readily available in the public sphere. The increasing digital presence of most people, via postings on digital networks, is available for review to any entity that would take the trouble of exploring the details of the presence. This process is well stated here:

Because most people are on their best behavior during the interview process, it can be hard for hiring managers or employers to tell. So they do the same thing your Bumble date does: they Google you.

In particular, they look at your Facebook, Instagram, LinkedIn, Twitter, and other social media profiles you have publicly available (Curtin, 2020).

In nearly half the cases of people being surveilled by an institution prior to hiring, the person was not selected based on the information that was revealed through the surveillance process. In situations such as this the institution remains in an especially powerful position to assess a person based on surveillance data. However, the increasing availability of tools of surveillance to people is beginning to turn the table on institutions which too are now being surveilled by people to assess the value of the institution.

P2I

As pointed out earlier, the rapid adoption of digital devices that can capture and circulate images and videos and increasing sophistication of the ways in which people can access data has allowed for the ability for people to be able to watch and assess institutions. This process takes on policy outcomes and can have economic impact when a single person or a small group of people can actually gather information about an institution and make that information accessible to many people who can collectively assess an institution. A key component of assessment in the in P2I context relies on the publication of the information that is gathered for a public assessment of activities of an institution. There is a presumption in the assessment process that the institution might not have wanted the information to be made public and the outcome of P2I surveillance is frequently the public display of actions of institutions that would present the institution in an unflattering light. Such public exposure of the institution can have long-standing effects that would never have happened unless the P2I process would have offered the assessment of the profile of the institution.

Since the effect of the P2I surveillance usually benefits the watcher, or the collective of watchers, the process of P2I surveillance is justified by the assessment it offers which leads to greater accountability on the part of the institution. When the "secrets" of the institution are exposed, it is normal to expect that the institution will act in ways to respond to the information that is exposed as a result of the P2I process. In free societies where people have relative freedom of behavior – taking out a camera and filming an event – the challenge for institutions not knowing when the P2I surveillance is occurring. In the case of surveillance initiated by an institution as in the case of the I2I and I2P, the watcher has certain obligations and expectations that the surveillance process be announced, albeit very inconspicuously, and the watched has a certain expectation that there is some form of surveillance going on. This tacit understanding between the watcher and the watched largely disappears with P2I because there is no predictability as to when a person may suddenly take out a smartphone and start to capture an event that may show an institution in a bad light. Institutions have responded to this in different ways, either by outright prohibiting the process of surveillance where the institution would not allow a person to carry a surveillance device such as a camera when within the premises of an institution or by assuming that the institution is being watched and thus adjusting the institutional behavior to present a favorable profile. Consider, for instance, the widespread use of body cameras among police in the USA which appears along with increasing P2I surveillance that assesses police behavior. The expectation was:

If police knew their every action was being recorded, the reasoning went, they would more likely be on their best behavior. If not, the cameras would at least capture any misconduct, making law enforcement more transparent and accountable (Matsakis, 2020).

It is the changed practices of institutions that becomes the sought-after outcome of the P2I process that is motivated by assessment. As stated in the 2020 case of the George Floyd recording referenced earlier, the rationale for capturing the event that leads to the death of the man is simply to show the World what was going on to expect to prevent such things from happening again. As stated in Chapter 5, P2I is motivated by a desire to seek security, but the line between security and assessment becomes tenuous because assessment can look like the process of securing the safety of people in the face of the power of the institutions. The ability to assess offers a different level of power to the people who are able to watch and measure the actions of institutions thus empowering the watcher in a way that has not been possible in the past. As such, it is this sense of power that also carries over to the P2P scenario.

P2P

The justification of P2P based on assessment of another person is applicable in some special situations and is a part of the overall logic for one person surveilling another person. As pointed out earlier, the primary justification for P2P surveillance has been based in the notion of security, but sometimes people want to discover the profile of another person to assess the potential for relationships. The process usually involves checking the digital network presence of a person before actually deciding whether to meet the person at all. This assessment can be done with the use of tools that would allow the exploration of the digital presence of the person. The importance of such P2P digital surveillance aimed at assessment is discussed by relationship advisors as in the case of the following from a Website that advises people on dating strategies:

Dating a guy with no social media is incredibly risky. It could be the best decision of your life, but it could also be the worst. You could end up married to the most grounded, down-to-earth man in the world OR you could end up in a body bag (Babe.net).

That form of P2P surveillance can extend to a face to face situation as well, although the digital tools make the process of P2P surveillance, especially amongst relative strangers, a much more feasible surveillance process. The goal of the surveillance is to learn more about the person, without any presumptions of threats to security. This form of surveillance reveals things such as favorite movies, books, and events. The information is frequently only used to determine whether it worthwhile to spend time with a person. Indeed, that assessment can also be done through a conversation, but the P2P process offers a sense of privacy to the voyeur (Fan Fiction).

The importance of this surveillance for assessment is borne out in the systems that have mushroomed that attempt to match two people of similar interests. Companies such as eHarmony have been around since the early 2000s when the notion of assessing a person was made into an algorithmic process where a person would volunteer data about the self for the privilege of a technological system that would analyze the data and offer a set of "matches" with other people where the logical process would assess the data and categorize into profile narratives. This is not P2P surveillance in the sense of one person watching another person, but it presumes that watching the data of another person is a socially permissible mechanism to make decisions about another person.

Although this justification for P2P surveillance does not have any overt presumptions about threats to security, it is still the case that assessment, security and trust can blend together without clear demarcations. The assessment through the P2P process offers information that can allow the watcher to make assumptions of trust which, if positive, can also have effects on the perceived threat to security. The demarcations between the constructs of assessment, security and trust can become an artificial process, but it is important to recognize the relationship to better understand the way in which P2P surveillance is conducted. I would argue that this form of surveillance would be one of the quickest growing categories of surveillance primarily because it is becoming increasingly possible to do this with the network of digital devices that are accumulating data about a person, and the ease with which the data can be retrieved. This data is becoming increasingly vital within relationships and can be used to assess the quality of a relationship, often leading to outcomes such as divorces. Consider the following:

A 2012 survey found that 92 percent of divorce attorneys reported an increase in the number of cases using evidence from smartphones in the previous three years. Another survey from the group found that 81 percent of divorce lawyers had seen an increase in cases involving social networking evidence over the previous five years (Pilon, 2015).

If the dissolution of a marriage is considered to be the outcome of assessing the quality of a relationship, then the P2P surveillance becomes justified because it allows for an evidence-based assessment of another person or a relationship.

Assessment is therefore a significant rationale for the practice of the different forms of surveillance. However, this process becomes especially important because in many of the cases, especially when the watcher is an institution, the data that is gathered takes on a certain commercial value and the data, and the person the data represents, can be bought and sold in a marketplace.

Surveillance and Commodification

In free market democratic systems there is always competition between institutions for attracting the attention of customers who often have choice in how they spend their resources. This is not only true for commercial interests but can be extrapolated to many different behaviors beyond consumptions. For instance, there is choice in political systems and people are usually free to choose leadership by making informed choices based on the information about the options to choose from. The combination of competition and attracting the attention of people has been the primary motivation for advertising that spans the commercial for toothpaste to the political advertising for Presidential candidates in a country like the USA. The key to attracting attention is the development of appropriate messages that will resonate with the target audience persuading the individual members of the audience to behave in a particular way. As any basic instructions on persuasion would say, the key to successful persuasion is a good assessment of the audience. For a long period of time, this assessment relied on social scientific methods such as market research using questionnaires and interviews where the marketer would be able to extrapolate the characteristics of the audience based on aggregate data collected from presumably representative samples. The extrapolated information would then be used in designing messages that are expected to attract a particular category of the audience. This mechanism offered reasonable results, but the messenger had to work with generalities about the audience without being able to "drill down" into smaller segments of the audience. The opportunity of utilizing surveillance as assessment offered a way to get increasing granular about the audience, thus yielding desirable results in terms of targeted messaging. This is why surveillance, particularly I2P, justifies surveillance as assessment.

With I2P surveillance it is now possible for different institutions to collect data about a person. This is a process that has been accumulating over time as indicated earlier, and it is possible to create a profile of a person, focusing on the specific aspect of assessment that is of importance to an institution. The commercial institutions are able to create profiles where the assessment can lead to highly targeted marketing messages. Even in the early days of I2P data surveillance, in 2012, a major departmental store in the United States "identified 25 products that when purchased together indicate a woman is likely pregnant. The value of this information was that Target could send coupons to the pregnant woman at an expensive and habit-forming period of her life (Lubin, 2012)." This is an illustration of how the data about the customers became commodity that had financial value in helping to circulate an incentive to purchase products. This form of surveillance as assessment is a commercial endeavor and the surveilled data, when assessed to be valuable, yields profits for corporations that are in the business of packaging the surveilled data for buyers as pointed out here in 2016:

Once these companies collect the information, the data brokers package and sell it — sometimes to other brokers, sometimes to businesses — that then use the information to target ads to consumers. And it's a lucrative industry. One of the largest brokers, Acxiom, reported over $800 million in revenue last year (Naylor, 2016).

The process of assessment and commodification is not only restricted to the realm of influencing commercial behavior but can be applied to other vital behavior such as political participation in democratic societies. There have been ongoing concerns with the way in digital networks such as Facebook that has access to personal data, as a product of participants willing accepting surveillance as data collection, are able to influence voting behavior in American elections. The matter came to the fore front at the time of writing this book, in 2020, when there were concerns about the way data surveillance of people by institutions might have been utilized to present political messages that would be customized for the individual. Consider for instance the process where a person's name is considered sufficient data to triangulate information and, as stated by the *British Broadcasting Corporation* (BBC): "buying someone's name can lead to making guesses about their income, number of children and ethnicity - which is then used to tailor a political message for them (Wakefield, 2020)."

Such assessments of personal information are increasingly a part of living in the surveillance ecosystem that has developed worldwide. There are specific commercial interests in the process as well as interests of specific groups that would like to be able to influence the behavior of people by access to the information that is gathered through the surveillance process. When surveillance is justified by the notion of assessment there is also an interest in watching over a length of time. It is often more useful to know how an entity changes over time and then craft messages that would acknowledge the changes. The principle of surveillance over time can be applied to any number of elements of data for a person. For instance, individualized data about health can be used to track the changes in a person's physical and mental condition, and that information could be great value in offering the appropriate treatment or offer the appropriate personalized messages about the way in which the specific individual could take care of personal health. These messages would expectedly change with time and data is collected in a longitudinal manner since a person's age could easily lead to changes in health data. This temporality of the surveillance is especially important when the data shows abnormalities when there is deviation from the norm. At that point, some action is needed to address the deviation.

The need for action is a consequence of surveillance independent of the justification offered for surveillance. Acting on the basis of data is a consequence of surveillance notwithstanding the justification for surveillance. This key consequence of surveillance is creating an intervention to control the action of a person or institution based on the data about the entity. The next chapter examines the notion of control as a consequence of surveillance.

REFERENCES

Curtin, M. (2020, January 9). 54 Percent of Employers Have Eliminated a Candidate Based on Social Media. Time to Clean Up Your Feed (and Tags). *Inc.com*. https://www.inc.com/melanie-curtin/54-percent-of-employers-have-eliminated-a-candidate-based-on-social-media-time-to-clean-up-your-feed-and-tags.html

Dating a guy with no social media is the secret to either true love or a kidnapping, but probably true love. babe. (2018, October 8). https://babe.net/2018/10/08/dating-a-guy-with-no-social-media-is-the-secret-to-either-true-love-or-a-kidnapping-but-probably-true-love-81082

Gewirtz, D. (2013, October 28). Why do allies spy on each other? *ZDNet*. https://www.zdnet.com/article/why-do-allies-spy-on-each-other/

Google. (n.d.). Why you're seeing an ad - Ads Help. *Google*. https://support.google.com/ads/answer/1634057?hl=en

InkLove904. (n.d.). *FanFiction*. https://www.fanfiction.net/u/3935242/InkLove904

Lubin, G. (2012, February 16). The Incredible Story Of How Target Exposed A Teen Girl's Pregnancy. *Business Insider*. https://www.businessinsider.com/the-incredible-story-of-how-target-exposed-a-teen-girls-pregnancy-2012-2

Luong, M. (2012, October 30). College Admissions using social media to evaluate applicants. *Collegiate Times*. http://www.collegiatetimes.com/news/virginia_tech/college-admissions-using-social-media-to-evaluate-applicants/article_e8c06d44-a3d8-5786-b9cf-ff6b17edbb8d.html

Matsakis, L. (2020). Dating a guy with no social media is the secret to either true love or a kidnapping, but probably true love. *babe*. https://babe.net/2018/10/08/dating-a-guy-with-no-social-media-is-the-secret-to-either-true-love-or-a-kidnapping-but-probably-true-love-81082

Naylor, B. (2016, July 11). Firms Are Buying, Sharing Your Online Info. What Can You Do About It? *NPR*. https://www.npr.org/sections/alltechconsidered/2016/07/11/485571291/firms-are-buying-sharing-your-online-info-what-can-you-do-about-it

Pilon, M. (2015). Divorced by Data | Backchannel. *Wired*. https://www.wired.com/2015/06/divorced-by-data/

Pines, G. (2021, May 3). A History of the Passport. *Travel*. https://www.nationalgeographic.com/travel/features/a-history-of-the-passport/

Singer, N. (2013, November 9). They Loved Your G.P.A. Then They Saw Your Tweets. *The New York Times*. https://www.nytimes.com/2013/11/10/business/they-loved-your-gpa-then-they-saw-your-tweets.html

Wakefield, J. (2020, November 27). Your data and how it is used to gain your vote. *BBC News*. https://www.bbc.com/news/technology-54915779

Winerman, L. (2004). Psychological sleuths--Criminal profiling: the reality behind the myth. *Monitor on Psychology*. https://www.apa.org/monitor/julaug04/criminal#:~:text=How%20does%20profiling%20work%3F,murderer%20Jack%20the%20Ripper's%20personality

Chapter 7
The Consequences of Watching:
Controlling the Watched

ABSTRACT

The outcome of surveillance is the ability to use the narratives to understand how an entity behaves. This information offers the opportunity to predict. With the ability to predict comes the opportunity to anticipate the future. Surveillance allows for controlling some aspects of the future. This applies to all the contexts of surveillance discussed.

INTRODUCTION

As suggested as the primary theme of the book, the product of surveillance is numerous different forms of data collected often over a length of time. Independent of the motivation of the collection of information, the data become available for analysis. As suggested in Chapter 2, this information makes up Big Data which creates the narrative profile. This profile is the foundation for most of the consequences of surveillance. It is not the case that the data remains in disparate pieces, but there are specific mechanisms of Big Data analysis that can be used to construct a multi-faceted profile of the person. In this chapter I explore one of the key consequences of the availability of profiles – the ability to control the entity which has been watched and profiled. I begin with a brief overview of the way control has been manifest in our lives with the emergence of systems that can create a "control society." I then offer the connection between control and prediction, suggesting that once there is a sense of control, it is also possible to predict the events that might happen, knowing how well behavior and attitudes can be controlled by manipulation based on the knowledge of the narratives. I then elaborate on the ways in which control and prediction works within the four contexts of surveillance.

Control in Society

History demonstrates that in a structured social system those in power attempt to retain their position of power. This tendency can have many different motivations, but the power offers an opportunity to control the behavior of those who are lower in the power hierarchy. The notion of control is central in any social system because it allows the powerful to retain power and to impose a specific description of the World to everyone the powerful are able to control. In horrific moments of human history, as in the case of the Holocaust during World War 2 of the 1940s and during the terrifying year of 2020 when a pandemic raged across the World, the powerful in societies had tried their best to retain control on people and spaces. The murder of the Jews in the Holocaust was possible because the fascist leaders of Germany under the Nazi rule were able to control the occupied people and territories by sheer military power of terrorizing people as documented in numerous historical treatises. During the pandemic of 2020, the leaders of the United States were unable to control the behavior of the people in the USA leading to America leading the World in deaths from the pandemic in 2020. The example from 2020 is more telling of the way in which control can be considered in the context of surveillance. The example from Nazi Germany demonstrates power that emanates through the barrel of a gun where freedom of choice is eliminated, and any resistance is met with violence thus scaring the powerless from resisting control. The example in the USA demonstrates that controlling human behavior – the simple act of wearing a mask to stem the flow of the disease – can become a challenge in the absence of any direct power to mandate a behavior. In such cases a different form of control is needed that relies more on surveillance than on the display of the power of the gun.

This distinction is important because it also points towards the bifurcations int the theoretical evolution in the way control is imagined in societies. Earlier I discussed the importance of the work of Foucault in understanding surveillance. As a quick reminder, the French thinker presented the notion of being "docile" in the face of a Panopticon system of surveillance. There was no longer the need to discipline and punish those who offended the powerful, but it was sufficient to remind the powerless that they were being watched. That very information is sufficient to control the behavior of the watched entity. This argument by Foucault placed the process of surveillance in the realm of control as opposed to the realm of discipline and punishment. The threat of disciplining via punishment remained in place but the need for punishment would reduce because discipline would be maintained by the watched – and the watched would voluntarily control behavior so as not to attract punishment. The consequence of surveillance therefore is gaining a sense of agreement with the powerful, in the absence of brute force, to agree with what the watcher desires.

Such agreement creates an ordered society where resistance disappears in the face of the demands of the powerful. Writing in the mid-1900s Italian author Antonio Gramsci calls this process hegemony (Gramsci, 1975). Although Gramsci was writing at a time when the World was facing several challenges such as Fascism in Italy and Germany, the increasing distance between the Communist nations and the Democratic nations and the World caught between two wars, his key idea was that the powerful in societies are able to create a worldview – an ideology made up of the ideas of the powerful – and the hegemonic process results in the rest of society agreeing with the worldview. In this situation, there need not be a direct display of power in societies but most people simple acquiesce to a set of practices because they find little space for arguing with the practice. Such practices may not even be beneficial to the person, but the behavior stems from a desire to remain docile and in compliance. This outcome is precisely the consequence of surveillance where the profiles of the watched offer specificity to the watched helping to create a society where control can be exercised to a great deal of precision as I will illustrate here.

It is also this transformation that French writer Gilles Deleuze calls the "societies of control" in moving the conversation away from the "societies of discipline" of Foucault. In the Deleuzian sense of control the focus of control are individuals as opposed to the masses and he states:

The numerical language of control is made of codes that mark access to information, or reject it. We no longer find ourselves dealing with the mass/individual pair. Individuals have become "dividuals," and masses, samples, data, markets, or "banks."

Although writing in 1992, before the rapid integration of digital surveillance in societies, Deleuze was beginning to point towards a key aspect of the relationship between the notion of control and data. In the first quarter of the Twenty-First Century, it is the access to information, or the access to the profile based on surveillance that offers the opportunity of control. Consequently, thinkers such as Foucault, Gramsci and Deleuze, amongst others, demonstrate the intimate relation between the obsession of the powerful to find mechanisms to control the behavior of the entities in a social system. This control, however, is connected with the ability to predict what an entity may do in the future, especially when direct and overt force is not being used to exercise control.

Making Predictions

The scholars who have written about control and society have often approached the issue from a theoretical perspective offering a critique of the consequences of a controlled society. The actual process of control is often not discussed in detail. However, when considered in the context of the methods of surveillance, the process of controlling a society becomes vitally important. It is also the case that the key aspect of control is observed behavior of people. The goal of control is to attenuate behavior in a way that it is aligned with the expectations of those in power. The theories of hegemony suggest that if there is agreement on a set of behaviors then it is likely that the people will do that behavior. The key to the process is the level of likelihood that most people will participate in a behavior and it is possible to predict that likelihood using information about the people who are expected to perform the behavior.

It is possible to make a statistically informed prediction that a certain kind of behavior would be performed by a group of people based on the information available about the group. The premise for this form of prediction is couched in theories that suggest that behavior is the result of a large range of factors such as attitudes, opinions, beliefs, dogmas, demographic attributes, and past behavior. These are usually measurable elements and there is a large network of industries that attempt to measure these elements with the hope of predicting behavior. For instance, democratic societies often rely on political surveys, or polls, that attempt to measure and predict the way in which people would vote. In large democratic countries such as India and the USA these polls take on a sacrosanct value as there is a rush to predict the winners of elections. This prediction is based on data that has been collected by the polling companies that specialize in collecting information from a representative sample of people to estimate the will of the population from which the sample is selected.

Prediction needs data. The process of collecting the data is a process of watching. It may not be the case that the watching is done covertly, but without watching it would be impossible to collect the data and make the vital predictions. For a long period of time, the process of data collection has relied on a survey methodology that attempts to make statistically valid predictions about the behavior of a large based on a sample selected from the group. The sampling process was unavoidable because there would often not be enough resources to watch every member of the group. Typically, the sample would volunteer to answer a set of questions and the data would then be used to make the predictions, within appropriate margins of error. This process started in earnest with the innovation of George Gallup as stated here:

Most modern polls derive from the Gallup method, invented by American George Gallup; This method involves sampling a randomly selected, statistically average group of people. Gallup's first poll, in 1932, correctly predicted a local election in Iowa. Four years later, Gallup went against a more respected straw poll conducted by the Literary Digest, which saw more than two million people return surveys. Based on that data, Literary Digest predicted Roosevelt's opponent, Alf Landon, would win. The Literary Digest was wrong, and Gallup was right; Roosevelt won in a landslide (Rhodes, et. al., 2019).

This description underscores the importance of data in prediction and how the data could well lead to incorrect predictions. The failure in predictions often stems from the fact that the data has to be utilized for estimating to a large group. The process of surveillance in the Twenty-First Century offers certain variations to the process where the prediction can be granulated to smaller groups where the estimates are less prone to error.

Surveillance can offer several major advantages over the polling process. First, with the existing and emerging forms of surveillance it is now possible to watch far more people than was possible with the polling process; secondly, it is possible to watch the larger number of people continuously over extended periods of time and finally, it is possible to watch many more aspects of the watched than what could have been done with the traditional polling process. These factors result in the production of the familiar Big Data which can now potentially drill down to a specific individual. It is no longer the case that it is necessary to generalize to an individual from the characteristics of the group the person may belong to, but it might be possible to watch and analyze exactly what an individual may be doing. The various mechanisms of surveillance produce the vast amounts of data about a single individual and it is now possible to actually predict the behavior of a group by knowing the characteristics of the individuals who make up the group. Prediction in such cases become much more precise as long as there are mechanisms to make sense of the data.

The combination of the data and advanced computing capabilities is now making it possible to take the data at a very granular level and draw conclusions. For instance, there are instances where data scientists are attempting to use machine learning tools to analyze the data and offer predictions where the computing process can be focused on the appropriate data to be able to draw conclusions of future behavior as in the case of the research emerging from places such as the University of Maryland in the USA (Subrahmanian & Kumar, 2017). The concern with the details of the data and its volume is being tackled by developing algorithms, or computation routines, that can parse the data and make precise predictions. In 2015 a team at the Massachusetts Institute of Technology developed a set of computation routines that was used to predict human behavior based on a large set of data points where the data points represented different aspects of the entity for which a prediction was needed. It was reported:

It's fairly common for machines to analyze data, but humans are typically required to choose which data points are relevant for analysis. In three competitions with human teams, a machine made more accurate predictions than 615 of 906 human teams. And while humans worked on their predictive algorithms for months, the machine took two to 12 hours to produce each of its competition entries (Goldhill, 2015).

The quick predictions offer the space for control where the surveillance data can be processed at great speed to create the individualized profiles that would become the foundations for prediction. This process has been around for a while. Predicting behavior based on generalized profiles has been a part of institutions such as law enforcement for a long period of time in certain societies; thus a person of color may be considered to be more likely to commit a crime in a society where they do not wield power, just as predictions are made about people of a particular religion precisely because they belong to a religious group. However, the process of surveillance changes the basis for predictions, where it is no longer belongingness to a group that matters, but the actual behavior of a person is brought into consideration for predictions. Consider the following:

With the goal of personality recognition in terms of analyzing user activity within Facebook, we collected information about the personality traits of users and their profiles on Facebook, hence we flourished an application using API Facebook. The participants of this study are 100 volunteers of Facebook users. We asked the participants to respond the NEO personality questionnaire in a period of 1 month in May 2012. At the end of this questionnaire, there was a link that asked the participants to permit the application to access their profiles. Based on all the collected data, classifiers were learned using different data mining techniques to recognize user personality by their profile and without filling out any questionnaire (Souri et al., 2018).

The strength of the process described here lies in the fact that the people who participated in the study did not have to do too much, such as answer a questionnaire, to offer the data for the predictions. When scaled up to larger populations, it could be possible to collect sufficient information from individuals to be able to make predictions at the level of the individual as in the case of the following example:

DeepSense's CEO, Amarpreet Kalkat, explains that DeepSense is fundamentally different from other AI services in that it doesn't focus merely on aggregating, cleaning and structuring data. Rather, it focuses on using the data it collects to make predictions. Employers thus aren't merely looking backward to figure out if you have something to hide-- they're getting a sense of how you'd act in situations that haven't even happened yet (Thibodeaux, 2017).

The ability to predict and control is thus dependent on the amount and quality of data available to the watcher and that process is specific to each category of surveillance. Each category has different motives for exercising control but eventually a shared consequence is the desire to watch, predict and attenuate what the watched entity could do next.

I2I

The spying context of I2I has historically been able to predict the actions of enemy troops. Given the importance of spying, militaries have always attempted to understand the logic of the adversaries and then best anticipate the move the opponent will make. The work of human spies during war time has primarily been ferreting out the information that could be used to predict the behavior of militaries. That notion extends to I2I surveillance of "friendly" nations as well where the consequence of I2I surveillance is also being able to anticipate how a friendly nation would behave even in peace time. The ability to predict, based on surveillance data, then allows an institution to plan its own activities that would lead to controlling the "enemy" to do much harm. The ability to effectively control another institution is deeply embedded in the data that the surveillance offers, and the analytic methods brought to bear on the data. For instance, one iconic surveillance institution is the Government Communications Headquarters (GCHQ) of Britain that gathers data on communication between different friendly and adversarial entities. During World War 2 the GCHQ had a special set up in Bletchley Park where data analysts would work on coded communication by the Germans. Although there were some doubts about the extent of the contribution of the data gathering and analysis done at Bletchley Park, the work of the people at the location was to predict the movement of the enemy troops so that the Allied troops were able to deal with the Axis with clear prior knowledge. The work of GCHQ continues and the ability to predict based on data has been used in other conflicts that directly involved Britain such as the conflict with Argentina over the Falkland Islands in 1982. It has been noted that, "GCHQ was able to intercept and break Argentine messages, British commanders were able to know within hours what orders were being given to their opponents, which offered a major advantage in the battle at sea and in retaking the islands (Corera, 2020)." There are other such agencies across the world where the nation as an institution is able to conduct surveillance with the express intention of controlling the activities of the watched institution at best, or adjust the activities of the watcher based on the surveillance data.

The same principle applies to other institutions such as private corporations working to make a profit. The ability to predict the activities of a competitor is of great value, not only to thwart the next action of the competition, but to decide internal policy within the institution that is watching. This principle of gathering data to predict the competitor's moves is well stated in a 2014 article:

Former American Airlines CEO Bob Crandall tells Fuld that he encouraged employees at all levels to "watch the competition" and pass along every bit of information no matter how small or how irrelevant it seems at the time. "It's like running a national intelligence network," Crandall says. "If you are running it right, everyone is aware that anything and everything is important, and lots of information trickles up to management. For example, if a ticket agent in Chicago hears from an agent at another airline that the rival airline is looking for additional gate space, she should tell the local manager, who calls the division head, who feeds it up the line. Senior management could then make some guesses about what the rival is up to and could either add flights to use existing gates more intensively or take other action to blunt the success of whatever the rival might do (Yakowicz, 2014)."

This simply points towards the desired outcome of I2I surveillance where the information can become valuable in ensuring success for the watcher while controlling the possible actions of the watched. This notion of data for predicting behavior becomes more sharpened when the watched is not a large entity such as a nation or corporation or a single person.

I2P

The surveillance of a person by an institution has nearly always been designed to predict and control the behavior of the person. From the time that monarchs and states have been able to watch a person, the institutions have been able to leverage the information gathered about the person to influence how the person would behave. The process of watching may not always be a legally sanctioned or an overt process, but as long as there is information about a person, it is possible to predict what the person would do. Over time, the information about a person has become increasingly elaborate and the profile of a person is built on the basis of specific person-level information without the need to classify the person into a specific group to estimate the prediction based on group belongingness. Now institutions know exactly what the person's behavior would be by compiling the data about the person from many different sources.

The possibility of prediction of the behavior of a person stems from several data sets that the process of surveillance gathers about a person. As I have suggested earlier in the book, many different kinds of information are gathered in the process of I2P surveillance based on the reach of the institution doing the watching. An authoritarian state with high levels of technological capability could have far more of a capacity to predict compared to a society where the institutions are weaker and there are fewer abilities to surveil. In all cases the possibility of prediction of the behavior of a person is grounded in understanding the "independent" variables that define the person in terms of demographics, attitudes, past behavior to best estimate, for that person, based on the person's individualized profile, what the person may do next. The most tricky aspect of this process is accurately gauging the reason why a person might behave in a particular way. Even though attitudes and beliefs can be gathered through the process of asking questions and observing the statements made by a person in public and private settings, there is still a gap in answering the "why" question related to the behavior of a person. Once that question can be adequately answered the control would almost automatically stem from attenuating the way a person thinks. This has been the subject of dystopic futures in novels such as *1984* where there is a specially telling moment when the level of the surveillance by an institution is revealed when it becomes clear that the state not only knows all of the measurable and observable aspects of a person but the deeper thoughts of a person. Consider the following:

"You asked me once," said O'Brien, "what was in Room 101. I told you that you knew the answer already. Everyone knows it. The thing that is in Room 101 is the worst thing in the world (Orwell, 1950).

The quote of the person who is about to torture the protagonist mentions the "worst thing in the world," suggesting that it is different for each person who is taken to the room. The ability of an institution to know what the worst thing is for a person is moving to a fictitious point where the process of I2P surveillance reveals the deepest secrets of a person's mind. That information can then be the leverage to control the person.

On a more real note, there are many aspects of the control. When the institution doing the surveillance, the controlled behavior is frequently related to the logic of security as discussed in Chapter 5. However, there are other institutions that are also watching the person as discussed earlier in the book with the objective of assessing the person. In such cases the control is related to more mundane behavior such as making a purchasing decision or voting for a candidate in a democratic system. Yet, the concern with prediction and control is paramount because the data gathered via I2P surveillance allows for customizing messages that would target the person to influence the behavior of the person. Consider for instance, the way in which a private corporation was able to gather data about people and use that information to craft messages that would be directed to specific persons to alter political opinion and eventual voting behavior. In the case of Cambridge Analytica, the corporation was able to use the personal data collected via a game on Facebook and the psychometric data offered sufficient personal information to be able to gauge the political attitudes of the person and develop messages that would use the attitude information to suggest a behavior that would be advantageous to a specific institution.

Indeed, the process of designing customized messages is the key to controlling behavior in free societies where a person may have a choice in terms of what they do. The goal of controlling behavior based on I2P data is to influence that choice and direct the person towards making choices which may not necessarily be advantageous to the person but would benefit the institution that is conducting the surveillance.

This process extends to the historical process of advertising with increasing access to personal data. In the first quarter of the Twenty-First Century anyone who has used the network to seek information using popular search engines such as Google is accustomed to the fact that a search based on a specific interest, such as the search for air fare prices often results in advertising directed at the person for hotels at the destination. This is the result of a technological process, "Online targeted advertisements use data from your browser to make marketing more personalized. Special algorithms then look at your website visits and searches over time to predict your preferences and show ads you may be interested in (Dangerfield, 2018)." The data being referred to are called "cookies" that refer to the activities that a person does using the computer when going to a network to seek information. That activity in turn produces "search data" that indicates what the person is interested in and the combination of these kinds of information become available to the institutions which can then analyze the information to create the messages that hope to influence behavior. The institutions typically have the ability to parse through the volumes of Big Data and create the messages. This process requires sufficient access to resources to analyze and predict placing the institution in a significant position of power over the person. The matter becomes different when the surveillance is done by a person and the watched entity is an institution. The power dynamics tend to shift in P2I surveillance when the person can hope to predict and control the behavior of institutions.

P2I

The notion of control changes in the cases of surveillance when the watcher is a person. The traditional relationships of power that often offer an intrinsic power to institutions over people or over other institutions break down when the watcher is a person, especially watching an institution. There are far fewer mechanisms of controlling the behavior of a government or a large corporation when the change is called for a person. Furthermore, when the watcher is an institution, as discussed all through this book, there are elaborate systems of watching that are put in place in a planned way. These infrastructures of surveillance, from the cameras in a departmental store to the way in which passengers are watched when using public transport, are put in place with significant cost and with a great deal of ongoing support. For instance, in 2012 it was estimated that different institutions in Britain spent nearly $800 Million on cameras to watch the people in public places. Naturally, people do not have such resources to surveil institutions in a systematic and regular way. Consequently, much of P2I surveillance occurs on the spur of the moment and could be a singular event and whatever control of institutional behavior, or response from an institution has to happen in response to such accidental and opportunistic moments of P2I surveillance that has been discussed so far. Overall, the P2I process has not been considered to be a mechanism to control institutional behavior.

The control consequence of P2I is derived from a unique aspect of P2I which does not usually happen with situations when surveillance is done by institutions. The product of the P2I surveillance, such as a video shot by a teenager as in the case of the George Floyd incident discussed earlier, is usually considered the intellectual property of the person who captures the images and thus the content is available for the watcher to use as the person wishes. In many cases these images are then circulated though digital networks. The person may not have the elaborate resources of an institution, such as a police department, but in free societies where there is adequate access to the Internet, images gain power by circulation and acceptance in the public sphere.

The controlling power of P2I is derived precisely from this process of "viralization" where a single image or a short video may become so popular that it derives its power from the fact that millions may have watched the image and thus the P2I surveillance conducted by a single person can become data available to millions. Consider for instance the case of the video that was captured by a passenger on a United Airlines flight in 2018 where a passenger on the flight captured the video of another passenger being forcibly removed from the flight. The captured video was distributed by the person on the Twitter network resulting in thousands watching the video in a short period of time and thousands more propagating the video through other networks (Victor & Stevens, 2017). In a short while the video received so many views that the institution – United Airlines – was compelled to respond. At that moment, I would argue, the person who had captured the video and distributed it, had gained control on the institution eliciting a response. There are other such instances, where institutions find themselves being controlled because of the anticipation of P2I surveillance where the institutions have to face an altered reality of accountability where the actions of the institution is under observation calling for the institution self-controlling its behavior to avoid the negative outcome of being "caught in the act" of doing something that could be considered to be incorrect.

This ability to control institutions has been increasingly recognized and P2I surveillance can become more systematic and organized with intervening institutions making it more convenient for people to watch institutions. The result of the watching is often systematically distributed, forcing the surveilled institution to respond. Earlier I had discussed the example of an institution such as TripAdvisor which offers a powerful example of the way in which intervening institutions facilitate control over other institutions. For instance, in the case of TripAdvisor, which was established in 2000 as a way to gather information from individuals about their experience within the hospitality industry such as hotels, restaurants, airlines and other travel products, the key to the process is that the reviews, which is the product of a person surveilling the quality of an institution such as a hotel, are made available by TripAdvisor to anyone who wants to find information on that particular hotel. This trend has had a significant impact in controlling how a hotel or restaurant conducts itself. Since bad reviews can have significant financial implications, institutions are quick to either correct their mistakes or are compelled to respond to what is being said about them. Sometimes there are concerns over the validity and motive of the reviews, but in general institutions such as TripAdvisor offer a structured approach to P2I surveillance where institutions begin to recognize the significance of the P2I process and remain alert with the goal of controlling their actions.

The value of organized P2I has resulted in most industries facing some form of the P2I process where people are in a position to surveil institutions. When institutions become aware of the process and see that there is both things to be gained and lost by neglecting to respond to the surveillance, there is an automatic move towards self-control of their behavior. In the case of P2I the power to control is primarily derived from the fact that it becomes difficult for institutions to ignore the voice of a person, especially when many unconnected people are simultaneously doing P2I surveillance on the same institution and the outcome of the surveillance is becoming available to a large number of people. The power inequity between people and institutions is disrupted in P2I surveillance because the person watching is continuing to find power through connection with other people.

The situation is a little different with P2P surveillance where the power dynamics shift and control over another person becomes connected with the P2P data and the pre-existing power relations in the context of controlling behavior.

P2P

The notion of control takes on a different notion when it is brought down to an interpersonal relational level with many different vectors of power that work between people. In order to understand the notions of control in the P2P surveillance it is useful to consider the surveillance process through the ways in which normative levels of control can be imposed in interpersonal relationships. The notion of control as a psychological trait that is manifest in behavior took on special attention among researchers in the 1960s and 1970s when different theoretical models were suggested to explain the way in which the need to control manifests in the relationship that a person has with the World that the person lives in. For instance, in 1966 the fundamental interpersonal relations orientation (FIRO) perspective addressed the issue of the need for control where individuals would have the desire to control a situation or a person just as some people are willing to be controlled and are "trusting, respectful, obedient, and willing to serve (Griffin, 2019)." The suggested theories were backed up by research and a systematic understanding of the mechanism of control in interpersonal relationships was crystalized leading to efforts to measure the levels of control a person was willing to exercise and endure. In 1979 researchers were able to develop a reliable questionnaire that would measure, "individual differences in the general level of motivation to control the events in one's life (Burger, 1979)." Utilizing the scale, and through experimental research there was an interest in examining, "the relationship between individual differences in desire for control and interpersonal interaction style (Burger, 1990)." Studies such as these demonstrated that the variability of attitudes towards control had a role in interpersonal relationships and they were manifest in many different contexts such as parent-child, partners, and several other interpersonal relationships (Aaron, et. al., 1992; Cook 1993).

The existing research offers a way to understand the consequence of surveillance in the P2P context where the surveillance results in controlling the behavior of the other person in the relationship. This aspect shows up in the various scenarios of P2P where one person is covertly or openly watching another person. The motivation to watch could be offering security (see Chapter 5) or to assess the quality of the person (see Chapter 6) but the fact that the watched may have a sense of being watched leads to attenuating behavior. Indeed, there is a slew of advice available from legal counsel, especially divorce lawyers, advising a person to watch out for signs of P2P surveillance and offering advice on what to do to avoid surveillance or confront the watcher.

Consider for instance the advice from a law firm in North Carolina, where I live: "If you feel your spouse should be punished for violating your privacy, and especially if you think that your spouse may be a danger to you or to others, you can seek criminal penalties or civil remedies." In such situations the outcome of the P2P surveillance, when discovered, is a new set of behavior on the part of the partner. The same group also offers the advice when a person is 'caught' via P2P surveillance: "Admit to any wrongdoing and seek counseling to repair the damage to your relationship." This is an example that relates the process to the notion of the Panopticon and the production of the docile subject of Foucault. Because P2P surveillance results in the controlling non-normative behavior, a person eventually falls in line with the normative expectations of the relationships.

The movement towards a specific norm is an important way in which P2P surveillance leads to controlling behavior. People usually want to remain within the normative expectation and the increasing prevalence of P2P surveillance is leading to controlling the behavior of another person. The early research of the late-Twentieth Century offers an understanding on why a person may want to control another human being in an interpersonal relationship, and that desire to control manifests in the way various ways in which the control is exercised via P2P surveillance.

Profile and Control

Creating a complete profile of the watched can be considered essential in every instance of surveillance where the result of the process is increased control over the visible and measurable behavior of the watched. It is impossible to assess the efficacy of control until there is some noticeable change. In the world imagined by Foucault, where the subjects of surveillance have become docile, control has been obtained through the Panopticon process. However, until that dreaded docility is obtained, control has to be measured against a particular form of behavior that might have been seen before the surveillance was started. For instance, there is evidence to suggest that the tendency to shop lift reduces when a person knows that there is active surveillance (Hayes & Downs, 2011). However, the effectiveness of the control is predicated upon the accuracy and detail of the profile of the watched entity.

Amplifying and elaborating the profile is directly related to another consequence of surveillance. To achieve control, it is necessary to invade the privacy of the watched. Right from the early days of surveillance, and as suggested frequently in this book, the concern with privacy has become increasingly important as there have been greater inroads of surveillance systems in the everyday lived practices of institution and people. The next chapter explores the ways in which surveillance is resulting in reconsidering the notions of privacy.

REFERENCES

Aron, A., Aron, E. N., & Smollan, D. (1992). Inclusion of other in the self-scale and the structure of interpersonal closeness. *Journal of Personality and Social Psychology*, *63*(4), 596–612. doi:10.1037/0022-3514.63.4.596

Burger, A. (1979). *Desirability of Control Scale*. Measurement Instrument Database for the Social Sciences. https://www.midss.org/content/desirability-control-scale

Cook, W. L. (1993). Interdependence and the interpersonal sense of control: An analysis of family relationships. *Journal of Personality and Social Psychology*, *64*(4), 587–601. doi:10.1037/0022-3514.64.4.587

Corera, G. (2020, October 19). Bletchley Park's contribution to WW2 'over-rated'. *BBC News*. https://www.bbc.com/news/uk-54604895

Dangerfield, K. (2018, March 29). Facebook, Google and others are tracking you. Here's how to stop targeted ads. *Global News*. https://globalnews.ca/news/4110311/how-to-stop-targeted-ads-facebook-google-browser/

Goldhill, O. (2015). An algorithm can predict human behavior better than humans. *Quartz*. https://qz.com/527008/an-algorithm-can-predict-human-behavior-better-than-humans/

Hayes, R., & Downs, D. M. (2011, July 22). Controlling retail theft with CCTV domes, CCTV public view monitors, and protective containers: A randomized controlled trial. *Security Journal*. https://link.springer.com/article/10.1057/sj.2011.12

Mitra, A., & Khosrowshahi, Y. (2018, March 29). Facebook, Google and others are tracking you. Here's how to stop targeted ads. *Global News*. https://globalnews.ca/news/4110311/how-to-stop-targeted-ads-facebook-google-browser/

Rhodes, C. (2019, January 11). *A brief history of opinion polls*. Museum of Australian Democracy at Old Parliament House. https://www.moadoph.gov.au/blog/a-brief-history-of-opinion-polls/#

Souri, A., Hosseinpour, S., & Rahmani, A. M. (2018, August 22). Personality classification based on profiles of social networks' users and the five-factor model of personality. *Human-centric Computing and Information Sciences*. https://hcis-journal.springeropen.com/articles/10.1186/s13673-018-0147-4

Subrahmanian, V. S., & Kumar, S. (2017, February 3). Predicting human behavior: The next frontiers. *Science*. https://science.sciencemag.org/content/355/6324/489

Thibodeaux, W. (2017, November 3). This Artificial Intelligence Can Predict How You'll Behave At Work Based on Social Media. *Inc.com*. https://www.inc.com/wanda-thibodeaux/this-artificial-intelligence-can-use-social-media-to-tell-hiring-managers-about-your-personality.html

Victor, D., & Stevens, M. (2017, April 10). United Airlines Passenger Is Dragged From an Overbooked Flight. *The New York Times*. https://www.nytimes.com/2017/04/10/business/united-flight-passenger-dragged.html

Yakowicz, W. (2014, July 28). How to Anticipate Your Competitors' Next Moves. *Inc.com*. https://www.inc.com/will-yakowicz/great-ceos-keep-rivals-close.html

Chapter 8
The Consequences of Watching:
Redefining Privacy

ABSTRACT

The discussion of surveillance invariably leads to an assessment of the idea of privacy. This is a construct that has been widely debated over time, with some of the early aspects of privacy taking shape in Britain. Later, a Supreme Court judge in America argued for privacy as the right to be "left alone." Over time, the concept has seen transformations with the focus on defining what aspects of the narrative can be considered to be protected. Eventually, every context of surveillance such as I2P and P2I has slightly different considerations of privacy.

INTRODUCTION

Other than surveillance, a major component of this book is the notion of privacy. All through the previous chapters I have hinted at the issue of privacy in the various examples and explanations. It is important to understand the ways in which surveillance works in everyday life before beginning to reconsider the way in which an understanding of privacy is transforming. This chapter focuses entirely on the issue of privacy.

After a brief introduction, I offer a review of the idea of privacy as it has manifest itself over history. This review offers a current description of privacy, followed by the analysis of privacy within the four contexts of surveillance.

To begin with, privacy must be considered in its relationship with the profiles and narratives that become the outcomes of surveillance. Perhaps the most debated outcome of the production of profiles has been the concern with the erosion of a sense of privacy. The product of surveillance is a profile – a story about an entity. The concern is over the way in which the profile can be used to control, and entity as discussed in the last chapter. There is little doubt that the profile offers powerful opportunities of control and the question is whether the use of the profile to manifest the control violates the sense of privacy.

A Brief History of Privacy

There are numerous aspects of this term that has opened it up for discussion throughout the history of human civilization that predates the current concerns with the erosion of privacy with expanded surveillance. Early references to the importance of privacy can be traced to ancient texts including the religious texts of the major religions in the World. There are references to way in which privacy should be conceptualized is also available in the texts related to politics and policy in early civilizations of the World and in the more modern times there has been a greater emphasis on the way in which privacy needs to be codified and often protected.

Religious documents such as the Bible, Geeta, Quran all have references to the notion of privacy where a person has the expectation to be left undisturbed. For instance, a commentator stated the following about privacy and how it is manifest in the Bible:

First, biblical privacy is more about protecting modesty than it is about being able to do what you want without anybody knowing. Modesty compels you to keep your good deeds covered rather than proclaim them on the corner (cf. Matthew 6). Modesty also compels you to keep your body covered, rather than flaunt it (cf. The Bible) (Bayly, 2018).

The issue of keeping the analog body private has been a part of a human desire in many different ways. Muslims would also find such references in the interpretation of the Quran where one commentary claims:

The sanctity of one's bodily privacy is well recognised in Islamic Law. The Quran (24:58) demarcates certain periods in a day which are times of privacy for an individual, and indicates the need for prior permission before one may enter the private sphere of another. These periods are before the prayer at dawn, during the afternoon where one rests, and after the night prayer. This verse also calls upon children who have not yet reached the age of puberty to get accustomed to asking for permission before entering rooms apart from their own (Marda and Acharya, 2014).

Here too the notion of the body is central as would be expected in times when the analog body would be center of attention. This is also why the early thinking of surveillance focused on the body of the watched as compared to the other aspects of a person that are available for surveillance in the Twenty-First Century. This focus on the body is also the reason that the attacks of privacy and the very basis of "being human" is related to keeping the body private by the simple act of covering the body with clothes. Cruelty towards humans often begins with disrobing the body and taking out that very fundamental aspect of privacy. Throughout history, persecution has involved the public humiliation of people through the process of stripping a person of clothes – records go back to the ancient times to events that go on contemporaneously. The notion of the privacy of the body, and the frequent attacks on it, is also seen in the records of the Greek civilization where Pericles is said to have remarked on privacy and surveillance in a speech after the Peloponnesian War:

The freedom which we enjoy in our government extends also to our ordinary life. There, far from exercising a jealous surveillance over each other, we do not feel called upon to be angry with our neighbour for doing what he likes, or even to indulge in those injurious looks which cannot fail to be offensive, although they inflict no positive penalty. But all this ease in our private relations does not make us lawless as citizens (Thucydides, 399 BCE).

In this segment of the speech there is a clear call to honor the private aspect of the citizens of Athens, albeit within the extremely limited definition of who was considered a citizen. The vital issue is that a reference to privacy permeates ancient texts indicating the centrality of the matter in human civilization as codified in social, political, and religious texts. With time, there has been increasing integration of the words in the ancient texts and the development of specific legal codes related to privacy. This is evident in some of the texts that offer advice on ways of life in Hindu texts. For instance, one commentator suggests:

By way of illustration the house building regulations prescribed by it are largely informed by the recognition of a need for privacy. To begin with, a person's house should be built at a suitable distance from a neighbor's house, to prevent any inconvenience. In addition the house's doors and windows should ideally not face a neighbours doors and windows directly. The occupants of the house should ensure the doors and windows are suitably covered. Furthermore, in the absence of a compelling justification, interference in a neighbour's affairs is penalised. Juxtaposed to religious texts that often perceived privacy as a concept driven by the imperative of purity, the Arthashastra is reflective of a secular connotation of privacy (Ahesh and Acharya, 2014).

Indeed, the references to the Hindu notions of privacy is invoked with the debate over the gigantic project of enumerating the information of all Indians was undertaken. Urgent questions about privacy came up as the project was being developed leading to decisions by the Supreme Court of India and one of the judges invoked the Bhagwat Gita to suggest that there was something fundamentally flawed in the way in which the identification scheme had the potential to become unrighteous (Krishna, 2017).

The codification of the notion of privacy, its importance, and its protection, becomes elaborated in the West with the centrality of the English Common Law. Much of the religious and ancient texts point towards the importance of privacy in human civilization but none has gone so far as to establish a right to privacy where there are legal guarantees that an entity has the right, like the right to life, to a clearly described sense of privacy. Moving forward from the ancient period, there have been significant reforms that have changed the relationship between people and the those who govern over people but a clear reference to privacy has eluded such transformations. Consider for instance the comments of a historian who examines the notion of privacy in history:

The English Parliament presented a bill of rights to King William and Queen Mary in 1689. It stands with the Magna Carta as the cornerstone of English liberty. Among other things, it referred to true, ancient, and indubitable rights and liberties of the people. The French have included a declaration of the rights of man and citizens in their constitutions since 1789, guaranteeing the freedoms of speech, religion, and the press and personal security. The right of privacy is implicit in these rights. None of these proclamations prevented individuals and groups from discriminating against those who chose certain religions and political beliefs, but, in the broadest sense, these discriminations were not illegal. The fact that they existed gave emphasis to the need some felt to keep their personal lives private (Shank, 1986).

The key to the treatise above is the "implicit" nature of the reference to privacy. It is simply assumed that privacy is part of the overall package of rights. This may have worked in a period where the threats to privacy were also less widespread and its violation immediately evident without many covert ways of surveillance. The tools used to invade privacy at the scale of contemporary Big Data did not exist and there were far more urgent matters to be considered. Indeed, the conversations about the keen interest in privacy is sometimes considered to be triggered by the development of technologies: "History of privacy makes clear that there is a strong relationship between privacy and the development of technology (Holvast, 2009)." To a large degree, this connection motivates one of the significant moments in the discussion of privacy in the USA with the treatise offered by American lawyers Samuel Warren and Louis Brandeis. The work was published in *The Harvard Law Review* in December 1890 and there are certain striking aspects of the commentary (Brandeis, 1890). The treatises hark back to the British Common Law and connects the issues of privacy with the emerging attacks on information about people. In a way, the treatise is as much about privacy as it is about surveillance, albeit a I2P form of surveillance. Consider, for instance, the concern with the way in which the media was a part of the surveillance process when Brandeis was writing:

Instantaneous photographs and newspaper enterprise have invaded the sacred precincts of private and domestic life; and numerous mechanical devices threaten to make good the prediction that "what is whispered in the closet shall be proclaimed from the house-tops." For years there has been a feeling that the law must afford some remedy for the unauthorized circulation of portraits of private persons; and the evil of invasion of privacy by the newspapers.

The statements about the newspapers of the 1890s could be transplanted to the elaborate methods of surveillance discussed earlier in this book. However, emerging out of this conversation, and occasional legal arguments, is a sense that privacy has to deal with the right to be left alone. This way of looking at privacy was starting to enter the legal space in the United States where the questions of surveillance was being connected with the rights of privacy. In the split decision on the case of Olmsted vs. United States in 1928 there were four judges out of the nine who had dissenting opinions. Eventually, Olmstead was convicted of bootlegging but as a dissenting judge, Brandeis stated:

The protection guaranteed by the Amendments is much broader in scope. The makers of our Constitution undertook to secure conditions favorable to the pursuit of happiness. They recognized the significance of man's spiritual nature, of his feelings, and of his intellect. They knew that only a part of the pain, pleasure and satisfactions of life are to be found in material things. They sought to protect Americans in their beliefs, their thoughts, their emotions, and their sensations. They conferred, as against the Government, the right to be let alone—the most comprehensive of rights and the right most valued by civilized men. To protect that right, every unjustifiable intrusion by the Government upon the privacy of the individual, whatever the means employed, must be deemed a violation of the Fourth Amendment. And the use, as evidence in a criminal proceeding, of facts ascertained by such intrusion must be deemed a violation of the Fifth.

I use the lengthy quote to illustrate the complications that begin to arise with the adoption of technologies of surveillance, in the case of Olmstead it was wiretapping of phone conversations, and the debates about privacy. The deliberations continue to take different pathways and are suspended during the two World Wars, but the matter again comes to global attention after World War 2

The combination of the abuses and invasions to privacy in World War 2 and the increasing growth of surveillance in the post-War period led to continuing global conversations about privacy and the United Nations took a role in the protection of privacy as a part of a larger effort to protect human rights. As stated by a commentator:

From the second part of the 20th century several international legal documents acknowledged the right to privacy as a first generation fundamental human right, which protection then appeared in the national legislations of the countries adopting these documents. These documents do not give further guidance on what privacy is, it is the case law of courts safeguarding these regulations which defines the exact content of privacy and the aspects of life which can be considered private (Luckas, 2019).

The key to these conversations of privacy is the ambiguity related to the notion of privacy while there was a fundamental commitment to protect it. Different documents have found different ways to protect the nebulous idea of privacy. For instance, the 2020 adoption by the European Union (EU) the *Charter for Fundamental Rights* includes

Article 7 which states, "Everyone has the right to respect for his or her private and family life, home and communications." This comes close to a specific description of privacy that includes:

1. Everyone has the right to respect for his private and family life, his home and his correspondence.
2. There shall be no interference by a public authority with the exercise of this right except such as is in accordance with the law and is necessary in a democratic society in the interests of national security, public safety or the economic well-being of the country, for the prevention of disorder or crime, for the protection of health or morals, or for the protection of the rights and freedoms of others.

It is important to note that this document refers primarily to "public authority" and does not explicitly refer to private institutions that are a significant part of P2I surveillance. However, this document of the Twenty-First Century and everything that has preceded it allows for the summarization of some of the key aspects of privacy.

Describing Privacy

The history of the discussions of privacy offer some key descriptors of privacy as it stands in the first quarter of the Twenty-First Century. It is quite likely there will be further changes in response to new circumstances facing people and institutions. For instance, the terrorist attacks on the USA on September 11, 2001, the adoption of a universal biometric system in India starting in 2009, the pandemic of 2020 have all had impacts on the way privacy can be described. However, most commentators agree that there are a few key elements of human life that is expected to remain private: the human body, the space it resides in, the data associated with the body/space, and the correspondence the body has with the World around.

When connected to each other, these elements of privacy can be cast as a story about the entity. As I have shown in the book thus far, an identity narrative or a profile is made up of many aspects of an entity – the analog presence of the entity and its location in space which refer to the "body" and "territory" as suggested by privacy advocates. This narrative also includes the data about the body, much of which is digitized. The narrative/profile of the entity remains in the combination of the body and its data and much of surveillance has been to watch the body and its data. Thus, the consequence of surveillance is to gain greater information about the narrative of the entity.

The way in which the idea of privacy has transformed over time demonstrates that the core relationship between three issues: 1) surveillance, 2) keeping a narrative private and 3) legal protection of privacy. The combination of circumstantial pressures such as terrorism and pandemics are opening up the spaces for greater surveillance. These are both legal spaces where surveillance can be mandated as in the way information was being collected at the time of the pandemic in 2020 as well as the space of public discourse where surveillance became acceptable after the attacks in New York in 2001. The collected information is constantly attempting to construct a narrative of the watched entity that is simultaneously complete and dynamic. This need to obtain the narrative threatens privacy and leads to the consequence of surveillance: shifts in concerns over privacy in each of the four contexts of surveillance.

I2I

Privacy in the institutional setting takes on a legal aspect that is well defined by national and international laws which help to protect institutions from being watched. These laws can also be mobilized when privacy has been invaded and institutions have specific recourses to combat the invasion. These incursions into privacy as a result of surveillance takes on broadly two forms, as discussed so far, the watching of the physical aspect of an entity as well as watching the intangible aspect of the entity. In the case of I2I surveillance the purpose of the watching is to precisely invade the privacy and gather information about the narrative of the entity that is produced at the intersection of all the information that is collected. It is also the case that if the surveillance is discovered ad the invasion of privacy gets too egregious then the watched can respond in a variety of ways.

In the case of private institutions, the most significant protection against the intrusion of privacy are laws that deal with Intellectual Property (IP). These are international laws that protect institutions, and special professions, against the stealth of their creation. Embodied in laws of patent, copyright, trademark and know how, these are laws that offer opportunities to seek legal recourse when it becomes clear that their private institutional narrative has been compromised as a result of surveillance by a competitor. There are numerous instances such conflicts where one institution has utilized some form of surveillance to dig into the IP of a competitor and gained advantages by surreptitiously collecting inside information. In most cases, the result of the invasion of IP becomes visible when the information collected by surveillance is used by an institution in the public sphere. For instance, one of the most visible and expensive such battle over IP infringement of the early Twenty-First Century has been between two giant corporations: "Apple and Samsung settled a seven-year legal fight on Wednesday, ending the most prominent case in a series of lawsuits over smartphone patents over the last decade (O'Connell, 2018)." Although the legal process did not eventually have a huge impact on the kinds of products that became available in the marketplace, the lawsuit demonstrated how the invasion of privacy can become a high-stakes affair when corporate institutions are involved in in I2I surveillance.

The situation becomes a little different when the institutions are not only corporate units usually working for profit. When states and governments enter into the fray of collecting IP or collecting military information, the rules change and the invasion of privacy as a consequence of surveillance becomes more complicated. Indeed, the response to such invasions can lead to outright conflict between nations. The I2I surveillance conducted by nation states is considered illegal and nations can take action against each other when privacy has been breached. Consider for instance the ways in which allegations have been brought about China and its state apparatus for I2I surveillance leading to the collection of the IP narratives of corporations. Indeed, the continuing concern with the ways in which IP is being accessed by other nations has led to the conflation of the IP interests with the national security interests of nations as institutions. For instance, in the case of the

United Sates, it has been noted that, "intellectual property started getting systematically treated as a national security threat to the United States. The scope of the threat is broadly conceived to include hacking, trade secret theft, file sharing, and even foreign students enrolling in American universities. In each case, the national security of the United States is claimed to be at risk, not just its economic competitiveness (Intellectual Property Theft 2016)." This tendency towards treating the invasion of privacy as a risk to a nation opens up different ways in which institutions can respond to such I2I surveillance.

This form of surveillance and the need for information continues constantly and institutions are increasingly more proactive about protecting their narratives from being watched and analyzed. The entire industry of cybersecurity has emerged as a result of the constant threats on digital data and it devolves into a "cat and mouse" game where private information is sought by institutions while institutions attempt to constantly patch the holes through which the watcher can enter. For instance, in 2020, there were reports of I2I surveillance of US private and government institutions where a significant amount of private information was obtained by those who were able to break into the systems. Indeed, it was stated:

If the Russia connection is confirmed, it will be the most sophisticated known theft of American government data by Moscow since a two-year spree in 2014 and 2015, in which Russian intelligence agencies gained access to the unclassified email systems at the White House, the State Department and the Joint Chiefs of Staff (Sanger, 2020).

It is important to note that in the case of I2I breach of private information there may be a semblance of power equity between the institutions where retaliatory surveillance is possible. Thus, if one institution is collecting the narrative of another institution then the victim can retaliate through legal recourse, military options or just counter-invasion of privacy. This balance, however, changes in the case of invasion of privacy as a consequence of I2P surveillance.

I2P

The issue of privacy is most often discussed in the context of the I2P surveillance since this is where the power inequity is considered to be most pronounced. The institutions usually have much greater power than a person, and as pointed out earlier, the institutions often have the motivation based in security and assessment to gather the narratives about people. The consequence is the loss of privacy. This particular aspect of institutional invasion of privacy has become especially important for two key reasons – the increasing covertness of the way in which I2P surveillance occurs and the completeness of the narrative given the amount of information that is being collected and shared amongst institutions about people.

Spying on people has been a part of the way in which institutions have retained control on power and subdued oppositions and challenges to power. It is usually known when an institution is watching a person or a group of people. Assumptions of protection of privacy are abandoned by people whenever there is action that could be considered disruptive to the status quo of an institution. Those who were opposing the institution were fully aware of the fact that their actions would be watched and thus secrecy was a part of the assumed way of life by the people who knew they were being watched by the institution. This presumption changes when the technologies of I2P surveillance expands to the extent that the methods become ubiquitous and "disappear from sight." The process of the I2P surveillance becomes so commonplace that the watched essentially "forgets" that they are being watched and people go about their lives without paying attention to the methods by which they are being watched. This form of surveillance allows for invasion of privacy in a manner where the process is persistent but invisible. Consider the claim that some TVs made in China have a "backdoor" to collect information about the viewer:

Shutterstock application security engineer John Jackson and security researcher "Sick Codes" found after investigating for three months that it is possible to access the file system of Android-based TCL smart TV through an undocumented TCP/IP port via Wi-Fi. Then, hackers can overwrite, collect, or delete files without the need for password or any security clearance(Robles, 2020).

It will require careful investigation to verify whether the allegation is genuine, but this illustrates the way in which institutions are able to enter personal spaces and potentially collect information in a way where the person forgets that information is being collected every time the person uses a tool such a smart speaker or types in words into a search engine on the Internet. The curious aspect of this form of surveillance is not necessarily covert in the sense that it is being done in secrecy but cover only because the tools and the processes have become a fabric of everyday life in the Twenty First Century. This becomes evident in some of the sociological research that suggests that people in certain age groups are less concerned about the privacy issues and are willing to accept the fact that their information is available to others, including institutions. For instance, a study in 2010 claimed:

Results suggested that most people regardless of gender enter full name, facial pictures, hometown and e-mail addresses in their profiles. However, males are more likely than females to disclose mobile phone number, home address and instant messaging (IM) screen names. Consistent with the past literature, youth, especially between the ages of 18 and 22, seem unaware of the potential dangers they are facing when entering real personal and contact information in their profiles while accepting friendship requests from strangers. Recommendations for future research include investigating the levels of awareness young people have when disclosing information about themselves that can potentially harm them in more ways than one (Taraszow et al., 2010).

Studies such as this demonstrate the fact that the invasions of privacy in the I2P context is increasingly becoming normalized.

This acceptance leads to the second aspect of the invasion of privacy in the I2P context – the granularity of the personal information that is being collected. A fairly large list develops when considering the variety of institutions that are collecting narrative information on the different aspects of a person. This was discussed earlier in the book and the concern remains over the level of institutional protection that is offered for the data. In some countries that data is better protected but such protections could be diminished in the face of circumstantial pressures where the private narratives are shared between institutions without overt notice to the individual. Consider, for instance, the way in which the travel to United States requires the sharing of traveler information with the US government as stated:

(2) INFORMATION.—A passenger and crew manifest for a flight required under paragraph (1) shall contain the following information:

(A) The full name of each passenger and crew member.

(B) The date of birth and citizenship of each passenger and crew member.

(C) The sex of each passenger and crew member.

(D) The passport number and country of issuance of each passenger and crew member if required for travel.

(E) The United States visa number or resident alien card number of each passenger and crew member, as applicable (US Government, 1978).

The government document elaborates on the ways in which this information would be shared. Other such situations arise when information needs to be shared between entities for smooth operation of everyday life practices and the private information becomes a commodity that is essential for the functioning of the institutions that essentially serve the people.

In the case of the I2P context, the consequence of surveillance is the constant invasion of the privacy of a person. The reverse happens when people are able to create narratives about institutions using information that is gathered via P2I surveillance.

P2I

The concern of privacy for a person or a group of people who are subject to surveillance has been a matter of debate since institutions have historically had the power to watch people. The possibility of people watching institutions is a comparatively recent process in 2021. Additionally, what is private for an institution is also different from what a person might consider to be private. The privacy of an institution is often connected with its ability to do its tasks and its overall goals. A profit-making corporation would want to protect its market advantage and thus is more concerned with the consequences of the I2I surveillance as opposed to people watching the institution. The I2I process could involve people but such people would be working for another institution and is thus a part of the I2I process. Much of the P2I process is subsumed in the I2I process except in the Twenty First century when the P2I surveillance has become widespread and institutions now have lesser abilities to keep things out of public scrutiny because the people are watching.

The matter for the institutions is not as much about keeping their entire narrative private but to ensure things that happen with an institution remain contained within a limited domain and do not enter the public sphere without the institutions having any control on the narrative. An institution is at great risk of losing public face if the secrets of the institution become exposed to a large audience, especially if that happens as a consequence of P2I surveillance. There is increasing set of evidence for this process as more people are purposefully or accidentally watching institutions and gathering the institutional narrative and making it public. Such wide circulation of the narratives leads to institutions becoming more careful about the way in which the institution would respond when a narrative becomes public. Consider for instance the situation faced by United Airlines when P2I surveillance propagated an event that happened in an aircraft. Without the P2I surveillance, the narrative of the event might have remained confined to the few people who witnessed the event and their immediate contacts. The story would not certainly have been witnessed by a very large international audience without the P2I technologies available in 2007. However, once the relatively private narrative became public, the institution had to quickly adapt to the exposure of the private narrative. In analyzing the situation, it was stated:

United's initial response attempted to downplay this offensive act (relying primarily on differentiation and mortification, but not really apologizing for this offensive act). This stance provoked outrage and ridicule. This study applies image repair theory (Benoit, 2015) to the discourse in this case study. United's CEO, Oscar Munoz, was forced to offer a "do-over," stressing mortification and corrective action that were actually directed to the offensive act. United finally arrived at the proper response, but it came too late to realize its full potential (Benoit, 2018).

This incident of 2007 demonstrated that things could not be kept private for institutions as long as there was some form of P2I surveillance going on.

Other than responding to narratives that have become public, the other response to increasing loss of the privacy of institutions has been the quest for greater transparency so that allegations of obstruction and opaqueness cannot be brought towards an institution. This is the case where institutions such as law enforcement would voluntarily use cameras to keep a record of its work that can be made public. This response, particularly for institutions that work directly with people, is the increasing transparency of information where the question of institutional privacy becomes unimportant, because some institutions such as those belonging to the government in free societies cannot claim to have private information. Consider for instance the various laws that govern the release of information about the government to the public. The Freedom of Information Act of 1967 in the USA, the similar act of 200 in UK and the Right to Information Act of 2005 in India all have the same stated purpose that was enumerated in the Indian version of the act:

The basic object of the Right to Information Act is to empower the citizens, promote transparency and accountability in the working of the Government, contain corruption, and make our democracy work for the people in real sense. It goes without saying that an informed citizen is better equipped to keep necessary vigil on the instruments of governance and make the government more accountable to the governed. The Act is a big step towards making the citizens informed about the activities of the Government (Government of India, 2005).

It is not just a coincidence that these acts, particularly those in the UK and India, are emerging at a point where the process of P2I is expanding and it is becoming increasingly important for institutions to become proactive about making things public as conveniently as possible. The consequence of P2I is not necessarily a threat to privacy as much as it is a need on the part of institutions to manage the narrative by making things more public than before. This is the power that the person has brought to the P2I context. This power continues in the P2P situation where the questions of privacy become some more complex.

P2P

The loss of privacy that results as the consequence of P2P surveillance is the most tricky in terms of the enumerating the kinds of personal narratives that become available to others and the mechanisms that can be used to. To a large degree, as indicated earlier in the book, the bulk of P2P surveillance occurs in the context of people who know each other – parents, siblings, partners, friends etc. The target of surveillance is also very precise and there are clear reasons for the watcher to remain covert. There is also limited access to institutional and legal recourses to challenge the invasion even if the surveillance is discovered by the watched. The process is also very contextual because the description of privacy, and determining what narrative is private becomes related to the context and the culture within which the surveillance occurs. Although there is always an attempt to standardize descriptions of privacy, as illustrated earlier in this chapter, there is also evidence that privacy could be interpreted differently in different cultures and might even be differentially interpreted within a small social group. As a consequence, the privacy laws that refer to the institutional invasion of privacy are governed by specific nations where each set of law is somewhat different from other nations. However, at the cultural level there are differences based on the culture, for instance, it has been illustrated that people in collectivist cultures are more trusting of others than those in individualistic cultures. Studies have shown that the nature of privacy is also differently constructed in different cultures, for instance, one study reported: "results demonstrate an overall lack of awareness of privacy issues and less concern about privacy in India than has been found in similar studies conducted in the United States (Kumaraguru and Cranor, 2006)."

Such differences in the way in which privacy is constructed leads to confusion about the way in which the invasion of privacy can be conceptualized within the P2P context. The key would be to understand the specific dynamics of narrative exchange within the specific contexts of the group which could be as small as a dyad – two people. The impact on invasion of privacy will depend on the existing patterns of narrative exchange within the group, and the invasion occurs only when the group norms are violated. This is further complicated by the fact that the group norms could change with the introduction of new technologies. Consider, for instance, the popularity of tools that keep an eye on a private home by offering automations that is often promoted as creating a smart home which has been described as: "the integration of technology and services through home networking for a better quality of living." These kinds of technologies with array of cameras in the home begins to create an invasion of privacy which becomes acceptable because it fulfils the purpose of providing security and the people being watched are also often the people who set up the watching process. These situations complicate the way in which privacy works in these P2P situations, and it is possible that some members of the group under self-surveillance may not be fully willing to participate in the watching process but have to acquiesce to the group decision. Consider, for instance, a report that claimed:

In-home video cameras can help you keep an eye on your pets or kids—baby monitors come in sharp night vision, after all. Other camera wanters cite surveillance as a crime deterrent or a way to capture evidence if someone does break in. With the possible benefits, those who don't want a camera in their living space often struggle to articulate their discomfort with being watched—to quote one husband, "it's weird and makes me feel weird (Withers, 2019)."

Situations such as these are being reported anecdotally and points towards the uneven acceptance of the invasion of privacy in the P2P context. This is something that will continue to become a point of debate as different people involved in the P2P scenario develop different levels of acceptance of the way in which narratives become available to other people in the group.

All of these different contexts of surveillance lead to a reconstruction of how privacy would be constructed as narratives become available to different watchers.

Re-Constructing Privacy

With the rapid expansion of surveillance justified by providing security (Chapter 6) and assessing the value of the watched (Chapter 7) there will be inevitable erosion of privacy as it had been imagined in the period before surveillance became widespread. That earlier version of privacy is being constantly reconstructed through a debate between the importance of retaining a stable sense of privacy and the advantages that surveillance offers. In this dialog surveillance is not just the notions of covert watching but the ways in surveillance happens at the overt level with corporations collecting data about search terms used on the Internet or a group of friends using applications that help to locate each other's phones. These are different forms of surveillance, but each comes with the added conveniences. Tracking of search terms allows the user to get targeted and relevant information whereas the phone tracking ensures that a group can locate each other quickly. This is the shape of the new privacy where the person or an institution may be willing to rethink the idea of privacy where a diminished privacy may be an acceptable option just as increased surveillance may be acceptable to allow for a more smoother conduct of everyday life in the future.

The next chapter explores some of the tendencies that can be expected in the future of surveillance based on the trends seen at the beginning of a new decade in 2021.

REFERENCES

About Right to Information Act 2005. Right to Information. 2005 Privacy Laws in Different Countries and How to Comply With Them. (2021, May 7). *WebsitePolicies.com*. https://www.websitepolicies.com/blog/privacy-laws-in-different-countries

Ancient History Sourcebook. (n.d.). *Thucydides (c.460/455-c.399 BCE): Pericles' Funeral Oration from the Peloponnesian War (Book 2.34-46). pericles.* http://www.wright.edu/~christopher.oldstone-moore/pericles.htm

Bayly, J. (2018, May 12). Is the Right to Privacy Biblical? *Warhorn Media.* https://warhornmedia.com/2016/04/27/is-right-privacy-biblical/

Benoit, W. L. (2018). Crisis and Image Repair at United Airlines: Fly the Unfriendly Skies. *STARS.* https://stars.library.ucf.edu/jicrcr/vol1/iss1/2/

Holvast, J. (2009). History of Privacy. In V. Matyáš, S. Fischer-Hübner, D. Cvrček, & P. Švenda (Eds.), *The Future of Identity in the Information Society. Privacy and Identity 2008. IFIP Advances in Information and Communication Technology* (Vol. 298). Springer. doi:10.1007/978-3-642-03315-5_2

Identifying Aspects of Privacy in Islamic Law. (n.d.). *Centre for Internet & Society.* https://cis-india.org/internet-governance/blog/identifying-aspects-of-privacy-in-islamic-law

Intellectual property theft and national security: Agendas and assumptions. (2016, March 17). *Taylor & Francis*. https://www.tandfonline.com/doi/full/10.1080/01972243.2016.1177762?scroll=top&needAccess=true

Krishna, G. (2017, September 28). Right to Privacy and the Bhagavad Gita. *Rediff*. https://www.rediff.com/news/column/right-to-privacy-and-the-bhagavad-gita/20170928.htm

Kumaraguru, P., & Cranor, L. (2006). Privacy in India: Attitudes and Awareness. In G. Danezis & D. Martin (Eds.), Lecture Notes in Computer Science: Vol. 3856. Privacy Enhancing Technologies. PET 2005. Springer. https://doi.org/10.1007/11767831_16.

Locating Constructs of Privacy within Classical Hindu Law. (2014). *Centre for Internet & Society*. https://cis-india.org/internet-governance/blog/loading-constructs-of-privacy-within-classical-hindu-law

Lukacs, A. (2016). *What is Privacy? The History and Definition of Privacy*. Academic Press.

O'Connell, M. E. (2018). Enhancing the Status of Non-State Actors Through a Global War on Terror? *NDLScholarship*. https://scholarship.law.nd.edu/law_faculty_scholarship/94

Privacy and Islam. From the Quran to data protection in Pakistan. (n.d.). *Taylor & Francis*. https://www.tandfonline.com/doi/abs/10.1080/1360080830701532043#:~:text=Islam%20gives%20great%20importance%20to,'%20(24%3A27)

Robles, C. J. (2020, November 16). Millions of TCL Smart TV May Be Affected by 'Backdoor' Security Flaw - Here's How to Protect Your TV. *Tech Times*. https://www.techtimes.com/articles/254197/20201115/tcl-smart-tvs-backdoor-security-flaw-experts-find-heres-protect.htm

Sanger, D. E. (2020, December 13). Russian Hackers Broke Into Federal Agencies, U.S. Officials Suspect. *The New York Times*. https://www.nytimes.com/2020/12/13/us/politics/russian-hackers-us-government-treasury-commerce.html

Taraszow, T., Aristodemou, E., Shitta, G., Laouris, Y., & Arsoy, A. (2010, January 1). Disclosure of personal and contact information by young people in social networking sites: An analysis using Facebook profiles as an example. *Latest TOC RSS*. https://www.ingentaconnect. com/content/intellect/mcp/2010/00000006/00000001/art0000

US Government (1994). TITLE 49—TRANSPORTATION.

Withers, R. (2019, November 11). When Couples Can't Agree on Surveillance in the Home. *Slate Magazine*. https://slate.com/ technology/2019/11/relationship-disputes-surveillance-cameras.html

Chapter 9
Looking to the Future

ABSTRACT

The future of surveillance is simply more of it. No entity has any incentive to reduce the level of surveillance. It has value to the watcher. What is expected to change is the amount and the way in which it is done. Trends in the cultural, social, economic, and political landscapes will have an influence on the way in which the different contexts of surveillance will proceed. In addition, it is expected that the technologies of surveillance will get more efficient, making the processes more accessible and invisible to the surveilled.

INTRODUCTION

I have offered a specific look at the process and consequences of surveillance in our everyday lives with a focus on the way in which surveillance is connected with the creation of narratives. The stories of the "lives" of people and institutions have increasingly become relevant to other people and institutions leading to the four main contexts of surveillance as the entities create narratives of each other. Given the focus on narratives, the future of surveillance can also be examined through the same lens to understand how the narratives would be impacted in the future. I consider the importance of the narratives in understanding the future of surveillance since the process of surveillance will have to stay in step with the trends expected in the way in which the narratives would shift with time. Consider for instance the way in which the new technologies have offered aspects of recording the stories that did not exist before some of the tools became available. Many who subscribe to a product called "Google Timeline" and have the GPS active on their smartphones with the Android software receive periodic updates from Google about the places the smartphone, and the person connected to the phone, has visited within a time period. This is a part of the personal narrative which could well be lost with time, but the tracking tool makes it a part of the narrative of a person. Thus, the narrative itself changes with time.

In this chapter I first consider some of the key ways in which the narrative may shift in the future and then consider the ways in which surveillance could transform to stay relevant for the narrative shifts. The narrative shifts are connected with the trends in lived practices and one key component of these practices is related to the cultural space that people and institutions are inserted in. Later in the chapter I would argue that there are other vectors that would impact the lived practices such as the political, economic, and technological contexts, but I begin with what can loosely be labelled "cultural/social."

Cultural/Social

It would be an understatement to state that the cultural and social spaces that most people in the World live in has seen some radical changes starting in the early 1900s. Major global conflicts of two World Wars, realignment of identity narratives with new found freedoms for long-oppressed segments of society including women, disappearance of traditional power structures such as the colonial systems, emergence of new structures of family and increasing fragmentation of monolithic cultures brought the World to the early 2000s when it was becoming clear that the dominant cultural and social motivators were being replaced by a more fractured and provisional notion of culture where not any single set of everyday lived practices could claim dominance because everyday life was constantly being reshaped. It also becomes clear in the 2000s that everyday lived practices – the things we do – is the product of a large set of determinants of which the cultural aspect is only one. There are other interconnected influences such as the political system, economic system, and the tools that are commonplace which also shapes our practices.

It is these practices that are also make up the notion of "culture" as suggested by some scholars where the idea of culture has been released from a focus on "high" culture to the understanding of "popular" culture where the identity narrative of an entity is the product of the things that a person would do, or the things that an institution would consider to be its primary activities. In the future, the change would most likely be in this segment where different people would find that they do different things and thus create the narratives that will be tracked by the processes of surveillance.

The first aspect of the change would most likely be a greater fracturing of the different cultures that make up a specific shared space such as a nation. This tendency becomes increasingly possible from the vantage point of 2021 where the World is seeing sharp divisions. For instance, the events in January 2021 leading up to the finalization of the American Presidential elections of 2020 demonstrate that sharp divisions are becoming evident in the American cultural space which has its political manifestations. People in the USA, and across the World, are increasingly creating a well-defined, or "narrow," narrative identity that is sharply different from the narrative identity of others. These identities are defined by specific cultural practices that are distinctly different from the way others live their life. Consider for instance the question of taking a vaccine to protect against the spread of the virus that consumed the World in 2020. Many have rejected the vaccine that became available in 2021 using the logic: "Americans evaluate decisions to vaccinate themselves or their children, those who strongly embrace Christian nationalism—close to a quarter of the population—will be much more likely to abstain, potentially prolonging the threat of certain illnesses (Andrew L. Whitehead, 2020)." It is such specific behavior patterns that become the defining characteristics of the cultural space and the narratives of the future where behavior is intimately connected with beliefs that are increasingly divergent.

It is quite likely that the World will be looking at greater fragmentation of practices where specific cultural practices will constantly be vying for dominance. No single set of practices may be able to claim and retain privilege for too long in what scholars have earlier called a "post-modern" condition of culture where the stable and universal "truths" become contested and abandoned. Identities based on the stabilities of meanings and truths become replaced with provisional identities that seem to shift with circumstances making it very difficult to discover and describe a singular identity that can be surveilled and "filed" as the identity of the entity. In other words, people and institutions are constantly changing, making it increasingly difficult to know what the identity narrative could be at any moment in time and how that narrative will shift in the future as new circumstances come up.

The pandemic of 2020 has been a good indicator of this process where people and institutions debated about the identity that was centered on the use of the mask. Although there was sufficient evidence to suggest that the use of a mask could slow down the spread of the virus, there were communities of people across the World who rejected the use of the mask using arguments about how the face covering did not align with their narrative of the World they lived in. Indeed, the conflict between alternative narratives about the mask extended to other identity narrative related to religion and politics in some parts of the World. The concern for surveillance is identifying the narrative that is relevant at any moment in time and be able to use the narrative to be able to be able to predict future action of the entities that subscribe to the narrative which implicates all the other practices of the entity. One of the keys such lived practice are the economic activities of an entity.

Economic

By economic lived practices I refer primarily to the things people and institutions do to make and spend money. There are wild variations in these practices based on numerous factors such as place where the people and institutions are located, the political practices of the place, the access to resources available to the entities and such elements that tend to shift with time. However, based on the trends in the first quarter of the 2000s there are indicators that suggest the process of making money for a large segment of the global population of people and institutions will rely on the use of digital technologies that are quickly becoming ubiquitous for large portions of the World. The digitization of the mechanisms of earning revenue would release the dependence on place when it comes to how people work. In the West, the process of 'telecommuting' for people became popular early in the 2000s and environmental influences have made the process increasingly attractive. This has a significant impact on the personal narratives of an individual. The process of "outsourcing" became especially popular in the 2000s when large Multi-National Corporations (MNC) chose to send work away from the West to the rising economies of the East. For instance, numerous companies began to set up locations in India which offered affordable and talented workers who readily worked with Western companies and MNCs because they offered lucrative options. Now the narratives of the people in South Asia became spread across a large space from Delhi to San Francisco as the same person would have multiple presences across different places because the economic imperatives demanded the elasticity in the identity narrative.

Even the kind of work that people would do would become variegated, making it important to track these narratives to understand how the economic activities of earning money are changing. These changes are likely to become more entrenched as global events shape the work of people. In the first quarter of the 2000s, perhaps one of the most significant global events has been the pandemic of 2020 where people were forced to alter their economic practices to respond to the threat to good health. One of the most remarkable change in the economic practice was the "work from home (WFH)" process where people were quarantined and restricted to their homes by lockdowns and curfews and those who could WFH were largely spared the economic calamity that was faced by the those whose work required a "real" presence and not just digital work. It is quite likely that the future would be place where the process of earning revenue may get disconnected from the place where the real body resides. This poses some challenges to surveilling the data and the body when the data may become globalized and the

167

body can disappear into hidden spaces as long as there is access to the global networks. These tendencies also influence the spending practices of the future.

Just as MNCs have spread out globally to find affordable and efficient labor, people and institutions have also realized that there are vast differences between the cost of services and products based on space and method of spending. For instance, things can be ordered using the network from digital dealers and the real products would arrive nearly anywhere in the World. Both people and institutions can take advantage of a global marketplace usually with few restrictions where people and institutions can do economic activities. In such cases it becomes challenging to create the narrative of economic practices because of the large disconnect between the real body as a target of surveillance and the economic activity data that the body is producing.

This disconnect will most probably increase in the future for the segment of the global population who have the resources to participate in the global marketplace. This participation will not just be a factor of financial power – wealth – but would also be closely connected with the ability to negotiate the global marketplace using the available and emergent systems. Thus, it will not necessarily need great amounts of wealth to be able use a semi-smart phone to access an online store and be able to order a product to be delivered to the place. Yet, this activity would generate a large amount of narrative information all of which can be surveilled and used to construct the narratives that can have predictive value in thinking of future of economic activities.

Predicting the future of economic activities is a gigantic industry by itself in the free-market capitalist systems because much of everything else depends on how the economic narrative develops and is presented to the people. The important aspect from the perspective of surveillance of narratives is to understand the overall economic narrative that is available in the public sphere and how people and institutions would be responding in their economic narrative. In addition to the narrative, there are some measurable realities about the economic state of a person or institution that would shape the activities and narratives. For instance, at various points in the first quarter of the Twenty-First Century the World has seen economic downturns that have been marked with loss of the ability to engage in economic activities. Such phases shape the economic system and influences the economic activities.

In spite of the expected variation in the economic health of people and institutions, there is evidence to suggest that much of the economic activities will be happening in the digital space. The use of "cash" as the mechanism for economic transaction, especially for people, may reduce further in the future. This tendency for a "cash less" system is the result of different conditions that arise. Consider for instance the situation in India, the second most populated country in the World with nearly a billion people, when in 2016 the Government of India made vast amounts of paper bills illegal tender and kickstarted a move to digital systems of economic transactions. In a similar way the pandemic of 2020 led to the development of systems of "touch less" payments that would allow people to conduct transactions while maintaining safe physical distance from others. Such moments have increasingly led to situations where some economic transactions can only be done using digital tools. The growth of home delivery of goods often requires a payment that might only be possible in a digital way. The emergent form of transactions is increasingly moving to digital platforms.

This tendency in economic practices has a profound impact on surveillance as the focus of watching shifts to creating the economic narrative of an entity by analyzing the economic data generated by transactions. With the increasing reliance on digital systems for economic activities, the surveillance data would grow in volume and it could be possible to trace the entire life history of the watched entity in terms of the digital economic data produced by the watched. That narrative can then be connected with other narratives such as the political activities of the watched. Much of the political activities have also increasingly moved to digital platforms.

Politics

Political activities since the end of the World War 2 was dominated by the rivalry between the two superpowers – Russia and America – as they competed for influence in every part of the World. This cold war defined much of global politics and spilled over into regional issues such as those in the South America, Middle East, South Asia, and Asia. Within this backdrop, much of the political activities were conducted by nation states that were the institutions that would be engaged in surveilling each other. This alignment was dismantled in the late 1980s with the diminishing influence of the Soviet block of countries and the gradual disbanding of the block itself. Additionally, in the early 1990s and going on for the next 20 years there was the emergence of the non-state entities that took on important political and military importance such as the emergence of entities such as Al Qaeda and ISIS which waged war against the West, particularly the United States. The nature of war changed to terrorism where the target of conflict was not necessarily the military, but civilians as demonstrated in numerous attacks on urban centers such as New York, London, Madrid, Jerusalem, Mumbai, and Delhi. This also altered the way in which surveillance worked with the watched entity becoming far more difficult to isolate and watch. The eventual discovery of the Al Qaeda leader, Osama Bin Laden, who was hiding out in Pakistan demonstrated the way in which the nature of conflict and politics would change.

Simultaneously in the early part of the Twenty-First Century there was the increasing appearance of nationalist populist movements in many parts of the World where the people of the nations selected leaders who represented a ultra nationalist position that would border on isolationism, retreat from global affairs, and producing a privileged class within nations that would dominate the national and global politics. In such cases the leadership would need to remain vigilant of the people in their own nations to continue to retain power, within the guise of a democratic system, or sometimes even by willing to abandon the democratic system as was the case of the one-term American President Donald Trump. These tendencies create a different set of requirements for institutional surveillance which is far more inward looking as compared to observing the political activities of the enemies outside national borders.

This trend in politics is likely to continue because even in democratic countries the people are increasingly dependent on political information that has transferred to the digital realm where digital networks are beginning to dominate the information space. When considering political history, there has often been a focus on considering the politics of people in leadership because much of the narratives are built around leaders and politicians. This is history that was narrated in biographies, documents, and the institutional media. The access to digital information, particularly from the non-institutional authors, will change the way politics would operate in the future.

A good example of the centrality of the digital networks appeared in the way in which the beacon of American democracy was called into question in 2021 when a mob of thousands attempted to disrupt the peaceful transition of power from Trump to Biden. This mob was made up of common people who fully believed in a series of political falsehoods that were constructed by a few unethical authors and then distributed through digital networks. Yet these lies became the "reality" for those who attempted to capture the politicians within the US Capitol Building in Washington, DC. This act, and other such acts such as the persecution of Muslims in some parts of India and the persecution of Hindus in some parts of Pakistan, or the clashes in Hong Kong that dominated the period of latter part of the 2010s represent the future of political action where the information for making political decisions would come through digital networks without any verification of the authenticity of the information. This process will require a different kind of surveillance that is not only watching the people who make up the political leadership but also the ways in which different political narratives are being distributed in the public sphere with the use of emergent technologies.

Technologies

There are several technological changes that futurists have pointed towards for the next decades. Amongst them, some are relevant to the way in which surveillance of narratives could evolve over time. The first tendency is the greater availability of digital devices within large parts of the global population. It is no longer the case that the people of the countries that have been labelled as "developed" are the only ones with access to digital devices. For instance there are projections that indicate that the number of cell phones worldwide will go over

17 billion by 2024. Not only will there be an explosion of devices, but these will also be connected to the global network.

There is no doubt that the reach of the Internet is constantly expanding. Much like other utilities such as electricity, data access is becoming increasingly ubiquitous. The pandemic of 2020 and the accompanying restrictions to movement accelerated the reach of the network. Many different tools including traditional cables to satellite connections were rapidly developed to send data to hard to reach places. This access to the network will also come with some specific benefits and burdens. While the access will allow people to connect, it is also the case that the access will remain in the control of institutions such as private corporations or the government. This pattern of ownership could have some significant impact on the way in which the access is regulated.

The combination of the ubiquitous digital device and persistent connection to the Internet will also foster a reliance on centralized depository of data. Although there are some discussions about the possible growth of "edge" computing, the reliance on the centralized data storage, often called the "cloud," is not expected to diminish. People and institutions will increasingly rely on the cloud to store data as well as to analyze the data. This transformation will allow for the digital device to become more of a conduit for the cloud as opposed to a self-contained computing device. Thus, as any user of voice assistants on smartphones know, many of the systems ceases to function without access to the Internet. This shifting of the data storage and processing demands to the cloud will allow for the shrinking of the size of digital devices which can now be implemented in many different things.

The incorporation of the fundamental digital device, the multiprocessor or the chip, into things will allow for the growth of the Internet of Things (IoT) where everyday objects will be connected to the Internet, even if the object has no digital characteristics. The ability to develop an IoT system will continuously generate data about the thing and the people who use it.

All of these changes would lead to the generation of enormous amounts of digital data that would be made up of different kinds of information that could include discursive data such as the utterances of a person to numeric data that records all the measurable attributes of a person or institution. This data will be analyzed in many different ways to extract narratives that will be extremely detailed as tools based in Artificial Intelligence (AI) are brought to bear on the data to extract as much information as possible. When such databases get connected to each other the narratives become even more detailed and it is these narratives that will become the substance of surveillance in all the different contexts. Each of the four contexts of surveillance is expected to develop in different ways within the emerging cultural, political, economic, and technological contexts.

I2I

Looking at the situation in 2021 there is a realignment of the global order with sharp divides between nations along with the populist movements in democratic countries such as India and America, the rise of life-long political leadership in countries such as Turkey and Russia and the growing influence of China across the globe. Superimposed on that are the threats of domestic and international terrorism. These conditions will call for increasing drive towards watching what nations and non-state groups are doing. The primary argument for I2I will be national security to keep a watch on the way in which various institutions can pose a threat to any nation. This process will most likely rely increasingly on collecting data about other countries through advanced technological means where the need will be to deploy technologies by nations to create the threat narratives that face a country. These methods would utilize the available and emergent technologies to disrupt national systems and collect national data. This form of I2I is sometimes also called cyber warfare where the line between "war" and "spying" gets increasingly blurred since the process of conducting the surveillance can actually be disruptive enough that it becomes tantamount to war. Consider for instance the events in 2018 as explained here:

In June 2018, a cyber espionage campaign by Chinese group of hackers targeting two United States-based satellite firms was exposed, whose fundamental motive was to seize military and civilian communications of the victim nations. The hackers intentionally infected the systems, along with regulating the satellite to change the positions of the orbiting devices and disrupt data traffic (Hore, et. al. 2021).

Although the situation is characterized as actions of hackers – a term that has often been romanticized within the technology community as amateurs on the edges of technology – in the case of China it is actually institutional technologists who have a specific aim to watch and disrupt. The outcome of such I2I processes will be increasing vulnerability of data which becomes the currency of I2I systems. This trend was demonstrated again in 2020 when it became clear that the United States became the subject of I2I data intrusion as reported here:

The attackers penetrated federal computer systems through a popular piece of server software offered through a company called SolarWinds. The threat apparently came from the same cyberespionage campaign that has afflicted cybersecurity firm FireEye, foreign governments and major corporations. The system is used by hundreds of thousands of organizations globally, including most Fortune 500 companies and multiple U.S. federal agencies, which are now scrambling to patch their networks (Johnson, 2021).

This particular example also points towards another trend that would operate at the commercial level where the increasing economic competition between private corporations, and in some cases states see the increasing need to watch each other to gain a market advantage.

The focus of the commercial I2I will also be data as there is fierce competition to produce goods and services that are quite similar but the corporations would want to maintain the market share by incorporating things that the competitor is doing. I discussed this earlier in the book and the institutions will find an increasing need to watch the innovations of the competitor, where the innovation is primarily data about the inventions and developments. There is increasing concern that the methods of industrial I2I will be on the rise and corporations may not be fully ready to address the concerns as pointed out here:

Companies are investing in R&D to secure competitiveness in their fields but efforts to counter industrial espionage does not match these actions resulting in serious monetary damages. Industrial espionage cases regarding intellectual property is on the rise due to this indifferent attitude of companies (IEEE).

The processes then get connected with the changes in the way industry is operating with increasing reliance on the IoT and other interconnected tools that make data vulnerable for covert observation. This is a condition that some have warned of in thinking of the Factory of the Future (FOF) as stated here: "The increasing degree of connectivity in factory of the future (FoF) environments, with systems that were never designed for a networked environment in terms of their technical security nature, is accompanied by a number of security risks that must be considered (Sanger, 2020)." The key to the process is the interconnection between system and the incorporation of the systems with the global network. The future I2I process will constantly seek ways to infiltrate the databases to gain commercial advantage. In the murky World of interconnections and attacks on data it might even be the case that attributing the I2I surveillance to a specific institution might become difficult as was the case in 2020 when one of the major developers of the vaccine for COVID-19 were not even sure who was surveilling them and what form of data was accessed as reported here:

The two companies said they had been informed by the EMA "that the agency has been subject to a cyber attack and that some documents relating to the regulatory submission for Pfizer and BioNTech's COVID-19 vaccine candidate" had been viewed. Such documents could be extremely valuable to other countries and companies rushing to develop vaccines, experts said (Stubbs, 2020).

The ability of institutions to utilize technologies to surveil each other can also be used effectively to watch people and it is quite likely that the I2P process will follow some of the trends that may be seen in the I2I processes.

I2P

The future of I2P will also be influenced by the need for institutions, both state and commercial, to gather data on people. The changes in social systems will perhaps produce new perceived sources of threat where specific groups of people would be considered to be of greater risk triggering greater amounts of surveillance. The contexts will keep changing because the threats will depend on the dominant hegemonic systems where the state as an institution could assume that certain categories of people pose a greater risk. For instance, in the USA, the events of 2020 described earlier, from the murder of George Floyd to the attacks on the US Capitol in 2021 produced new threat centers and law enforcement has declared that there are new groups of people who need to be watched more carefully. Consider for instance the following situation where the Federal Bureau of Investigation was following specific people connected with the militia by surveilling the data that the perpetrators were producing:

Throughout the summer, there was chatter in the militia world about clandestine meetings going on to discuss "constitutional flashpoints" – when and how the various factions might take a coordinated stand on pet issues such as gun rights, lockdowns and mask mandates, or the imagined invasion of leftist "looters and rioters." But the movement is diffuse, and rife with infighting and suspicion. One militia leader said he stopped attending big gatherings because they often turned into "bravado" about revolution in a room that's likely under surveillance (Allam, 2020).

Societal changes other than threats of violence would also trigger greater deals of I2P surveillance where many different kinds of data about a person would become the focus of state watching to understand how a person might become a threat to others or to oneself. The pandemic of 2020, and threats of future pandemics [] has triggered situations where different kinds of data about a person is being connected together to ostensibly reduce the severe outcomes of such public health events and perhaps even prevent things from getting completely out of control.

A notion of "contact tracing" that remained within the specialized work of public health systems suddenly became prominent as some countries demonstrated that the process of I2P surveillance had favorable outcomes with respect to the pandemic of 2020. For instance, one of the most successful mechanism of I2P worked in Taiwan where the I2P surveillance became a matter of survival and a collaborative event as stated here:

The whole country voluntarily partnered with the government to create a protean network of databases in which information flows both from the bottom up and from the top down. To make new online and offline tools for fighting the virus, "hacktivists," developers and citizens have been collaborating with the government on vTaiwan, a sort of online democracy town hall and brainstorming site. One tool, for example, prevented a run on face masks by mapping where the stocks were and allocating them wherever they were most needed. By involving people in the solutions, rather than just dictating policies to them, the process is transparent and inspires trust, even civic pride (Kluth, 2020).

The nature of I2P will perhaps change as people begin to see the usefulness of sharing data. This change will also be accelerated by the fact that more people will be generating more data. Turning again to the context of the global pandemic of 2020, there was a need to restrict movement, and some people were able to work from home (WFH) and this process required new levels of digital involvement where different types of data would now be digitized and be available in the cloud. This caused some concerns about the level of personal data that was becoming available to commercial institutions that were facilitating the WFH process. In the early days of the pandemic, when many people had to adopt virtual meetings there was concern that the meeting data, which was now all digital, would become available to institutions. For instance, there was a concern in the West about a corporation that became leaders in providing a platform for digital video communication: "The California-based firm has come under heavy scrutiny after three U.S. and Hong Kong-based activists said their accounts had been suspended and meetings disrupted after they tried to hold events related to the anniversary of China's Tiananmen Square crackdown (Goh, 2020)." Although such suspicions needed greater verification, it was the case that in December 2020, the FBI did lodge a complaint against Zoom:

FBI agents in a criminal complaint unsealed Friday in a Brooklyn federal court, highlights the often-hidden threats of censorship on a forum promoted as a platform for free speech. It also raises questions about how Zoom is protecting users' data from governments that seek to surveil and suppress people inside their borders and abroad (Drew Harwell, 2020).

The temptation of collecting data of people to control behavior would be an ongoing tendency in the I2P context. This process would be facilitated by the fact that people are disclosing data at an unprecedented rate, and the IoT and cloud technologies are distributing the data across the networks which is open observation by the institutions that provide services to people. However, the access to data generation tools by people, and the simultaneous access to data collection tools would also have an impact on the two contexts of surveillance where the person is the watcher: P2I and P2P.

P2I and P2P

There would most likely be two major factors that would alter the way in which the P2I process would evolve in the future. The first is technological where the access to digital devices that are connected to the network would explode. As indicated earlier there will be billions of such devices that would have the capability of creating and distributing messages. Additionally, the familiarity with such devices will also change and more people, of many different strata of society, will be able to use these devices thus gaining a voice in the public sphere. In the 1980s scholars such as Spivak had asked whether the subaltern has a voice and even when Websites were beginning to become popular it was clear that many segments of society who were traditionally silenced were gaining a voice (Mitra, 2001). This phenomenon has been on the rise as the newer generations such as the millennials have emerged as digital natives whose familiarity with the technologies have become a natural part of their lived experience. These are the people, armed with their digital devices, who are now the watchers in the P2I context of surveillance. They will be able to capture any moment they want and circulate their narrative bits, narbs, instantly for many to see. Alternatively, in the P2P context they will be able to keep a record of their surveillance findings for appropriate use when they want to use the narrative. Their access to multitude of narratives would become ubiquitous and these permanent narratives would circulate endlessly within the cloud making things tricky for who they are watching, either institutions or other people.

The second key factor that will drive the change is the cultural imperative. In a World that celebrates increasing diversity many marginalized segments are beginning to be empowered because of the access to the technologies. This results in greater accountability for institutions which might have been the reason for the marginalization to begin with. People in the oppressed groups can now point out the inequities with greater emphasis and to a wider audience when such inequities are meted out by institutions. In this book, I have frequently used the example of the George Floyd killing demonstrating how that P2I surveillance resulted in a global call for greater equities in the way law enforcement treats minorities in different cultural and political systems. Such P2I surveillance could increasingly increase posing challenges for institutions whose "hidden" narratives of unequitable treatment may begin to come to light because of the P2I surveillance. The process would also begin to take on global relevance because the cloud cannot be easily regulated and when narratives that result from P2I surveillance reach the cloud, institutions often lose control on the narratives. This process began to gain attention as early as the early 2010s when events such as the uprisings in Egypt, sometimes called the Arab Spring, became known to the World because of people captured the institutional actions and created the people's narrative that triggered worldwide attention. This "viralization" of the narratives that result from P2I surveillance would possibly be the most notable feature of the suture of P2I.

A similar trend could also be noted in the P2P surveillance where the inequitable distribution of power in more intimate social units – families, couples, friends – could be challenged as more people are able to watch each other. The results could take different forms in the future. On one hand there could be greater degree of accountability on the part of people in the social units to explain their actions to each other. Domestic oppression could take on a different form where the narratives captured through P2P surveillance can call on people to be able to interrogate the actions of those with whom there are intimate connections. Such challenges could result in greater equity within intimate groups.

The P2P process could also leak into the cloud and the public sphere where the narratives produced from the P2P surveillance ends up entering the public sphere with possible results that can vary from mere embarrassment of seeing a unflattering picture on digital networks to more severe consequences. Consider for instance the following outcome of a narrative that results from P2P surveillance:

Do as I say, not as I do.

A Massachusetts teenager who publicly shamed her mother for attending the Capitol riot said her mom was "brainwashed" by the MAGA movement and lied to her — telling her daughter she was going to visit an out-of-town doctor.

Helena Duke, 18, went viral Thursday after she tweeted a video of a woman being punched in the face during the violent pro-President Trump protests in Washington, DC, Wednesday, with the caption: "hi mom remember the time you told me I shouldn't go to BLM protests bc they could get violent...this you?" (O'Neill, 2021).

There could be a trend in situations such as this where the line between the contexts of surveillance begins to get blurred in the future with many of the different forms of surveillance, as categorized in this book, may become further variegated creating unexpected outcomes of great consequence.

Looking to the future it would appear that the processes of surveillance will only expand with new technologies being deployed at all levels of surveillance. This would most likely be coupled with the increasing need to do surveillance by all different entities from institutions to people. The combination of social and cultural shifts and the ubiquity of tools that can be used for surveillance will produce a condition where all the motivations of surveillance will become important to all the different groups who can be watchers. The prevalence of surveillance would become so commonplace and persistent that it is likely that it will simply disappear from sight. People and institutions would simply expect to be surveilled and it could call into question the theories that Foucault had suggested – the docility of the people being watched. It might be that it would no longer matter that one is being surveilled and entities would act in the way they would want. This became evident in the riots at the US Capitol in 2021 when the criminals who stormed the building were not deterred by the fact that they knew they would be captured on numerous cameras, and their digital presence would be investigated. The process of surveillance as deterrence to "bad" behavior may become increasingly irrelevant, especially as different segments of society feel empowered. The question that could become important would focus on the relevance of surveillance itself and its original motives will begin to shift.

Increasingly, surveillance will be about narratives where the process would be geared towards the collection of narratives about entities and creating detailed profiles where the watcher would know much about the watched. Even though the power relations between the watched and the watcher may begin to alter, the fact will remain that there will be elaborated narratives some of which could become instantly available in the public space given that watchers would have access to the tools that would circulate the narratives in the public space. The watched may not even care about the narratives that are out there, and counter-narratives will be generated and circulated based on counter-surveillance leading to a constant regression of the "truth" as has been suggested in the 1990s by scholars who argued for the instability of meaning as multiple narratives offer multiple structures of reality that will compete for audience attention and credibility. It is precisely the numerous mechanisms of surveillance that will create this situation of a heteroglossia of voices that will clamor of relevance. The eventual reality will be akin to the condition that was described in the book *1984* written in 1949 where the proverbial "Big Brother" is always watching using the "telescreen" and just like the people in the novel, there will be eventual normalization of the presence of the cameras and other watching systems.

Many are concerned with this eventuality and groups across the World, in 2020s, are concerned about privacy and truth and are seeking ways to combat this rhizomatic panopticon. In the last chapter, I offer some indications of how it might be possible to live within a system where narratives become currency and how that wealth can be managed by people and institutions.

REFERENCES

Allam, H. (2020, October 9). Michigan Domestic Terror Plot Sends Shockwaves Through Militia World. *NPR*. https://www.npr.org/2020/10/09/922319136/michigan-domestic-terror-plot-sends-shockwaves-through-militia-world

Andrew, L., & Whitehead, S. L. P. (2020). How Culture Wars Delay Herd Immunity: Christian Nationalism and Anti-vaccine Attitudes. *SAGE Journals*. https://journals.sagepub.com/doi/full/10.1177/2378023120977727

Classification of Industrial Espionage Cases and Countermeasures. (n.d.). *IEEE Xplore*. https://ieeexplore.ieee.org/abstract/document/9070418?casa_token=zWIFW1iZd9YAAAAA%3AdRLYU2a75mXDF51AygKVh-1_SGYkzbyvbmfsIqGx-LIEp728c5ZKzznwftUnbxIHyorXKyFceg

Drew Harwell, E. N. (2020, December 19). Federal prosecutors accuse Zoom executive of working with Chinese government to surveil users and suppress video calls. *The Washington Post*. https://www.washingtonpost.com/technology/2020/12/18/zoom-helped-china-surveillance/

Goh, B. (2020, June 11). U.S. lawmakers ask Zoom to clarify China ties after it suspends accounts. *Reuters*. https://www.reuters.com/article/us-zoom-video-commn-privacy-idUSKBN23I3GP

Hore, S., & Raychaudhuri, K. (2021). Cyber Espionage—An Ethical Analysis. In M. K. Sharma, V. S. Dhaka, T. Perumal, N. Dey, & J. M. R. S. Tavares (Eds.), *Innovations in Computational Intelligence and Computer Vision. Advances in Intelligent Systems and Computing* (Vol. 1189). Springer. doi:10.1007/978-981-15-6067-5_5

Johnson, K. (2021, January 6). U.S. formally links Russia to massive 'ongoing' cyber attack; scope of hacking unclear. *USA Today*. https://www.usatoday.com/story/news/politics/2021/01/05/u-s-formally-links-russia-massive-cyberattack-hack-ongoing/6552803002/

Kluth, A. (2020). *Bloomberg.com*. https://www.bloomberg.com/opinion/articles/2020-04-22/taiwan-offers-the-best-model-for-coronavirus-data-tracking

Mitra, A. (2001). Marginal Voices in Cyberspace. *SAGE Journals*. https://journals.sagepub.com/doi/10.1177/1461444801003001003

O'Neill, J. (2021, January 8). Teen shames 'brainwashed' mom who got punched in face at Capitol riot. *New York Post*. https://nypost.com/2021/01/08/teen-shames-mom-who-got-punched-in-face-at-capitol-riot/

Stubbs, J. (2020, December 9). Hackers steal Pfizer/BioNTech COVID-19 vaccine data in Europe, companies say. *Reuters*. https://www.reuters.com/article/ema-cyber/hackers-steal-pfizer-biontech-covid-19-vaccine-data-in-europe-companies-say-idINKBN28J21V

Chapter 10
Living While Being Watched

ABSTRACT

The process of surveillance has now become a part of our everyday lives. It is futile to expect that an entity would not be surveilled. It is also quite likely that there will be interest in greater opportunities to surveil others. In these situations, there needs to be better awareness of the ways in which surveillance occurs and to remember that the object of surveillance is the narrative, which is to some extent in the control of the surveilled entity. At the same time, the watcher needs to consider what needs to be watched and make the appropriate arrangements of watching. In the end, the key to surveilling is to do it in a stealthy way, without it being discovered that surveillance is happening.

INTRODUCTION

The processes of surveillance in contemporary societies is not about to suddenly disappear but is expected to increase and be more pervasive in everyday life. The consequent questions of privacy as discussed in this book will also remain in the forefront, perhaps with heightened legal arrangements for the protection of an altered sense of privacy. There may also be technologically efficient modes of watching where the fact that one is being watched recedes out of sight. However, for people and institutions who remain aware of the processes of surveillance there may be new tendencies to both watch and to evade watching.

In this chapter I reiterate the importance of narrative and how it is constructed by the subject as well as by others watching the subject. I then offer a set of pragmatic concerns related to the decision of engaging in surveillance and understanding the different ways in which we can be cognizant of the surveillance we all experience. This awareness applies to an overall understanding of the technologies and the systems of surveillance and knowing when and how to be aware of the surveillance process. Most importantly, it is to remember that true surveillance is a covert process and the most important thing for the future watcher is to do it without coming into view.

I would suggest that within the four contexts of surveillance that I have laid out here, the common factor is the narrative. The object of surveillance is eventually the story related to the entity being watched. This story is the combination of all the elements I have suggested earlier ranging from the mundane act of purchasing vegetables with a credit card at a grocery store to complex acts of subterfuge to conceal a nuclear testing by a nation. All these acts of people and institutions make up the narrative and any conversations about surveillance will need to focus on how much of the narrative is being captured through the process of surveillance. In the dystopia of *1984* George Orwell had painted a picture where every aspect of a person's life story is under observation and the idealized surveillance system is indeed like the 1988 film called *The Truman Show* where a person's entire life story is pre-designed by a television network and the life story becomes an endless serialized TV show for the voyeuristic pleasure of the audience. The film offers a glimpse into the way in which institutions might be able to create an environment where every aspect of the story of the person is controlled and surveilled without any knowledge by the individual. Indeed, the narrative of the person is so well managed that the person never even realizes that the narrative is indeed being managed. This makes the narrative crucial. Any entity that can capture the narrative, and eventually manage the progression of the narrative gains immense power over the entity whose narrative is being managed.

The conversations about surveillance and the issue of privacy need to consider that eventually what needs to be managed by the watcher is which aspect of the narrative is available to surveillance. The dystopic perspective is that every aspect of the narrative is available to be seen. While science "fiction" may lead to such consequences, it is still possible, in free democratic societies, that narratives can be managed to allow for some concealment of parts of the narrative. This centrality of the life story is also recognized by the watcher whose goal is to observe every aspect of the life story and erode away the means of concealment and management. It is therefore a tug of war between how much of the story must be hidden and how much gets revealed.

At the same time, there also needs to be attention paid to how the narrative is actually generated. People and institutions do things – these are the lived practices – and a record of these events could easily be the basis of the narrative that is being surveilled. Simultaneously the narrative is the product of the level of the choice in constructing and circulating a narrative. In some cases a person or institution might have a significant of choice and in some other cases the choice might be very reduced as discussed in the next two sections.

The Personal Narrative

In a system where there is sufficient knowledge that one is being watched, it is possible to take on the "docility" suggested by Foucault and create a narrative that complies with the "normal" and thus the watcher finds no reason to censure or pay additional attention to the surveilled entity. This is a condition where the watched entity retains agency on the construction of the narrative and can utilize that agency to the comply, defy, or create a false narrative that is designed to be surveilled.

The complete resignation to compliance with the expectations of the watcher is the dystopic future where a person or institution abandons choice and feels that the pervasive surveillance demands compliance. Earlier in the book I have offered examples from fiction where protagonists would do exactly what they are expected to do and are constantly aware that they have only limited control on their own narratives. In such cases a grand narrative for a society or system is in place and the only option is to comply because anything else would lead to retributions. This is the condition where no one can veer from the expected norms of behavior especially since they know that they are constantly being watched. This compliance was witnessed during the pandemic of 2020 when some societies demanded compliance with certain norms such as the use of the mask and anyone caught veering from it would be punished. Consider for instance the way in which a city in France adopted the surveillance cameras to detect people who were not in compliance:

Many artificial intelligence (AI) innovations are being adopted worldwide in the rush to stop the spread of Covid-19, and use of these tools, under emergency laws, has raised the alarm about possible invasions of privacy.

The French surveillance system does include an automatic alert to city authorities and police where breaches of the mask and distancing rules are spotted (BBC, 2020).

Knowledge of the system is akin to the original concept of the Panopticon where a person has lost agency on the narrative of the self and must comply to avoid possible punitive action from the watcher. Indeed, this example is derived from a democratic "free" society whose history is steeped in defiance of authoritarian monarchies and often considered one of the birthplaces of the notion of personal liberty.

When faced with the loss of control on the narratives, one option is to defy and create an alternative narrative that would also be observed by the watcher. The consequences of creating a defiant narrative may not be good for the watched, but that act of defiance might actually become the only way in which the watched can feel empowered in the face of persistent monitoring of their narratives. This is the way in which the surveilled offers a narrative to the watcher leading to a crisis on the part of the watcher about the proper response to the narrative. There are numerous examples of this process where surveillance may show that a person or institution is actively creating a narrative that goes against the grain of the expected norms of a social system. Consider the attack on the US Capitol in 2021 when the insurrectionists actually utilized the fact that they were under I2P surveillance by cameras and through monitoring of voices in digital networks and created a defiant, albeit contestable narrative. The extended quote below demonstrates the way in which narratives of defiance can be created for the watcher and then circulated with the full knowledge that the narrative is being surveilled:

One of the defining images of the Capitol siege was of a man dangling from the balcony of the Senate chamber. Clad in black and with a helmet over his head, he might have been hard to identify even after he paused to sit in a leather chair at the top of the Senate dais and hold up a fist.

But Josiah Colt made it easy. He posted a video to his Facebook page moments later, bragging about being the first to reach the chamber floor and sit in Nancy's Pelosi's chair (he was wrong). He used a slur to describe Pelosi and called her "a traitor."

A little later, the 34-year-old from Boise, Idaho, posted again. This time, he sounded more anxious. "I don't know what to do," Colt said in a video he'd soon delete but not before it was cached online. "I'm in downtown D.C. I'm all over the news now."

Colt was far from the only one documenting the insurrection from within last Wednesday in Washington. Many in the mob that ransacked the Capitol did so while livestreaming, posting on Facebook and taking selfies, turning the seat of American lawmaking into a theater of real-time — and often strikingly ugly and violent — far-right propaganda (Coyle, 2021).

While such narratives of opposition can be created in the face of persistent surveillance there is another way in which agency can be exercised to create narratives.

Earlier in the book, in reference to the I2I context of surveillance I had used the example of the Indian nuclear program which created a deceptive narrative for the American satellites which were watching the nuclear test site in India. This is a strategy that could well become the norm as there is greater concern with the way narratives are being surveilled. With agency on the creation of narratives given the tools available to many people it is possible to create a false narrative. Consider for instance a relatively ubiquitous tool called the Virtual Private Network (VPN) that makes Internet services believe that you are in a particular location, e.g., America, whereas one is physically in Brazil. While VPN is an useful tool to access resources that are restricted to specific physical places it is also a way of confusing surveillance systems that attempt to create a narrative by examining the Internet Protocol (IP) address of a digital device assuming that the real person using the device is located in the place indicated by the IP address of the device. However, VPN hides that part of the narrative as stated here:

There are many reasons to hide yourself online. IP addresses can be used to discern your physical location, and can sometimes do so with remarkable accuracy. These addresses also act like personal identifiers, a little like a phone number, letting advertisers and adversaries track you online. They can also be used to launch targeted attacks against you.

You may even be hiding from a watchful or oppressive government. Journalists are especially likely to hide their IP addresses when they're reporting in dangerous areas or on sensitive subjects. Of course, I'm not encouraging anyone to break local laws, but I do want people to know how to keep themselves safe, should the need arise (Max Eddy is a Software Analyst, 2018).

There are thus different ways in which one can retain control on the surveilled narrative. Yet, there are moments when that control is completely lost because the narrative is actually created by others where the watched entity has no sense of agency.

The Story Told by Others

While the life stories of people and institutions are frequently narrated by the entities there are numerous cases where the entities do not have any control on the narratives. Agency disappears because others actually capture and tell stories. These stories might not be the product of surveillance, but merely captured and circulated without the intent of "watching" but these narratives become a part of the corpus of information that can be used to construct the narrative that becomes the object of surveillance. These are narratives that remain a part of everyday life, especially in the age of access to technologies, which can either not be avoided or are essential for the conduct of everyday life. These are narratives that are captured by people and institutions about other people and institutions and remain essential for the functioning of many aspects of current way of life. These may come about as a result of changes in the way that life activities function as things change.

These are narratives that include many different aspects of life, and I will highlight a few to illustrate this process. A vital aspect of the narrative is the financial narrative of a person or an institution. The increasing digitization of everyday financial activities require the construction of a financial representation. In the face of enormous changes such as demonetization in India in 2016, the adoption of work from home practices across the World in 2020 and move to digital consumer activities using tools of online shopping a large amount of data is being accumulated about financial behavior. Consider for instance the 2016 situation in India where the government made a unilateral and surprise decision to declare that some of the paper money in India would no longer be legal tender. As result, a country that relied heavily on a "cash" economic system was catapulted into the digital age of online transaction. Within four years, by 2020, independent of the location and status, a person could perform most of the essential functions of everyday economic life using a smartphone and several different forms of online platforms for economic activity. Every single such activity would be recorded and stored. Other than disengaging from economic activity, most people in India did not have a choice to not create a financial narrative. People had lost agency on the narrative, and there was no way to not have the narrative if one wanted to live a normal life. These narratives may not be immediate objects of surveillance but when needed such narratives could be drawn up to start watching a person or institution.

A similar situation can also be traced for the narratives related to the health of a person. The pandemic of 2020 demonstrated that there is a constant need to capture the whereabouts of a person and the health-related behavior of people to control the spread of the disease. New narratives needed to be constructed, where a person would have no choice about the narrative and lost agency. These narratives became required parts of everyday life to be able to live through the narrative. History will tell if such loss of narratives would become a part of everyday life even after the pandemic may have been brought under control. For instance, many academic institutions made it a requirement that every member of the institution tell a tiny life story every day to be allowed access to essential resources. In such cases the data would not necessarily be used for surveillance but can readily be accessed if it were necessary to construct the narrative of a person. Here too the person loses agency on the narrative.

A final instance where a person loses agency occurs when an entity, usually a person, would be in a situation where "friendly" watchers would unwittingly construct and circulate narratives that eventually become a part of the life story that is the object of surveillance. Since the early days of digital networks such as Facebook, there have been instances where a picture captured and circulated by a friend becomes the narb that is included in the corpus of the surveilled narrative and can lead to unpleasant outcomes. In such cases the narrative is entirely out of control of the subject and it might be impossible for the subject to ever correct a narrative. This becomes a confusing realm of narrative production because the lines between deliberate surveillance and simple curiosity become blurred when the narrative which is produced as a result of curiosity suddenly becomes P2I surveillance with enormous consequences as was the case with the George Floyd situation. At another level, personal narratives that were circulated digitally could be the reason for institutional consequences because institutions would consider the data in making decisions. Consider for instance the way in which the perpetrators of the attack on the US Capitol of 2021 were censured for their act of insurrection:

A day after the riots, a direct marketing production company posted a statement on its website: "Navistar Direct Marketing was made aware that a man wearing a Navistar company badge was seen inside the U.S. Capitol on January 6, 2021 during the security breach. After review of the photographic evidence the employee in question has been terminated for cause (O'Kane, 2021)."

This is a tendency that is likely to continue as there are more ways in which the narratives spin out of control and people and institutions have to struggle with keeping the narratives under control. As a result, there is greater need to understand the way in which the narratives would be used by other people and institutions. I have explained that process all through the book, but it is useful to summarize it to develop some preliminary strategies of action to manage how the narratives are used.

Who is Interested in the Narrative?

As indicated in this book, there are numerous entities that are interested in collecting narratives for different reasons. An important step in managing the narrative is to keep in sight the different interest groups who would be interested in constructing a surveilled narrative. As shown in the book, people, and institutions, have different groups who want to collect the narratives. The four categories of surveillance show that for institutions there are other institutions who seek out the story of their competition – be it military or financial. Thus institutions need to remain vigilant and continuously monitor the ways in which their stories could be examined by other institutions. This could mean periodic survey of the way in which the narratives are protected and watch for different ways in which narratives may be surveilled. Most institutions do that in a regular way to protect their interests from prying eyes. There are different ways in which institutions, large and small, can exercise this protection. Consider the following advice for small businesses:

A simple video monitoring plan for the front entrance and back entrance or loading dock will yield information about who is coming and going into and out of your business premises occasionally, regularly, legally and illegally. A card-swipe access system for your company's sensitive areas creates an electronic trail that can be audited and analyzed at any time, far superior to the memory of the person at the security desk (Cardenas, 2017).

There can be much more elaborate ways of monitoring intrusion, but the premise of such steps is to acknowledge that institutions are surveilled. It is a mistake to think that an institution is immune to surveillance and that awareness that other institutions would not be watching could be led to expensive outcomes.

This awareness could be extended to conditions where institutions must also be conscious of the fact that they are being watched by people as well. The increasing empowerment of people with digital tools, as discussed earlier, should sensitize institutions to the fact that they could become subjects of surveillance by people at a moment's notice. This may not necessarily translate to a docility on the part of institutions, but it must mean a persistent awareness that mistakes and transgressions on the part of an institution can become public rapidly. There needs to be strategies to address the outcome of such inevitable P2I surveillance where the institutions must assume that their narratives are being watched.

The same strategies apply to people when they are the subject of surveillance. As the book makes clear, there are numerous groups interested in the narrative of individuals. There is an uncanny similarity with the Panopticon model in the current technologically-facilitate all around surveillance of a person where the narratives are actively sought. Much like the institutions, when people become complacent about surveillance there is the inevitability that their narratives become accessible to many. Therefore, there is a constant need to "look around" and see the different entities that are constantly watching a person. The pervasive nature of this surveillance often makes it "disappear from sight," but as indicated in this book, that ubiquity of surveillance is precisely what makes it successful and alarming.

While people and institutions attempt to understand who may be interested in the narratives, it is also the case that the people and institutions are also constantly seeking narratives through the process of surveillance. Thus an important aspect of managing the process of surveillance is also decide whose narratives would be sought by those who are in the act of surveilling others.

Does Anyone Need to be Watched?

The fact that surveillance processes have become so elaborated with the "Pan" part of the theoretical "Panopticon" expanded to the extent that nearly any entity can be watched, it is important to consider how to decide about who needs to be watched. From a privacy-centric perspective, it can be argued that in open and free societies, no person should be the subject of surveillance; and in an idealized place free of conflict or competition, it can be argued that no institutions should be the subject of surveillance. However, as the practice of everyday surveillance happens as discussed in this book, there is constant surveillance with the attempt to create useful narratives. In such cases and given the reach of the "opticon" decisions need to be made about what entities should attract enhanced watching.

The decision of who to watch can be sought in the motivations of surveillance – security and assessment. Those entities that can be perceived to be a threat are often selected to be the subjects of surveillance. The tricky aspect of this process is arriving at an acceptable description of what is considered a threat. There can be multiple descriptions that may shift with time and circumstances. Certain institutions could suddenly be perceived as a threat when the relationships change or there are points of inflexion with vital events. For instance, the attack on America in 2001 catapulted groups such as the Al Qaeda to a heightened threat level requiring special surveillance of similar groups. The pandemic of 2020 made certain categories of people, those with reduced immune responses, subjects of special surveillance to ensure the safety of their health. Instances such as these demonstrate that there can be a need to collect specific sets of narratives at different moments in time. These needs lead to the development of specific surveillance systems that would create the most complete narrative of the selected threat.

Simultaneously, narratives are needed when there is a call for increased assessment of certain entities. In this case the subjects of surveillance alter based on the requirements of assessment. There may not be a specific threat profile attached to a narrative, but there may be a curiosity about the narrative to understand what the narrative says about the entity. This is a more benign process of surveillance where the watcher is principally interested in knowing more of the value of the watched and as the watched entity goes through changes the focus of the surveillance shifts.

Overall, as described in this book who is being watched keeps on shifting, but there is always an argument that can be made for watching certain entities. When managing the surveillance process it is safest to assume that any entity is open for surveillance. In a similar way, there will increasingly be a need to identify who needs to be watched. This is especially true within the P2I and the P2P conditions.

Who Do You Want to Watch?

The rationale for watching from the perspective of the person is often based in the same logics as in the case of the institutional watcher – security and assessment. However, the nature of security and the kind of assessment is nuanced by the relationships that a person may have with other persons and institutions. Thus, if a person decides to engage in a personal act of surveillance there are some important aspects that need to be considered as to who would be watched and under what circumstances.

The focus of surveillance – who – in the case of the P2I and P2P is often determined by the access the watcher has with respect to the subject. Unlike institutions which often have financial and legal abilities to cast a far-reaching net on who can be watched, the personal watcher always remains somewhat limited in the scope of watching especially in the P2I context. However, within those limitations a reasonable rule of thumb is to watch institutions that can have a direct impact on the person. Thus the academic institution where the person pays to receive an education has a direct effect on the life of a person, similarly if a person is employed by an institution, that could become the focus of attention, there are also instances where a person may choose watch an institution that may have a vital impact for a short time, such as a hospital where a person is receiving care. Generally, such institutions can become the object of surveillance and a person may actually have sufficient resources to do such surveillance. On the other hand, there are many institutions that are of tangential value to the lived experience of a person, and there makes little sense to surveil such entities, and it could be difficult for a person to find the opportunity to watch institutions such as the military establishment of a country or other similar institutions where the surveilled narratives may be of little immediate value to the person. Finally, in the P2I context, a person might do opportunistic surveillance where a person could chance upon institutional events where the narrative may be of great import and is accidentally captured by the person, calling into question the acts of an institution. I would argue that such form of surveillance could be of great value in assessing how an institution operates and presents specific narratives that might call into question the institutional narrative. Such conditions, as in the case of the George Floyd incident, are particularly important moments of surveillance and a person might actually be the trigger for vital movements in society.

Selecting the target for P2P surveillance is a somewhat trickier prospect since there are frequent pre-existing relational contexts that need to be considered in such selection. These could be connections that are based in family, such as father and son, or connections that develop between people as in the case of romantic partners. One of the key considerations is the effect that P2P surveillance may have on these relationships. Especially if the nature of surveillance remains covert there are significant dangers to how an existing relationship would be transformed if and when the narratives discovered through surveillance become public or when the subject realizes that the person is a subject of a watching eye. Any pre-meditated P2P act must take into consideration how a target would respond to the P2P act. Consequently, the selection should be based on a basic risk assessment as to what are the risks related to the act of surveillance which must be balanced with what are the rewards gained from the narrative that emerges from the act of surveillance. To some degree the same principle should be applied when overt surveillance is done in the P2P situation where the subjects are aware of being watched. That awareness can lead to erosion of the relationships and could indeed become a barrier to forming relationships. Thus, it is especially important to consider the relationships when planning to conduct P2P surveillance.

Along with the considerations of who needs to be watched and who should be selected for watching comes the aspects of managing the technologies of surveillance when thinking of the ways in which narratives would be gathered as well as managing technologies if one wants to reduce the chance of being watched.

Managing the Technologies

When considering the managing of the surveillance, either as the watcher or as the watched the key concern has to deal with the tools of surveillance. The different tools have been discussed earlier in the book, but here I highlight some of the ways in which the tools can be managed to influence the narrative that is produced by the surveillance process. This management is predicated on the fact that the narrative is composed of data where the data is generated by the various tools and devices that are frequently used by people and institutions.

There is really no feasible way to operate in the society of the first quarter of the Twenty-First Century without generating data and needing access to data. Especially after the pandemic of 2020, the reliance of remote work facilitated by the digital network has produced gigantic amounts of data recording vast traces of the activity of people and institutions. As indicated in Chapter 9, this process is only going to become magnified in the future. The management of the narrative stems from acknowledging that the generation of data will not cease, but there may be ways in which the amount of data generated can be slightly minimized by strategies where people can alter behavior just slightly to reduce the data footprint. Consider, for instance, the process of making a small purchase, such as a cup of coffee at a coffee shop. Generally, a large number of customers choose to pay using some form of a cashless option. As indicated earlier, that payment is added to the corpus of data that composes the narrative of the person. This could be avoided by a payment where cash is used to complete the purchase. This act does not create a data point for the person because the transaction is not connected to the person and is only a part of the narrative of the institution which must show that the transaction has happened. In some cases, such as buying from the unorganized section of an economic system such as a street vendor, the cash transaction may not be the part of the narrative of any entity. The strategy is simply to reduce the digital traces and thus diminish the amount of data that is being added to the narrative.

The main step in this process is to recognize when and how data is being generated. This mindfulness is the key to managing the narrative. The tools for surveillance surround us and the access to surveillance tools is also widespread. It is important to recognize that the tools are constantly able to generate and circulate data and the management of the tools needs to be geared towards prioritizing data in terms of what could be considered from the perspective of both the watcher and the watched. The emerging surveillance system calls for familiarity with the data collection systems and being constantly mindful of the processes.

Being Aware

In *Alien Technology* I had made the argument that there is an increasing tendency for people to become alienated from the technologies that surround them because the tools have become so complicated that it is impossible for most people to fully understand how the tools work. On the other hand, the tools have also become ubiquitous – disappeared from sight until they do not function – making technologies a natural part of everyday life. In many cases people do not even notice the existence of the technologies until they stop working. For instance, in most of the developed nations availability of electricity is taken for granted until something happens to shut down the electrical grids. In many ways the crucial tools of surveillance – from institutional tracking systems to personal smartphone cameras – are becoming ubiquitous. Most people know of their existence or use the tools without always being connected with the consequences of using the tools. The notion of technological alienation suggests that there are different levels of alienation and most people are unaware of how the technology works or its intended and unintended outcomes as long as the tools perform in the way expected.

Yet, there are those in all societies who are aware of how the tools work. Indeed, there are several levels of alienation – some who are completely unaware to those who are experts. This stratification of alienation produces a system where the alienated remain powerless in the technological ecosystem as mere subjects of the system whereas those who understand and work with the technology can wield an unusual amount of power on the alienated. Even though the power is not usually abused, there are numerous instances, as in the case of surreptitious surveillance, where those "in the know" can watch the rest with the watched, because of their alienation, is completely unaware of what is going on around them. For instance, any departmental store in much of the World is now equipped with numerous surveillance cameras which the shoppers do not even notice, but those cameras could be constantly capturing the move of every person in the shop. Those who control the cameras are able to exercise power on those for whom the surveillance camera technology has become ubiquitous. This differentiation is an important factor to consider when managing the surveillance environment.

It is increasingly important to become aware and mindful of the surveillance systems that have become commonplace. Being alienated is a dangerous way to be because there is then little knowledge and understanding of exactly what kinds of narratives are being produced by others about a person or an institution. It is vital that people and institutions become aware of the ways in which their lives are being altered, and perhaps controlled, by the those who understand the surveillance technologies. This reduction of alienation would offer a way out of the "docility" that results from the realization that there is persistent surveillance but without fully recognizing how it happens and what it does. While resistance to surveillance to retain privacy may be becoming increasingly difficult, it does not mean that there should be direct acquiescence to surveillance.

There are indeed two possible pathways to the future of surveillance. One is the alienated population who have abandoned any ability to understand the surveillance process and have agreed that the only way to be is to constantly abandon privacy. The numerous dystopian futures describe this system demonstrating how the sense of freedom of the self can be rapidly eroded as the systems of surveillance completely overtake the individual liberty especially in the I2P and P2P situations. Here all narratives are exposed and always available for scrutiny by the unalienated who design and operate the systems of surveillance and the observed merely becomes subjects whose lives are open books to be read and analyzed the watcher.

This dystopia can be avoided by greater awareness of the systems of surveillance and the rationale and consequences of the surveillance process. Sometimes, the collective "good" may require a level of surveillance that must be put in place as in the case of securing the skies after the attack of 2001 in the USA and the global pandemic of 2020. The key to the success of such systems is an abundance of transparency about how and why the surveillance must be done. An informed public sphere can offer cooperation in the surveillance process because there is an understanding of the process. Simultaneously, when the level of alienation is reduced, there is greater degree of regulation of the surveillance process with the constant scrutiny of the balance between surveillance and the need to preserve a sense of privacy.

It is vital to keep an eye on the tension between levels of surveillance and the erosion of privacy. The future healthy society would be one where mindful people, with clear knowledge of the surveillance systems, becoming a part of deciding how the surveillance process must work for a greater level of benefit that goes beyond the narrow purposes of surveillance as is often the case now. As pointed out in this book, surveillance is not just about the tools and systems, but it is essentially a way of producing detailed narratives and this aspect of surveillance needs to be in sight as we create a more robust and productive surveillance society.

REFERENCES

BBC. (2020, May 4). Coronavirus France: Cameras to monitor masks and social distancing. *BBC News*. https://www.bbc.com/news/world-europe-52529981

Cardenas, H. (2017, November 21). How to Prevent Corporate Espionage. *Small Business - Chron.com*. https://smallbusiness.chron.com/prevent-corporate-espionage-48433.html

Coyle, J. (2021, January 11). A theater of propaganda: The Capitol, cameras and selfies. *AP News*. https://apnews.com/article/us-capitol-siege-social-media-e65c4283c48c8b57509ec6522ec578f6

Max Eddy is a Software Analyst. (2018, January 26). How to Hide Your IP Address. *PCMag India*. https://in.pcmag.com/old-encryption/102427/how-to-hide-your-ip-address

O'Kane, C. (2021, January 13). Some people are out of their jobs after images of them at Capitol riots appear online. *CBS News*. https://www.cbsnews.com/news/capitol-riots-people-lose-jobs/

Compilation of References

About Right to Information Act 2005. Right to Information. 2005 Privacy Laws in Different Countries and How to Comply With Them. (2021, May 7). *WebsitePolicies.com*. https://www.websitepolicies.com/blog/privacy-laws-in-different-countries

Allam, H. (2020, October 9). Michigan Domestic Terror Plot Sends Shockwaves Through Militia World. *NPR*. https://www.npr.org/2020/10/09/922319136/michigan-domestic-terror-plot-sends-shockwaves-through-militia-world

Althusser, L. (1977). *Lenin and philosophy, and other essays: transl.from the french by ben brewster*. Monthly Review Press.

Ancient History Sourcebook. (n.d.). *Thucydides (c.460/455-c.399 BCE): Pericles' Funeral Oration from the Peloponnesian War (Book 2.34-46). pericles*. http://www.wright.edu/~christopher.oldstone-moore/pericles.htm

Andrew, L., & Whitehead, S. L. P. (2020). How Culture Wars Delay Herd Immunity: Christian Nationalism and Anti-vaccine Attitudes. *SAGE Journals*. https://journals.sagepub.com/doi/full/10.1177/2378023120977727

Andrews, J. D. (1982). The structuralist study of narrative: its history, use and limits. In P. Hernadi (Ed.), *The horizon of literature* (pp. 99–124). The University of Nebraska Press.

Aron, A., Aron, E. N., & Smollan, D. (1992). Inclusion of other in the self-scale and the structure of interpersonal closeness. *Journal of Personality and Social Psychology*, *63*(4), 596–612. doi:10.1037/0022-3514.63.4.596

Barthes, R. (1975). *S/Z* (R. Miller, Trans.). McMillan.

Bayly, J. (2018, May 12). Is the Right to Privacy Biblical? *Warhorn Media*. https://warhornmedia.com/2016/04/27/is-right-privacy-biblical/

BBC. (2020, May 4). Coronavirus France: Cameras to monitor masks and social distancing. *BBC News*. https://www.bbc.com/news/world-europe-52529981

Benoit, W. L. (2018). Crisis and Image Repair at United Airlines: Fly the Unfriendly Skies. *STARS*. https://stars.library.ucf.edu/jicrcr/vol1/iss1/2/

Black, D., Berkenfeld, D., Silverman, L., & Corrado, M. (n.d.). Focal Length: Understanding Camera Zoom & Lens Focal Length: Nikon. *Nikon.* https://www.nikonusa.com/en/learn-and-explore/a/tips-and-techniques/understanding-focal-length.html

Brunon-Ernst, A. (2016). *Beyond Foucault: new perspectives on Bentham's Panopticon.* Routledge Taylor & Francis Group. doi:10.4324/9781315569192

Burger, A. (1979). *Desirability of Control Scale.* Measurement Instrument Database for the Social Sciences. https://www.midss.org/content/desirability-control-scale

Cardenas, H. (2017, November 21). How to Prevent Corporate Espionage. *Small Business - Chron. com.* https://smallbusiness.chron.com/prevent-corporate-espionage-48433.html

CBS Interactive. (2004). Abuse At Abu Ghraib. *CBS News.* https://www.cbsnews.com/news/abuse-at-abu-ghraib/

Cheng, A. (2019, November 21). Amazon Go Looks To Expand As Checkout-Free Shopping Starts To Catch On Across The Retail Landscape. *Forbes.* https://www.forbes.com/sites/andriacheng/2019/11/21/thanks-to-amazon-go-checkout-free-shopping-may-become-a-real-trend/#5dc1b9c5792b

Classification of Industrial Espionage Cases and Countermeasures. (n.d.). *IEEE Xplore.* https://ieeexplore.ieee.org/abstract/document/9070418?casa_token=zWIFW1iZd9YAAAAA%3AdRL YU2a75mXDF51AygKVh-1_SGYkzbyvbmfsIqGx-LIEp728c5ZKzznwftUnbxIHyorXKyFceg

Cook, W. L. (1993). Interdependence and the interpersonal sense of control: An analysis of family relationships. *Journal of Personality and Social Psychology, 64*(4), 587–601. doi:10.1037/0022-3514.64.4.587

Corera, G. (2020, October 19). Bletchley Park's contribution to WW2 'over-rated'. *BBC News.* https://www.bbc.com/news/uk-54604895

Coyle, J. (2021, January 11). A theater of propaganda: The Capitol, cameras and selfies. *AP News.* https://apnews.com/article/us-capitol-siege-social-media-e65c4283c48c8b57509ec6522ec578f6

Curtin, M. (2020, January 9). 54 Percent of Employers Have Eliminated a Candidate Based on Social Media. Time to Clean Up Your Feed (and Tags). *Inc.com.* https://www.inc.com/melanie-curtin/54-percent-of-employers-have-eliminated-a-candidate-based-on-social-media-time-to-clean-up-your-feed-and-tags.html

Dangerfield, K. (2018, March 29). Facebook, Google and others are tracking you. Here's how to stop targeted ads. *Global News.* https://globalnews.ca/news/4110311/how-to-stop-targeted-ads-facebook-google-browser/

Darrin. (2020, March 3). How To Catch a Cheater: Tips from a Private Investigator. *North American Investigations.* https://pvteyes.com/private-investigator-tips-on-how-to-catch-your-cheating-spouse/#:~:text=If%20you%20find%20that%20you,it%20gets%20to%20that%20point

Dating a guy with no social media is the secret to either true love or a kidnapping, but probably true love. babe. (2018, October 8). https://babe.net/2018/10/08/dating-a-guy-with-no-social-media-is-the-secret-to-either-true-love-or-a-kidnapping-but-probably-true-love-81082

Derek, M., & Yuen, C. (2014). *Deciphering Sun Tzu: how to read 'The art of war.* Oxford University Press.

Drew Harwell, E. N. (2020, December 19). Federal prosecutors accuse Zoom executive of working with Chinese government to surveil users and suppress video calls. *The Washington Post.* https://www.washingtonpost.com/technology/2020/12/18/zoom-helped-china-surveillance/

Driver, J. (2014, September 22). The History of Utilitarianism. *Stanford Encyclopedia of Philosophy.* https://plato.stanford.edu/entries/utilitarianism-history/

Elizabeth. (2019, April 29). What Is Focal Length in Photography? *Photography Life.* https://photographylife.com/what-is-focal-length-in-photography

Family Sharing. (2021). *Apple.* https://www.apple.com/family-sharing/

Fisher, W. R. (1984). Narration as Human Communication Paradigm: The Case of Public Moral Argument. *Communication Monographs, 51*(1), 1–22. doi:10.1080/03637758409390180

Fisher, W. R. (1985a). The Narrative Paradigm: An Elaboration. *Communication Monographs, 52*(4), 347–367. doi:10.1080/03637758509376117

Fisher, W. R. (1985b). The Narrative Paradigm: In the Beginning. *Journal of Communication, 35*(4), 74–89. doi:10.1111/j.1460-2466.1985.tb02974.x

Fisher, W. R. (1987). *Human Communication as Narration: Toward a Philosophy of Reason, Value, and Action.* University of South Carolina Press.

Foucault, M., & Sheridan, A. (2020). *Discipline and punish: the birth of the prison.* Penguin Books.

Gadamer, H. G. (1982). *Truth and method.* Crossword Publishing.

Galič, M., Timan, T., & Koops, B.-J. (2016, May 13). Bentham, Deleuze and Beyond: An Overview of Surveillance Theories from the Panopticon to Participation. *Philosophy & Technology.* https://link.springer.com/article/10.1007/s13347-016-0219-1

Gazizullin, A. (2016, March 5). The Significance of the 'Human Security' Paradigm in International Politics. *E.* https://www.e-ir.info/2016/02/29/the-significance-of-the-human-security-paradigm-in-international-politics/

Gewirtz, D. (2013, October 28). Why do allies spy on each other? *ZDNet.* https://www.zdnet.com/article/why-do-allies-spy-on-each-other/

Goettsche Partners. (2011). GP. *Amazon.* https://www.amazon.com/gp/product/B07MHCFCBG?tag=p00935-20&ascsubtag=07o0e56a6zGrXrHH0cJuHfY

Goh, B. (2020, June 11). U.S. lawmakers ask Zoom to clarify China ties after it suspends accounts. *Reuters*. https://www.reuters.com/article/us-zoom-video-commn-privacy-idUSKBN23I3GP

Goldhill, O. (2015). An algorithm can predict human behavior better than humans. *Quartz*. https://qz.com/527008/an-algorithm-can-predict-human-behavior-better-than-humans/

Google. (n.d.). Why you're seeing an ad - Ads Help. *Google*. https://support.google.com/ads/answer/1634057?hl=en

Guardian News and Media. (2009, April 17). Starwood sues Hilton for 'stealing trade secrets'. *The Guardian*. https://www.theguardian.com/business/2009/apr/17/industrial-espionage-hotel-industry-lawsuit

Hayes, R., & Downs, D. M. (2011, July 22). Controlling retail theft with CCTV domes, CCTV public view monitors, and protective containers: A randomized controlled trial. *Security Journal*. https://link.springer.com/article/10.1057/sj.2011.12

Holvast, J. (2009). History of Privacy. In V. Matyáš, S. Fischer-Hübner, D. Cvrček, & P. Švenda (Eds.), *The Future of Identity in the Information Society. Privacy and Identity 2008. IFIP Advances in Information and Communication Technology* (Vol. 298). Springer. doi:10.1007/978-3-642-03315-5_2

Hore, S., & Raychaudhuri, K. (2021). Cyber Espionage—An Ethical Analysis. In M. K. Sharma, V. S. Dhaka, T. Perumal, N. Dey, & J. M. R. S. Tavares (Eds.), *Innovations in Computational Intelligence and Computer Vision. Advances in Intelligent Systems and Computing* (Vol. 1189). Springer. doi:10.1007/978-981-15-6067-5_5

Identifying Aspects of Privacy in Islamic Law. (n.d.). *Centre for Internet & Society*. https://cis-india.org/internet-governance/blog/identifying-aspects-of-privacy-in-islamic-law

InkLove904. (n.d.). *FanFiction*. https://www.fanfiction.net/u/3935242/InkLove904

Intellectual property theft and national security: Agendas and assumptions. (2016, March 17). *Taylor & Francis*. https://www.tandfonline.com/doi/full/10.1080/01972243.2016.1177762?scroll=top&needAccess=true

Jany, L. (2020, May 27). Minneapolis police, protesters clash almost 24 hours after George Floyd's death in custody. *Star Tribune*. https://www.startribune.com/minneapolis-police-marchers-clash-over-death-of-george-floyd-in-custody/570763352/

Johns, L. (2014, July 11). A Critical Evaluation of the Concept of Human Security. *E*. https://www.e-ir.info/2014/07/05/a-critical-evaluation-of-the-concept-of-human-security/

Johnson, K. (2021, January 6). U.S. formally links Russia to massive 'ongoing' cyber attack; scope of hacking unclear. *USA Today*. https://www.usatoday.com/story/news/politics/2021/01/05/u-s-formally-links-russia-massive-cyberattack-hack-ongoing/6552803002/

Kelion, C. F. L. (2020, July 16). Coronavirus: Russian spies target Covid-19 vaccine research. *BBC News*. https://www.bbc.com/news/technology-53429506

Kelly, H. (2012). Police embrace social media as crime-fighting tool. *CNN*. Available at: https://www.cnn.com/2012/08/30/tech/social-media/fighting-crime-social-media

Kluth, A. (2020). *Bloomberg.com*. https://www.bloomberg.com/opinion/articles/2020-04-22/taiwan-offers-the-best-model-for-coronavirus-data-tracking

Krishna, G. (2017, September 28). Right to Privacy and the Bhagavad Gita. *Rediff*. https://www.rediff.com/news/column/right-to-privacy-and-the-bhagavad-gita/20170928.htm

Kumaraguru, P., & Cranor, L. (2006). Privacy in India: Attitudes and Awareness. In G. Danezis & D. Martin (Eds.), Lecture Notes in Computer Science: Vol. 3856. Privacy Enhancing Technologies. PET 2005. Springer. https://doi.org/10.1007/11767831_16.

Lin, L., & Purnell, N. (2019, December 6). A World With a Billion Cameras Watching You Is Just Around the Corner. *The Wall Street Journal*. https://www.wsj.com/articles/a-billion-surveillance-cameras-forecast-to-be-watching-within-two-years-11575565402#:~:text=The%20report%2C%20from%20industry%20researcher,little%20over%20half%20the%20total

Locating Constructs of Privacy within Classical Hindu Law. (2014). *Centre for Internet & Society*. https://cis-india.org/internet-governance/blog/loading-constructs-of-privacy-within-classical-hindu-law

Lubin, G. (2012, February 16). The Incredible Story Of How Target Exposed A Teen Girl's Pregnancy. *Business Insider*. https://www.businessinsider.com/the-incredible-story-of-how-target-exposed-a-teen-girls-pregnancy-2012-2

Lukacs, A. (2016). *What is Privacy? The History and Definition of Privacy*. Academic Press.

Luong, M. (2012, October 30). College Admissions using social media to evaluate applicants. *Collegiate Times*. http://www.collegiatetimes.com/news/virginia_tech/college-admissions-using-social-media-to-evaluate-applicants/article_e8c06d44-a3d8-5786-b9cf-ff6b17edbb8d.html

MacIntyre, A. (1981). *After virtue: A study in moral theory* (2nd ed.). The University of Notre Dame Press.

Magrath, R. D., Pitcher, B. J., & Gardner, J. L. (2009, February 22). Recognition of other species' aerial alarm calls: speaking the same language or learning another? *Proceedings. Biological sciences*. https://www.ncbi.nlm.nih.gov/pmc/articles/PMC2660948/

Masoner, L. (n.d.). Explore the Major Advances in the History of Photography. *The Spruce Crafts*. https://www.thesprucecrafts.com/brief-history-of-photography-2688527

Matsakis, L. (2020). Dating a guy with no social media is the secret to either true love or a kidnapping, but probably true love. *babe*. https://babe.net/2018/10/08/dating-a-guy-with-no-social-media-is-the-secret-to-either-true-love-or-a-kidnapping-but-probably-true-love-81082

Max Eddy is a Software Analyst. (2018, January 26). How to Hide Your IP Address. *PCMag India*. https://in.pcmag.com/old-encryption/102427/how-to-hide-your-ip-address

Mcleod, S. (2020, December 29). Maslow's Hierarchy of Needs. *Simply Psychology*. https://www.simplypsychology.org/maslow.html#:~:text=Maslow's%20hierarchy%20of%20needs%20is,hierarchical%20levels%20within%20a%20pyramid.&text=From%20the%20bottom%20of%20the,esteem%2C%20and%20self%2Dactualization

Mitra, A. (2001). Marginal Voices in Cyberspace. *SAGE Journals*. https://journals.sagepub.com/doi/10.1177/1461444801003001003

Mitra, A., & Khosrowshahi, Y. (2018, March 29). Facebook, Google and others are tracking you. Here's how to stop targeted ads. *Global News*. https://globalnews.ca/news/4110311/how-to-stop-targeted-ads-facebook-google-browser/

Morris, P. G. (2008). Exposure. *The New Yorker*. https://www.newyorker.com/magazine/2008/03/24/exposure-5

Naylor, B. (2016, July 11). Firms Are Buying, Sharing Your Online Info. What Can You Do About It? *NPR*. https://www.npr.org/sections/alltechconsidered/2016/07/11/485571291/firms-are-buying-sharing-your-online-info-what-can-you-do-about-it

Neuman, S. (2017, October 18). Officers Fired After Forcible Removal Of United Airlines Passenger. *NPR*. https://www.npr.org/sections/thetwo-way/2017/10/18/558469185/officers-fired-after-forcible-removal-of-united-airlines-passenger

Newsroom: About UPS. (n.d.). *About UPS-US*. https://www.pressroom.ups.com/pressroom/ContentDetailsViewer.page?ConceptType=PressReleases&id=1543925402585-887#:~:text=%E2%80%9CUPS%20drivers%20make%20an%20average%20of%20125%20stops%20each%20day.&text=It%20uses%20the%20UPS%20data,delivery%20or%20pickup%20point%20changes

O'Connell, M. E. (2005). Enhancing the Status of Non-State Actors Through a Global War on Terror? *NDLScholarship*. https://scholarship.law.nd.edu/law_faculty_scholarship/94

O'Connell, M. E. (2018). Enhancing the Status of Non-State Actors Through a Global War on Terror? *NDLScholarship*. https://scholarship.law.nd.edu/law_faculty_scholarship/94

O'Kane, C. (2021, January 13). Some people are out of their jobs after images of them at Capitol riots appear online. *CBS News*. https://www.cbsnews.com/news/capitol-riots-people-lose-jobs/

O'Neill, J. (2021, January 8). Teen shames 'brainwashed' mom who got punched in face at Capitol riot. *New York Post*. https://nypost.com/2021/01/08/teen-shames-mom-who-got-punched-in-face-at-capitol-riot/

Pilon, M. (2015). Divorced by Data | Backchannel. *Wired*. https://www.wired.com/2015/06/divorced-by-data/

Pilossoph, J. (2019, May 23). Column: Tracking your spouse's phone – peace of mind or lack of trust? *chicagotribune.com*. https://www.chicagotribune.com/suburbs/lake-zurich/ct-ppn-column-love-essentially-tl-0629-20170622-story.html

Pines, G. (2021, May 3). A History of the Passport. *Travel*. https://www.nationalgeographic.com/travel/features/a-history-of-the-passport/

Privacy and Islam. From the Quran to data protection in Pakistan. (n.d.). *Taylor & Francis*. https://www.tandfonline.com/doi/abs/10.1080/13600830701532043#:~:text=Islam%20gives%20great%20importance%20to,'%20(24%3A27)

Propp, V. (1968). *Morphology of the Folktale* (2nd ed.). University of Texas Press.

Pruitt, S. (2018, October 16). An Ode to the Massive Sears Catalog, Which Even Delivered Houses by Mail. *History.com*. https://www.history.com/news/sears-catalog-houses-hubcaps

Public Broadcasting Service. (n.d.). Voices from the "Dark Side": The CIA Torture Debate. *PBS*. https://www.pbs.org/wgbh/frontline/article/voices-from-the-dark-side-the-cia-torture-debate/

Rashid, F. Y. (2015, October 2). EMV sets the stage for a better payment future. *CSO Online*. https://www.infoworld.com/article/2988549/emv-deadline-fraud-time-bomb-is-ticking.html

Rhodes, C. (2019, January 11). *A brief history of opinion polls*. Museum of Australian Democracy at Old Parliament House. https://www.moadoph.gov.au/blog/a-brief-history-of-opinion-polls/#

Ricouer, P. (1984). Time and narrative (vol. 1; K. McLaughlin & D. Pellaur, Trans.). The University of Chicago Press.

Ricouer, P. (1977). The model of the text: Meningful action considered as text. In F. R. Dallmayr & T. A. McCarthy (Eds.), *Understanding and social inquiry* (pp. 316–334). The University of Notre Dame Press.

Ricouer, P. (1983). The narrative function. In J. B. Thompson (Ed.), *Paul Ricouer, hermeneutics and the human sciences: Essays on language, action, and interpretation* (pp. 274–296). Cambridge University Press.

Robles, C. J. (2020, November 16). Millions of TCL Smart TV May Be Affected by 'Backdoor' Security Flaw - Here's How to Protect Your TV. *Tech Times*. https://www.techtimes.com/articles/254197/20201115/tcl-smart-tvs-backdoor-security-flaw-experts-find-heres-protect.htm

Sahadi, J. (2013). What the NSA costs taxpayers. *CNNMoney*. https://money.cnn.com/2013/06/07/news/economy/nsa-surveillance-cost/index.html

Sanger, D. E. (2020, December 13). Russian Hackers Broke Into Federal Agencies, U.S. Officials Suspect. *The New York Times*. https://www.nytimes.com/2020/12/13/us/politics/russian-hackers-us-government-treasury-commerce.html

Shoham, D., & Liebig, M. (2016). The intelligence dimension of Kautilyan statecraft and its implications for the present. *Journal of Intelligence History*, *15*(2), 119–138. doi:10.1080/16161262.2015.1116330

Singer, N. (2013, November 9). They Loved Your G.P.A. Then They Saw Your Tweets. *The New York Times*. https://www.nytimes.com/2013/11/10/business/they-loved-your-gpa-then-they-saw-your-tweets.html

SneezSafe. (2021, May 18). *Our Way Forward*. https://ourwayforward.wfu.edu/students/sneezsafe/

Souri, A., Hosseinpour, S., & Rahmani, A. M. (2018, August 22). Personality classification based on profiles of social networks' users and the five-factor model of personality. *Human-centric Computing and Information Sciences*. https://hcis-journal.springeropen.com/articles/10.1186/s13673-018-0147-4

Stubbs, J. (2020, December 9). Hackers steal Pfizer/BioNTech COVID-19 vaccine data in Europe, companies say. *Reuters*. https://www.reuters.com/article/ema-cyber/hackers-steal-pfizer-biontech-covid-19-vaccine-data-in-europe-companies-say-idINKBN28J21V

Subrahmanian, V. S., & Kumar, S. (2017, February 3). Predicting human behavior: The next frontiers. *Science*. https://science.sciencemag.org/content/355/6324/489

Suman, S. (2015, October 26). Institutions: Meaning, Characteristics, Role and Other Details. *Economics Discussion*. https://www.economicsdiscussion.net/articles/institutions-meaning-characteristics-role-and-other-details/13121

Taraszow, T., Aristodemou, E., Shitta, G., Laouris, Y., & Arsoy, A. (2010, January 1). Disclosure of personal and contact information by young people in social networking sites: An analysis using Facebook profiles as an example. *Latest TOC RSS*. https://www.ingentaconnect.com/content/intellect/mcp/2010/00000006/00000001/art0000

Thibodeaux, W. (2017, November 3). This Artificial Intelligence Can Predict How You'll Behave At Work Based on Social Media. *Inc.com*. https://www.inc.com/wanda-thibodeaux/this-artificial-intelligence-can-use-social-media-to-tell-hiring-managers-about-your-personality.html

Todorov, T. (1977). *The Poetics of Prose*. Cornell University Press.

Trenholm, R. (n.d.). History of digital cameras: From '70s prototypes to iPhone and Galaxy's everyday wonders. *CNET*. https://www.cnet.com/news/photos-the-history-of-the-digital-camera/

UCL. (2018, May 17). *Kilmainham Gaol, Dublin: a 'panoptic' prison?* Bentham Project. https://www.ucl.ac.uk/bentham-project/who-was-jeremy-bentham/panopticon/kilmainham-gaol-dublin-panoptic-prison

US Government (1994). TITLE 49—TRANSPORTATION.

US Legal. (n.d.). Find a legal form in minutes. Person of Interest Law and Legal Definition. *USLegal, Inc.* https://definitions.uslegal.com/p/person-of-interest/

Victor, D., & Stevens, M. (2017, April 10). United Airlines Passenger Is Dragged From an Overbooked Flight. *The New York Times*. https://www.nytimes.com/2017/04/10/business/united-flight-passenger-dragged.html

Wakefield, J. (2020, November 27). Your data and how it is used to gain your vote. *BBC News*. https://www.bbc.com/news/technology-54915779

White, H. (1984). The question of narrative in contemporary historical theory. *History and Theory*, *23*(1), 1–33. doi:10.2307/2504969

Winerman, L. (2004). Psychological sleuths--Criminal profiling: the reality behind the myth. *Monitor on Psychology*. https://www.apa.org/monitor/julaug04/criminal#:~:text=How%20does%20profiling%20work%3F,murderer%20Jack%20the%20Ripper's%20personality

Withers, R. (2019, November 11). When Couples Can't Agree on Surveillance in the Home. *Slate Magazine*. https://slate.com/technology/2019/11/relationship-disputes-surveillance-cameras.html

Yakowicz, W. (2014, July 28). How to Anticipate Your Competitors' Next Moves. *Inc.com*. https://www.inc.com/will-yakowicz/great-ceos-keep-rivals-close.html

Your smart TV may be spying on you - and stopping it is against the law. The World from PRX. (n.d.). https://www.pri.org/stories/2015-02-13/your-smart-tv-may-be-spying-you-and-stopping-it-against-law

Zdanowicz, C., & Grinberg, E. (2018, April 10). Passenger dragged off overbooked United flight. *CNN*. https://www.cnn.com/2017/04/10/travel/passenger-removed-united-flight-trnd/index.html

Related References

To continue our tradition of advancing information science and technology research, we have compiled a list of recommended IGI Global readings. These references will provide additional information and guidance to further enrich your knowledge and assist you with your own research and future publications.

Abbas, R., Michael, K., & Michael, M. G. (2017). What Can People Do with Your Spatial Data?: Socio-Ethical Scenarios. In A. Marrington, D. Kerr, & J. Gammack (Eds.), *Managing Security Issues and the Hidden Dangers of Wearable Technologies* (pp. 206–237). Hershey, PA: IGI Global. doi:10.4018/978-1-5225-1016-1.ch009

Abulaish, M., & Haldar, N. A. (2018). Advances in Digital Forensics Frameworks and Tools: A Comparative Insight and Ranking. *International Journal of Digital Crime and Forensics, 10*(2), 95–119. doi:10.4018/IJDCF.2018040106

Ahmad, F. A., Kumar, P., Shrivastava, G., & Bouhlel, M. S. (2018). Bitcoin: Digital Decentralized Cryptocurrency. In G. Shrivastava, P. Kumar, B. Gupta, S. Bala, & N. Dey (Eds.), *Handbook of Research on Network Forensics and Analysis Techniques* (pp. 395–415). Hershey, PA: IGI Global. doi:10.4018/978-1-5225-4100-4.ch021

Ahmed, A. A. (2017). Investigation Approach for Network Attack Intention Recognition. *International Journal of Digital Crime and Forensics, 9*(1), 17–38. doi:10.4018/IJDCF.2017010102

Akhtar, Z. (2017). Biometric Spoofing and Anti-Spoofing. In M. Dawson, D. Kisku, P. Gupta, J. Sing, & W. Li (Eds.), Developing Next-Generation Countermeasures for Homeland Security Threat Prevention (pp. 121-139). Hershey, PA: IGI Global. doi:10.4018/978-1-5225-0703-1.ch007

Akowuah, F. E., Land, J., Yuan, X., Yang, L., Xu, J., & Wang, H. (2018). Standards and Guides for Implementing Security and Privacy for Health Information Technology. In Y. Maleh (Ed.), *Security and Privacy Management, Techniques, and Protocols* (pp. 214–236). Hershey, PA: IGI Global. doi:10.4018/978-1-5225-5583-4.ch008

Akremi, A., Sallay, H., & Rouached, M. (2018). Intrusion Detection Systems Alerts Reduction: New Approach for Forensics Readiness. In Y. Maleh (Ed.), *Security and Privacy Management, Techniques, and Protocols* (pp. 255–275). Hershey, PA: IGI Global. doi:10.4018/978-1-5225-5583-4.ch010

Aldwairi, M., Hasan, M., & Balbahaith, Z. (2017). Detection of Drive-by Download Attacks Using Machine Learning Approach. *International Journal of Information Security and Privacy*, *11*(4), 16–28. doi:10.4018/IJISP.2017100102

Alohali, B. (2017). Detection Protocol of Possible Crime Scenes Using Internet of Things (IoT). In M. Moore (Ed.), *Cybersecurity Breaches and Issues Surrounding Online Threat Protection* (pp. 175–196). Hershey, PA: IGI Global. doi:10.4018/978-1-5225-1941-6.ch008

AlShahrani, A. M., Al-Abadi, M. A., Al-Malki, A. S., Ashour, A. S., & Dey, N. (2017). Automated System for Crops Recognition and Classification. In N. Dey, A. Ashour, & S. Acharjee (Eds.), *Applied Video Processing in Surveillance and Monitoring Systems* (pp. 54–69). Hershey, PA: IGI Global. doi:10.4018/978-1-5225-1022-2.ch003

Anand, R., Shrivastava, G., Gupta, S., Peng, S., & Sindhwani, N. (2018). Audio Watermarking With Reduced Number of Random Samples. In G. Shrivastava, P. Kumar, B. Gupta, S. Bala, & N. Dey (Eds.), *Handbook of Research on Network Forensics and Analysis Techniques* (pp. 372–394). Hershey, PA: IGI Global. doi:10.4018/978-1-5225-4100-4.ch020

Anand, R., Sinha, A., Bhardwaj, A., & Sreeraj, A. (2018). Flawed Security of Social Network of Things. In G. Shrivastava, P. Kumar, B. Gupta, S. Bala, & N. Dey (Eds.), *Handbook of Research on Network Forensics and Analysis Techniques* (pp. 65–86). Hershey, PA: IGI Global. doi:10.4018/978-1-5225-4100-4.ch005

Aneja, M. J., Bhatia, T., Sharma, G., & Shrivastava, G. (2018). Artificial Intelligence Based Intrusion Detection System to Detect Flooding Attack in VANETs. In G. Shrivastava, P. Kumar, B. Gupta, S. Bala, & N. Dey (Eds.), *Handbook of Research on Network Forensics and Analysis Techniques* (pp. 87–100). Hershey, PA: IGI Global. doi:10.4018/978-1-5225-4100-4.ch006

Antunes, F., Freire, M., & Costa, J. P. (2018). From Motivation and Self-Structure to a Decision-Support Framework for Online Social Networks. In V. Ahuja & S. Rathore (Eds.), *Multidisciplinary Perspectives on Human Capital and Information Technology Professionals* (pp. 116–136). Hershey, PA: IGI Global. doi:10.4018/978-1-5225-5297-0.ch007

Atli, D. (2017). Cybercrimes via Virtual Currencies in International Business. In M. Moore (Ed.), *Cybersecurity Breaches and Issues Surrounding Online Threat Protection* (pp. 121–143). Hershey, PA: IGI Global. doi:10.4018/978-1-5225-1941-6.ch006

Baazeem, R. M. (2018). The Role of Religiosity in Technology Acceptance: The Case of Privacy in Saudi Arabia. In J. McAlaney, L. Frumkin, & V. Benson (Eds.), *Psychological and Behavioral Examinations in Cyber Security* (pp. 172–193). Hershey, PA: IGI Global. doi:10.4018/978-1-5225-4053-3.ch010

Bailey, W. J. (2017). Protection of Critical Homeland Assets: Using a Proactive, Adaptive Security Management Driven Process. In M. Dawson, D. Kisku, P. Gupta, J. Sing, & W. Li (Eds.), Developing Next-Generation Countermeasures for Homeland Security Threat Prevention (pp. 17-50). Hershey, PA: IGI Global. doi:10.4018/978-1-5225-0703-1.ch002

Bajaj, S. (2018). Current Drift in Energy Efficiency Cloud Computing: New Provocations, Workload Prediction, Consolidation, and Resource Over Commitment. In S. Aljawarneh & M. Malhotra (Eds.), *Critical Research on Scalability and Security Issues in Virtual Cloud Environments* (pp. 283–303). Hershey, PA: IGI Global. doi:10.4018/978-1-5225-3029-9.ch014

Balasubramanian, K. (2018). Hash Functions and Their Applications. In K. Balasubramanian & M. Rajakani (Eds.), *Algorithmic Strategies for Solving Complex Problems in Cryptography* (pp. 66–77). Hershey, PA: IGI Global. doi:10.4018/978-1-5225-2915-6.ch005

Balasubramanian, K. (2018). Recent Developments in Cryptography: A Survey. In K. Balasubramanian & M. Rajakani (Eds.), *Algorithmic Strategies for Solving Complex Problems in Cryptography* (pp. 1–22). Hershey, PA: IGI Global. doi:10.4018/978-1-5225-2915-6.ch001

Balasubramanian, K. (2018). Secure Two Party Computation. In K. Balasubramanian & M. Rajakani (Eds.), *Algorithmic Strategies for Solving Complex Problems in Cryptography* (pp. 145–153). Hershey, PA: IGI Global. doi:10.4018/978-1-5225-2915-6.ch012

Balasubramanian, K. (2018). Securing Public Key Encryption Against Adaptive Chosen Ciphertext Attacks. In K. Balasubramanian & M. Rajakani (Eds.), *Algorithmic Strategies for Solving Complex Problems in Cryptography* (pp. 134–144). Hershey, PA: IGI Global. doi:10.4018/978-1-5225-2915-6.ch011

Balasubramanian, K. (2018). Variants of the Diffie-Hellman Problem. In K. Balasubramanian & M. Rajakani (Eds.), *Algorithmic Strategies for Solving Complex Problems in Cryptography* (pp. 40–54). Hershey, PA: IGI Global. doi:10.4018/978-1-5225-2915-6.ch003

Balasubramanian, K., & K., M. (2018). Secure Group Key Agreement Protocols. In K. Balasubramanian, & M. Rajakani (Eds.), *Algorithmic Strategies for Solving Complex Problems in Cryptography* (pp. 55-65). Hershey, PA: IGI Global. doi:10.4018/978-1-5225-2915-6.ch004

Balasubramanian, K., & M., R. (2018). Problems in Cryptography and Cryptanalysis. In K. Balasubramanian, & M. Rajakani (Eds.), *Algorithmic Strategies for Solving Complex Problems in Cryptography* (pp. 23-39). Hershey, PA: IGI Global. doi:10.4018/978-1-5225-2915-6.ch002

Balasubramanian, K., & Abbas, A. M. (2018). Integer Factoring Algorithms. In K. Balasubramanian & M. Rajakani (Eds.), *Algorithmic Strategies for Solving Complex Problems in Cryptography* (pp. 228–240). Hershey, PA: IGI Global. doi:10.4018/978-1-5225-2915-6.ch017

Balasubramanian, K., & Abbas, A. M. (2018). Secure Bootstrapping Using the Trusted Platform Module. In K. Balasubramanian & M. Rajakani (Eds.), *Algorithmic Strategies for Solving Complex Problems in Cryptography* (pp. 167–185). Hershey, PA: IGI Global. doi:10.4018/978-1-5225-2915-6.ch014

Balasubramanian, K., & Mathanan, J. (2018). Cryptographic Voting Protocols. In K. Balasubramanian & M. Rajakani (Eds.), *Algorithmic Strategies for Solving Complex Problems in Cryptography* (pp. 124–133). Hershey, PA: IGI Global. doi:10.4018/978-1-5225-2915-6.ch010

Balasubramanian, K., & Rajakani, M. (2018). Secure Multiparty Computation. In K. Balasubramanian & M. Rajakani (Eds.), *Algorithmic Strategies for Solving Complex Problems in Cryptography* (pp. 154–166). Hershey, PA: IGI Global. doi:10.4018/978-1-5225-2915-6.ch013

Balasubramanian, K., & Rajakani, M. (2018). The Quadratic Sieve Algorithm for Integer Factoring. In K. Balasubramanian & M. Rajakani (Eds.), *Algorithmic Strategies for Solving Complex Problems in Cryptography* (pp. 241–252). Hershey, PA: IGI Global. doi:10.4018/978-1-5225-2915-6.ch018

Barone, P. A. (2017). Defining and Understanding the Development of Juvenile Delinquency from an Environmental, Sociological, and Theoretical Perspective. In S. Egharevba (Ed.), *Police Brutality, Racial Profiling, and Discrimination in the Criminal Justice System* (pp. 215–238). Hershey, PA: IGI Global. doi:10.4018/978-1-5225-1088-8.ch010

Beauchere, J. F. (2018). Encouraging Digital Civility: What Companies and Others Can Do. In R. Luppicini (Ed.), *The Changing Scope of Technoethics in Contemporary Society* (pp. 262–274). Hershey, PA: IGI Global. doi:10.4018/978-1-5225-5094-5.ch014

Behera, C. K., & Bhaskari, D. L. (2017). Malware Methodologies and Its Future: A Survey. *International Journal of Information Security and Privacy*, *11*(4), 47–64. doi:10.4018/IJISP.2017100104

Benson, V., McAlaney, J., & Frumkin, L. A. (2018). Emerging Threats for the Human Element and Countermeasures in Current Cyber Security Landscape. In J. McAlaney, L. Frumkin, & V. Benson (Eds.), *Psychological and Behavioral Examinations in Cyber Security* (pp. 266–271). Hershey, PA: IGI Global. doi:10.4018/978-1-5225-4053-3.ch016

Berbecaru, D. (2018). On Creating Digital Evidence in IP Networks With NetTrack. In G. Shrivastava, P. Kumar, B. Gupta, S. Bala, & N. Dey (Eds.), *Handbook of Research on Network Forensics and Analysis Techniques* (pp. 225–245). Hershey, PA: IGI Global. doi:10.4018/978-1-5225-4100-4.ch012

Berki, E., Valtanen, J., Chaudhary, S., & Li, L. (2018). The Need for Multi-Disciplinary Approaches and Multi-Level Knowledge for Cybersecurity Professionals. In V. Ahuja & S. Rathore (Eds.), *Multidisciplinary Perspectives on Human Capital and Information Technology Professionals* (pp. 72–94). Hershey, PA: IGI Global. doi:10.4018/978-1-5225-5297-0.ch005

Bhardwaj, A. (2017). Ransomware: A Rising Threat of new age Digital Extortion. In S. Aljawarneh (Ed.), *Online Banking Security Measures and Data Protection* (pp. 189–221). Hershey, PA: IGI Global. doi:10.4018/978-1-5225-0864-9.ch012

Bhattacharjee, J., Sengupta, A., Barik, M. S., & Mazumdar, C. (2018). An Analytical Study of Methodologies and Tools for Enterprise Information Security Risk Management. In M. Gupta, R. Sharman, J. Walp, & P. Mulgund (Eds.), *Information Technology Risk Management and Compliance in Modern Organizations* (pp. 1–20). Hershey, PA: IGI Global. doi:10.4018/978-1-5225-2604-9.ch001

Bruno, G. (2018). Handling the Dataflow in Business Process Models. In V. Ahuja & S. Rathore (Eds.), *Multidisciplinary Perspectives on Human Capital and Information Technology Professionals* (pp. 137–151). Hershey, PA: IGI Global. doi:10.4018/978-1-5225-5297-0.ch008

Carneiro, A. D. (2017). Defending Information Networks in Cyberspace: Some Notes on Security Needs. In M. Dawson, D. Kisku, P. Gupta, J. Sing, & W. Li (Eds.), Developing Next-Generation Countermeasures for Homeland Security Threat Prevention (pp. 354-375). Hershey, PA: IGI Global. doi:10.4018/978-1-5225-0703-1.ch016

Chakraborty, S., Patra, P. K., Maji, P., Ashour, A. S., & Dey, N. (2017). Image Registration Techniques and Frameworks: A Review. In N. Dey, A. Ashour, & S. Acharjee (Eds.), *Applied Video Processing in Surveillance and Monitoring Systems* (pp. 102–114). Hershey, PA: IGI Global. doi:10.4018/978-1-5225-1022-2.ch005

Chaudhari, G., & Mulgund, P. (2018). Strengthening IT Governance With COBIT 5. In M. Gupta, R. Sharman, J. Walp, & P. Mulgund (Eds.), *Information Technology Risk Management and Compliance in Modern Organizations* (pp. 48–69). Hershey, PA: IGI Global. doi:10.4018/978-1-5225-2604-9.ch003

Cheikh, M., Hacini, S., & Boufaida, Z. (2018). Visualization Technique for Intrusion Detection. In Y. Maleh (Ed.), *Security and Privacy Management, Techniques, and Protocols* (pp. 276–290). Hershey, PA: IGI Global. doi:10.4018/978-1-5225-5583-4.ch011

Chen, G., Ding, L., Du, J., Zhou, G., Qin, P., Chen, G., & Liu, Q. (2018). Trust Evaluation Strategy for Single Sign-on Solution in Cloud. *International Journal of Digital Crime and Forensics*, *10*(1), 1–11. doi:10.4018/IJDCF.2018010101

Chen, J., & Peng, F. (2018). A Perceptual Encryption Scheme for HEVC Video with Lossless Compression. *International Journal of Digital Crime and Forensics*, *10*(1), 67–78. doi:10.4018/IJDCF.2018010106

Chen, K., & Xu, D. (2018). An Efficient Reversible Data Hiding Scheme for Encrypted Images. *International Journal of Digital Crime and Forensics*, *10*(2), 1–22. doi:10.4018/IJDCF.2018040101

Chen, Z., Lu, J., Yang, P., & Luo, X. (2017). Recognizing Substitution Steganography of Spatial Domain Based on the Characteristics of Pixels Correlation. *International Journal of Digital Crime and Forensics*, *9*(4), 48–61. doi:10.4018/IJDCF.2017100105

Cherkaoui, R., Zbakh, M., Braeken, A., & Touhafi, A. (2018). Anomaly Detection in Cloud Computing and Internet of Things Environments: Latest Technologies. In K. Munir (Ed.), *Cloud Computing Technologies for Green Enterprises* (pp. 251–265). Hershey, PA: IGI Global. doi:10.4018/978-1-5225-3038-1.ch010

Chowdhury, A., Karmakar, G., & Kamruzzaman, J. (2017). Survey of Recent Cyber Security Attacks on Robotic Systems and Their Mitigation Approaches. In R. Kumar, P. Pattnaik, & P. Pandey (Eds.), *Detecting and Mitigating Robotic Cyber Security Risks* (pp. 284–299). Hershey, PA: IGI Global. doi:10.4018/978-1-5225-2154-9.ch019

Cortese, F. A. (2018). The Techoethical Ethos of Technic Self-Determination: Technological Determinism as the Ontic Fundament of Freewill. In R. Luppicini (Ed.), *The Changing Scope of Technoethics in Contemporary Society* (pp. 74–104). Hershey, PA: IGI Global. doi:10.4018/978-1-5225-5094-5.ch005

Crosston, M. D. (2017). The Fight for Cyber Thoreau: Distinguishing Virtual Disobedience from Digital Destruction. In M. Korstanje (Ed.), *Threat Mitigation and Detection of Cyber Warfare and Terrorism Activities* (pp. 198–219). Hershey, PA: IGI Global. doi:10.4018/978-1-5225-1938-6.ch009

da Costa, F., & de Sá-Soares, F. (2017). Authenticity Challenges of Wearable Technologies. In A. Marrington, D. Kerr, & J. Gammack (Eds.), *Managing Security Issues and the Hidden Dangers of Wearable Technologies* (pp. 98–130). Hershey, PA: IGI Global. doi:10.4018/978-1-5225-1016-1.ch005

Dafflon, B., Guériau, M., & Gechter, F. (2017). Using Physics Inspired Wave Agents in a Virtual Environment: Longitudinal Distance Control in Robots Platoon. *International Journal of Monitoring and Surveillance Technologies Research*, 5(2), 15–28. doi:10.4018/IJMSTR.2017040102

Dash, S. R., Sheeraz, A. S., & Samantaray, A. (2018). Filtration and Classification of ECG Signals. In C. Pradhan, H. Das, B. Naik, & N. Dey (Eds.), *Handbook of Research on Information Security in Biomedical Signal Processing* (pp. 72–94). Hershey, PA: IGI Global. doi:10.4018/978-1-5225-5152-2.ch005

Dhavale, S. V. (2018). Insider Attack Analysis in Building Effective Cyber Security for an Organization. In J. McAlaney, L. Frumkin, & V. Benson (Eds.), *Psychological and Behavioral Examinations in Cyber Security* (pp. 222–238). Hershey, PA: IGI Global. doi:10.4018/978-1-5225-4053-3.ch013

Dixit, P. (2018). Security Issues in Web Services. In G. Shrivastava, P. Kumar, B. Gupta, S. Bala, & N. Dey (Eds.), *Handbook of Research on Network Forensics and Analysis Techniques* (pp. 57–64). Hershey, PA: IGI Global. doi:10.4018/978-1-5225-4100-4.ch004

Doraikannan, S. (2018). Efficient Implementation of Digital Signature Algorithms. In K. Balasubramanian & M. Rajakani (Eds.), *Algorithmic Strategies for Solving Complex Problems in Cryptography* (pp. 78–86). Hershey, PA: IGI Global. doi:10.4018/978-1-5225-2915-6.ch006

E., J. V., Mohan, J., & K., A. (2018). Automatic Detection of Tumor and Bleed in Magnetic Resonance Brain Images. In C. Pradhan, H. Das, B. Naik, & N. Dey (Eds.), *Handbook of Research on Information Security in Biomedical Signal Processing* (pp. 291-303). Hershey, PA: IGI Global. doi:10.4018/978-1-5225-5152-2.ch015

Escamilla, I., Ruíz, M. T., Ibarra, M. M., Soto, V. L., Quintero, R., & Guzmán, G. (2018). Geocoding Tweets Based on Semantic Web and Ontologies. In M. Lytras, N. Aljohani, E. Damiani, & K. Chui (Eds.), *Innovations, Developments, and Applications of Semantic Web and Information Systems* (pp. 372–392). Hershey, PA: IGI Global. doi:10.4018/978-1-5225-5042-6.ch014

Farhadi, M., Haddad, H. M., & Shahriar, H. (2018). Compliance of Electronic Health Record Applications With HIPAA Security and Privacy Requirements. In Y. Maleh (Ed.), *Security and Privacy Management, Techniques, and Protocols* (pp. 199–213). Hershey, PA: IGI Global. doi:10.4018/978-1-5225-5583-4.ch007

Fatma, S. (2018). Use and Misuse of Technology in Marketing: Cases from India. *International Journal of Technoethics*, *9*(1), 27–36. doi:10.4018/IJT.2018010103

Fazlali, M., & Khodamoradi, P. (2018). Metamorphic Malware Detection Using Minimal Opcode Statistical Patterns. In Y. Maleh (Ed.), *Security and Privacy Management, Techniques, and Protocols* (pp. 337–359). Hershey, PA: IGI Global. doi:10.4018/978-1-5225-5583-4.ch014

Filiol, É., & Gallais, C. (2017). Optimization of Operational Large-Scale (Cyber) Attacks by a Combinational Approach. *International Journal of Cyber Warfare & Terrorism*, *7*(3), 29–43. doi:10.4018/IJCWT.2017070103

Forge, J. (2018). The Case Against Weapons Research. In R. Luppicini (Ed.), *The Changing Scope of Technoethics in Contemporary Society* (pp. 124–134). Hershey, PA: IGI Global. doi:10.4018/978-1-5225-5094-5.ch007

G., S., & Durai, M. S. (2018). Big Data Analytics: An Expedition Through Rapidly Budding Data Exhaustive Era. In D. Lopez, & M. Durai (Eds.), *HCI Challenges and Privacy Preservation in Big Data Security* (pp. 124-138). Hershey, PA: IGI Global. doi:10.4018/978-1-5225-2863-0.ch006

Gammack, J., & Marrington, A. (2017). The Promise and Perils of Wearable Technologies. In A. Marrington, D. Kerr, & J. Gammack (Eds.), *Managing Security Issues and the Hidden Dangers of Wearable Technologies* (pp. 1–17). Hershey, PA: IGI Global. doi:10.4018/978-1-5225-1016-1.ch001

Gamoura, S. C. (2018). A Cloud-Based Approach for Cross-Management of Disaster Plans: Managing Risk in Networked Enterprises. In S. Aljawarneh & M. Malhotra (Eds.), *Critical Research on Scalability and Security Issues in Virtual Cloud Environments* (pp. 240–268). Hershey, PA: IGI Global. doi:10.4018/978-1-5225-3029-9.ch012

Gao, L., Gao, T., Zhao, J., & Liu, Y. (2018). Reversible Watermarking in Digital Image Using PVO and RDWT. *International Journal of Digital Crime and Forensics, 10*(2), 40–55. doi:10.4018/IJDCF.2018040103

Geetha, S., & Sindhu, S. S. (2016). Audio Stego Intrusion Detection System through Hybrid Neural Tree Model. In B. Gupta, D. Agrawal, & S. Yamaguchi (Eds.), *Handbook of Research on Modern Cryptographic Solutions for Computer and Cyber Security* (pp. 126–144). Hershey, PA: IGI Global. doi:10.4018/978-1-5225-0105-3.ch006

Geethanjali, P. (2018). Bio-Inspired Techniques in Human-Computer Interface for Control of Assistive Devices: Bio-Inspired Techniques in Assistive Devices. In D. Lopez & M. Durai (Eds.), *HCI Challenges and Privacy Preservation in Big Data Security* (pp. 23–46). Hershey, PA: IGI Global. doi:10.4018/978-1-5225-2863-0.ch002

Ghany, K. K., & Zawbaa, H. M. (2017). Hybrid Biometrics and Watermarking Authentication. In S. Zoughbi (Ed.), *Securing Government Information and Data in Developing Countries* (pp. 37–61). Hershey, PA: IGI Global. doi:10.4018/978-1-5225-1703-0.ch003

Hacini, S., Guessoum, Z., & Cheikh, M. (2018). False Alarm Reduction: A Profiling Mechanism and New Research Directions. In Y. Maleh (Ed.), *Security and Privacy Management, Techniques, and Protocols* (pp. 291–320). Hershey, PA: IGI Global. doi:10.4018/978-1-5225-5583-4.ch012

Hadlington, L. (2018). The "Human Factor" in Cybersecurity: Exploring the Accidental Insider. In J. McAlaney, L. Frumkin, & V. Benson (Eds.), Psychological and Behavioral Examinations in Cyber Security (pp. 46-63). Hershey, PA: IGI Global. doi:10.4018/978-1-5225-4053-3.ch003

Haldorai, A., & Ramu, A. (2018). The Impact of Big Data Analytics and Challenges to Cyber Security. In G. Shrivastava, P. Kumar, B. Gupta, S. Bala, & N. Dey (Eds.), *Handbook of Research on Network Forensics and Analysis Techniques* (pp. 300–314). Hershey, PA: IGI Global. doi:10.4018/978-1-5225-4100-4.ch016

Hariharan, S., Prasanth, V. S., & Saravanan, P. (2018). Role of Bibliographical Databases in Measuring Information: A Conceptual View. In J. Jeyasekar & P. Saravanan (Eds.), *Innovations in Measuring and Evaluating Scientific Information* (pp. 61–71). Hershey, PA: IGI Global. doi:10.4018/978-1-5225-3457-0.ch005

Hore, S., Chatterjee, S., Chakraborty, S., & Shaw, R. K. (2017). Analysis of Different Feature Description Algorithm in object Recognition. In N. Dey, A. Ashour, & P. Patra (Eds.), *Feature Detectors and Motion Detection in Video Processing* (pp. 66–99). Hershey, PA: IGI Global. doi:10.4018/978-1-5225-1025-3.ch004

Hurley, J. S. (2017). Cyberspace: The New Battlefield - An Approach via the Analytics Hierarchy Process. *International Journal of Cyber Warfare & Terrorism*, *7*(3), 1–15. doi:10.4018/IJCWT.2017070101

Hussain, M., & Kaliya, N. (2018). An Improvised Framework for Privacy Preservation in IoT. *International Journal of Information Security and Privacy*, *12*(2), 46–63. doi:10.4018/IJISP.2018040104

Ilahi-Amri, M., Cheniti-Belcadhi, L., & Braham, R. (2018). Competence E-Assessment Based on Semantic Web: From Modeling to Validation. In V. Ahuja & S. Rathore (Eds.), *Multidisciplinary Perspectives on Human Capital and Information Technology Professionals* (pp. 246–267). Hershey, PA: IGI Global. doi:10.4018/978-1-5225-5297-0.ch013

Jambhekar, N., & Dhawale, C. A. (2018). Cryptography in Big Data Security. In D. Lopez & M. Durai (Eds.), *HCI Challenges and Privacy Preservation in Big Data Security* (pp. 71–94). Hershey, PA: IGI Global. doi:10.4018/978-1-5225-2863-0.ch004

Jansen van Vuuren, J., Leenen, L., Plint, G., Zaaiman, J., & Phahlamohlaka, J. (2017). Formulating the Building Blocks for National Cyberpower. *International Journal of Cyber Warfare & Terrorism*, *7*(3), 16–28. doi:10.4018/IJCWT.2017070102

Jaswal, S., & Malhotra, M. (2018). Identification of Various Privacy and Trust Issues in Cloud Computing Environment. In S. Aljawarneh & M. Malhotra (Eds.), *Critical Research on Scalability and Security Issues in Virtual Cloud Environments* (pp. 95–121). Hershey, PA: IGI Global. doi:10.4018/978-1-5225-3029-9.ch005

Jaswal, S., & Singh, G. (2018). A Comprehensive Survey on Trust Issue and Its Deployed Models in Computing Environment. In S. Aljawarneh & M. Malhotra (Eds.), *Critical Research on Scalability and Security Issues in Virtual Cloud Environments* (pp. 150–166). Hershey, PA: IGI Global. doi:10.4018/978-1-5225-3029-9.ch007

Javid, T. (2018). Secure Access to Biomedical Images. In C. Pradhan, H. Das, B. Naik, & N. Dey (Eds.), *Handbook of Research on Information Security in Biomedical Signal Processing* (pp. 38–53). Hershey, PA: IGI Global. doi:10.4018/978-1-5225-5152-2.ch003

Jeyakumar, B., Durai, M. S., & Lopez, D. (2018). Case Studies in Amalgamation of Deep Learning and Big Data. In D. Lopez & M. Durai (Eds.), *HCI Challenges and Privacy Preservation in Big Data Security* (pp. 159–174). Hershey, PA: IGI Global. doi:10.4018/978-1-5225-2863-0.ch008

Jeyaprakash, H. M. K., K., & S., G. (2018). A Comparative Review of Various Machine Learning Approaches for Improving the Performance of Stego Anomaly Detection. In G. Shrivastava, P. Kumar, B. Gupta, S. Bala, & N. Dey (Eds.), Handbook of Research on Network Forensics and Analysis Techniques (pp. 351-371). Hershey, PA: IGI Global. doi:10.4018/978-1-5225-4100-4.ch019

Jeyasekar, J. J. (2018). Dynamics of Indian Forensic Science Research. In J. Jeyasekar & P. Saravanan (Eds.), *Innovations in Measuring and Evaluating Scientific Information* (pp. 125–147). Hershey, PA: IGI Global. doi:10.4018/978-1-5225-3457-0.ch009

Jones, H. S., & Moncur, W. (2018). The Role of Psychology in Understanding Online Trust. In J. McAlaney, L. Frumkin, & V. Benson (Eds.), *Psychological and Behavioral Examinations in Cyber Security* (pp. 109–132). Hershey, PA: IGI Global. doi:10.4018/978-1-5225-4053-3.ch007

Jones, H. S., & Towse, J. (2018). Examinations of Email Fraud Susceptibility: Perspectives From Academic Research and Industry Practice. In J. McAlaney, L. Frumkin, & V. Benson (Eds.), *Psychological and Behavioral Examinations in Cyber Security* (pp. 80–97). Hershey, PA: IGI Global. doi:10.4018/978-1-5225-4053-3.ch005

Joseph, A., & Singh, K. J. (2018). Digital Forensics in Distributed Environment. In G. Shrivastava, P. Kumar, B. Gupta, S. Bala, & N. Dey (Eds.), *Handbook of Research on Network Forensics and Analysis Techniques* (pp. 246–265). Hershey, PA: IGI Global. doi:10.4018/978-1-5225-4100-4.ch013

K., I., & A, V. (2018). Monitoring and Auditing in the Cloud. In K. Munir (Ed.), *Cloud Computing Technologies for Green Enterprises* (pp. 318-350). Hershey, PA: IGI Global. doi:10.4018/978-1-5225-3038-1.ch013

Kashyap, R., & Piersson, A. D. (2018). Impact of Big Data on Security. In G. Shrivastava, P. Kumar, B. Gupta, S. Bala, & N. Dey (Eds.), *Handbook of Research on Network Forensics and Analysis Techniques* (pp. 283–299). Hershey, PA: IGI Global. doi:10.4018/978-1-5225-4100-4.ch015

Kastrati, Z., Imran, A. S., & Yayilgan, S. Y. (2018). A Hybrid Concept Learning Approach to Ontology Enrichment. In M. Lytras, N. Aljohani, E. Damiani, & K. Chui (Eds.), *Innovations, Developments, and Applications of Semantic Web and Information Systems* (pp. 85–119). Hershey, PA: IGI Global. doi:10.4018/978-1-5225-5042-6.ch004

Kaur, H., & Saxena, S. (2018). UWDBCSN Analysis During Node Replication Attack in WSN. In C. Pradhan, H. Das, B. Naik, & N. Dey (Eds.), *Handbook of Research on Information Security in Biomedical Signal Processing* (pp. 210–227). Hershey, PA: IGI Global. doi:10.4018/978-1-5225-5152-2.ch011

Kaushal, P. K., & Sobti, R. (2018). Breaching Security of Full Round Tiny Encryption Algorithm. *International Journal of Information Security and Privacy*, *12*(1), 89–98. doi:10.4018/IJISP.2018010108

Kavati, I., Prasad, M. V., & Bhagvati, C. (2017). Search Space Reduction in Biometric Databases: A Review. In M. Dawson, D. Kisku, P. Gupta, J. Sing, & W. Li (Eds.), Developing Next-Generation Countermeasures for Homeland Security Threat Prevention (pp. 236-262). Hershey, PA: IGI Global. doi:10.4018/978-1-5225-0703-1.ch011

Kaye, L. K. (2018). Online Research Methods. In J. McAlaney, L. Frumkin, & V. Benson (Eds.), *Psychological and Behavioral Examinations in Cyber Security* (pp. 253–265). Hershey, PA: IGI Global. doi:10.4018/978-1-5225-4053-3.ch015

Kenekar, T. V., & Dani, A. R. (2017). Privacy Preserving Data Mining on Unstructured Data. In S. Tamane, V. Solanki, & N. Dey (Eds.), *Privacy and Security Policies in Big Data* (pp. 167–190). Hershey, PA: IGI Global. doi:10.4018/978-1-5225-2486-1.ch008

Khaire, P. A., & Kotkondawar, R. R. (2017). Measures of Image and Video Segmentation. In N. Dey, A. Ashour, & S. Acharjee (Eds.), *Applied Video Processing in Surveillance and Monitoring Systems* (pp. 28–53). Hershey, PA: IGI Global. doi:10.4018/978-1-5225-1022-2.ch002

Knibbs, C., Goss, S., & Anthony, K. (2017). Counsellors' Phenomenological Experiences of Working with Children or Young People who have been Cyberbullied: Using Thematic Analysis of Semi Structured Interviews. *International Journal of Technoethics*, 8(1), 68–86. doi:10.4018/IJT.2017010106

Ko, A., & Gillani, S. (2018). Ontology Maintenance Through Semantic Text Mining: An Application for IT Governance Domain. In M. Lytras, N. Aljohani, E. Damiani, & K. Chui (Eds.), *Innovations, Developments, and Applications of Semantic Web and Information Systems* (pp. 350–371). Hershey, PA: IGI Global. doi:10.4018/978-1-5225-5042-6.ch013

Kohler, J., Lorenz, C. R., Gumbel, M., Specht, T., & Simov, K. (2017). A Security-By-Distribution Approach to Manage Big Data in a Federation of Untrustworthy Clouds. In S. Tamane, V. Solanki, & N. Dey (Eds.), *Privacy and Security Policies in Big Data* (pp. 92–123). Hershey, PA: IGI Global. doi:10.4018/978-1-5225-2486-1.ch005

Korstanje, M. E. (2017). English Speaking Countries and the Culture of Fear: Understanding Technology and Terrorism. In M. Korstanje (Ed.), *Threat Mitigation and Detection of Cyber Warfare and Terrorism Activities* (pp. 92–110). Hershey, PA: IGI Global. doi:10.4018/978-1-5225-1938-6.ch005

Korstanje, M. E. (2018). How Can World Leaders Understand the Perverse Core of Terrorism?: Terror in the Global Village. In C. Akrivopoulou (Ed.), *Global Perspectives on Human Migration, Asylum, and Security* (pp. 48–67). Hershey, PA: IGI Global. doi:10.4018/978-1-5225-2817-3.ch003

Krishnamachariar, P. K., & Gupta, M. (2018). Swimming Upstream in Turbulent Waters: Auditing Agile Development. In M. Gupta, R. Sharman, J. Walp, & P. Mulgund (Eds.), *Information Technology Risk Management and Compliance in Modern Organizations* (pp. 268–300). Hershey, PA: IGI Global. doi:10.4018/978-1-5225-2604-9.ch010

Ksiazak, P., Farrelly, W., & Curran, K. (2018). A Lightweight Authentication and Encryption Protocol for Secure Communications Between Resource-Limited Devices Without Hardware Modification: Resource-Limited Device Authentication. In Y. Maleh (Ed.), *Security and Privacy Management, Techniques, and Protocols* (pp. 1–46). Hershey, PA: IGI Global. doi:10.4018/978-1-5225-5583-4.ch001

Kukkuvada, A., & Basavaraju, P. (2018). Mutual Correlation-Based Anonymization for Privacy Preserving Medical Data Publishing. In C. Pradhan, H. Das, B. Naik, & N. Dey (Eds.), *Handbook of Research on Information Security in Biomedical Signal Processing* (pp. 304–319). Hershey, PA: IGI Global. doi:10.4018/978-1-5225-5152-2.ch016

Kumar, G., & Saini, H. (2018). Secure and Robust Telemedicine using ECC on Radix-8 with Formal Verification. *International Journal of Information Security and Privacy*, *12*(1), 13–28. doi:10.4018/IJISP.2018010102

Kumar, M., & Bhandari, A. (2017). Performance Evaluation of Web Server's Request Queue against AL-DDoS Attacks in NS-2. *International Journal of Information Security and Privacy*, *11*(4), 29–46. doi:10.4018/IJISP.2017100103

Kumar, M., & Vardhan, M. (2018). Privacy Preserving and Efficient Outsourcing Algorithm to Public Cloud: A Case of Statistical Analysis. *International Journal of Information Security and Privacy*, *12*(2), 1–25. doi:10.4018/IJISP.2018040101

Kumar, R. (2018). A Robust Biometrics System Using Finger Knuckle Print. In G. Shrivastava, P. Kumar, B. Gupta, S. Bala, & N. Dey (Eds.), *Handbook of Research on Network Forensics and Analysis Techniques* (pp. 416–446). Hershey, PA: IGI Global. doi:10.4018/978-1-5225-4100-4.ch022

Kumar, R. (2018). DOS Attacks on Cloud Platform: Their Solutions and Implications. In S. Aljawarneh & M. Malhotra (Eds.), *Critical Research on Scalability and Security Issues in Virtual Cloud Environments* (pp. 167–184). Hershey, PA: IGI Global. doi:10.4018/978-1-5225-3029-9.ch008

Kumari, R., & Sharma, K. (2018). Cross-Layer Based Intrusion Detection and Prevention for Network. In G. Shrivastava, P. Kumar, B. Gupta, S. Bala, & N. Dey (Eds.), *Handbook of Research on Network Forensics and Analysis Techniques* (pp. 38–56). Hershey, PA: IGI Global. doi:10.4018/978-1-5225-4100-4.ch003

Lapke, M. (2018). A Semiotic Examination of the Security Policy Lifecycle. In Y. Maleh (Ed.), *Security and Privacy Management, Techniques, and Protocols* (pp. 237–253). Hershey, PA: IGI Global. doi:10.4018/978-1-5225-5583-4.ch009

Liang, Z., Feng, B., Xu, X., Wu, X., & Yang, T. (2018). Geometrically Invariant Image Watermarking Using Histogram Adjustment. *International Journal of Digital Crime and Forensics, 10*(1), 54–66. doi:10.4018/IJDCF.2018010105

Liu, Z. J. (2017). A Cyber Crime Investigation Model Based on Case Characteristics. *International Journal of Digital Crime and Forensics, 9*(4), 40–47. doi:10.4018/IJDCF.2017100104

Loganathan, S. (2018). A Step-by-Step Procedural Methodology for Improving an Organization's IT Risk Management System. In M. Gupta, R. Sharman, J. Walp, & P. Mulgund (Eds.), *Information Technology Risk Management and Compliance in Modern Organizations* (pp. 21–47). Hershey, PA: IGI Global. doi:10.4018/978-1-5225-2604-9.ch002

Long, M., Peng, F., & Gong, X. (2018). A Format-Compliant Encryption for Secure HEVC Video Sharing in Multimedia Social Network. *International Journal of Digital Crime and Forensics, 10*(2), 23–39. doi:10.4018/IJDCF.2018040102

M., S., & M., J. (2018). Biosignal Denoising Techniques. In C. Pradhan, H. Das, B. Naik, & N. Dey (Eds.), *Handbook of Research on Information Security in Biomedical Signal Processing* (pp. 26-37). Hershey, PA: IGI Global. doi:10.4018/978-1-5225-5152-2.ch002

Mahapatra, C. (2017). Pragmatic Solutions to Cyber Security Threat in Indian Context. In R. Kumar, P. Pattnaik, & P. Pandey (Eds.), *Detecting and Mitigating Robotic Cyber Security Risks* (pp. 172–176). Hershey, PA: IGI Global. doi:10.4018/978-1-5225-2154-9.ch012

Majumder, A., Nath, S., & Das, A. (2018). Data Integrity in Mobile Cloud Computing. In K. Munir (Ed.), *Cloud Computing Technologies for Green Enterprises* (pp. 166–199). Hershey, PA: IGI Global. doi:10.4018/978-1-5225-3038-1.ch007

Maleh, Y., Zaydi, M., Sahid, A., & Ezzati, A. (2018). Building a Maturity Framework for Information Security Governance Through an Empirical Study in Organizations. In Y. Maleh (Ed.), *Security and Privacy Management, Techniques, and Protocols* (pp. 96–127). Hershey, PA: IGI Global. doi:10.4018/978-1-5225-5583-4.ch004

Malhotra, M., & Singh, A. (2018). Role of Agents to Enhance the Security and Scalability in Cloud Environment. In S. Aljawarneh & M. Malhotra (Eds.), *Critical Research on Scalability and Security Issues in Virtual Cloud Environments* (pp. 19–47). Hershey, PA: IGI Global. doi:10.4018/978-1-5225-3029-9.ch002

Mali, A. D. (2017). Recent Advances in Minimally-Obtrusive Monitoring of People's Health. *International Journal of Monitoring and Surveillance Technologies Research*, 5(2), 44–56. doi:10.4018/IJMSTR.2017040104

Mali, A. D., & Yang, N. (2017). On Automated Generation of Keyboard Layout to Reduce Finger-Travel Distance. *International Journal of Monitoring and Surveillance Technologies Research*, 5(2), 29–43. doi:10.4018/IJMSTR.2017040103

Mali, P. (2018). Defining Cyber Weapon in Context of Technology and Law. *International Journal of Cyber Warfare & Terrorism*, 8(1), 43–55. doi:10.4018/IJCWT.2018010104

Malik, A., & Pandey, B. (2018). CIAS: A Comprehensive Identity Authentication Scheme for Providing Security in VANET. *International Journal of Information Security and Privacy*, 12(1), 29–41. doi:10.4018/IJISP.2018010103

Manikandakumar, M., & Ramanujam, E. (2018). Security and Privacy Challenges in Big Data Environment. In G. Shrivastava, P. Kumar, B. Gupta, S. Bala, & N. Dey (Eds.), *Handbook of Research on Network Forensics and Analysis Techniques* (pp. 315–325). Hershey, PA: IGI Global. doi:10.4018/978-1-5225-4100-4.ch017

Manogaran, G., Thota, C., & Lopez, D. (2018). Human-Computer Interaction With Big Data Analytics. In D. Lopez & M. Durai (Eds.), *HCI Challenges and Privacy Preservation in Big Data Security* (pp. 1–22). Hershey, PA: IGI Global. doi:10.4018/978-1-5225-2863-0.ch001

Mariappan, P. B. P., & Teja, T. S. (2016). Digital Forensic and Machine Learning. In S. Geetha & A. Phamila (Eds.), *Combating Security Breaches and Criminal Activity in the Digital Sphere* (pp. 141–156). Hershey, PA: IGI Global. doi:10.4018/978-1-5225-0193-0.ch009

Marques, R., Mota, A., & Mota, L. (2016). Understanding Anti-Forensics Techniques for Combating Digital Security Breaches and Criminal Activity. In S. Geetha & A. Phamila (Eds.), *Combating Security Breaches and Criminal Activity in the Digital Sphere* (pp. 233–241). Hershey, PA: IGI Global. doi:10.4018/978-1-5225-0193-0.ch014

Mbale, J. (2018). Computer Centres Resource Cloud Elasticity-Scalability (CRECES): Copperbelt University Case Study. In S. Aljawarneh & M. Malhotra (Eds.), *Critical Research on Scalability and Security Issues in Virtual Cloud Environments* (pp. 48–70). Hershey, PA: IGI Global. doi:10.4018/978-1-5225-3029-9.ch003

McAvoy, D. (2017). Institutional Entrepreneurship in Defence Acquisition: What Don't We Understand? In K. Burgess & P. Antill (Eds.), *Emerging Strategies in Defense Acquisitions and Military Procurement* (pp. 222–241). Hershey, PA: IGI Global. doi:10.4018/978-1-5225-0599-0.ch013

McKeague, J., & Curran, K. (2018). Detecting the Use of Anonymous Proxies. *International Journal of Digital Crime and Forensics*, *10*(2), 74–94. doi:10.4018/IJDCF.2018040105

Meitei, T. G., Singh, S. A., & Majumder, S. (2018). PCG-Based Biometrics. In C. Pradhan, H. Das, B. Naik, & N. Dey (Eds.), *Handbook of Research on Information Security in Biomedical Signal Processing* (pp. 1–25). Hershey, PA: IGI Global. doi:10.4018/978-1-5225-5152-2.ch001

Menemencioğlu, O., & Orak, İ. M. (2017). A Simple Solution to Prevent Parameter Tampering in Web Applications. In M. Korstanje (Ed.), *Threat Mitigation and Detection of Cyber Warfare and Terrorism Activities* (pp. 1–20). Hershey, PA: IGI Global. doi:10.4018/978-1-5225-1938-6.ch001

Minto-Coy, I. D., & Henlin, M. G. (2017). The Development of Cybersecurity Policy and Legislative Landscape in Latin America and Caribbean States. In M. Moore (Ed.), *Cybersecurity Breaches and Issues Surrounding Online Threat Protection* (pp. 24–53). Hershey, PA: IGI Global. doi:10.4018/978-1-5225-1941-6.ch002

Mire, A. V., Dhok, S. B., Mistry, N. J., & Porey, P. D. (2016). Tampering Localization in Double Compressed Images by Investigating Noise Quantization. *International Journal of Digital Crime and Forensics*, 8(3), 46–62. doi:10.4018/IJDCF.2016070104

Mohamed, J. H. (2018). Scientograph-Based Visualization of Computer Forensics Research Literature. In J. Jeyasekar & P. Saravanan (Eds.), *Innovations in Measuring and Evaluating Scientific Information* (pp. 148–162). Hershey, PA: IGI Global. doi:10.4018/978-1-5225-3457-0.ch010

Mohan Murthy, M. K., & Sanjay, H. A. (2018). Scalability for Cloud. In S. Aljawarneh & M. Malhotra (Eds.), *Critical Research on Scalability and Security Issues in Virtual Cloud Environments* (pp. 1–18). Hershey, PA: IGI Global. doi:10.4018/978-1-5225-3029-9.ch001

Moorthy, U., & Gandhi, U. D. (2018). A Survey of Big Data Analytics Using Machine Learning Algorithms. In D. Lopez & M. Durai (Eds.), *HCI Challenges and Privacy Preservation in Big Data Security* (pp. 95–123). Hershey, PA: IGI Global. doi:10.4018/978-1-5225-2863-0.ch005

Mountantonakis, M., Minadakis, N., Marketakis, Y., Fafalios, P., & Tzitzikas, Y. (2018). Connectivity, Value, and Evolution of a Semantic Warehouse. In M. Lytras, N. Aljohani, E. Damiani, & K. Chui (Eds.), *Innovations, Developments, and Applications of Semantic Web and Information Systems* (pp. 1–31). Hershey, PA: IGI Global. doi:10.4018/978-1-5225-5042-6.ch001

Moussa, M., & Demurjian, S. A. (2017). Differential Privacy Approach for Big Data Privacy in Healthcare. In S. Tamane, V. Solanki, & N. Dey (Eds.), *Privacy and Security Policies in Big Data* (pp. 191–213). Hershey, PA: IGI Global. doi:10.4018/978-1-5225-2486-1.ch009

Mugisha, E., Zhang, G., El Abidine, M. Z., & Eugene, M. (2017). A TPM-based Secure Multi-Cloud Storage Architecture grounded on Erasure Codes. *International Journal of Information Security and Privacy*, 11(1), 52–64. doi:10.4018/IJISP.2017010104

Nachtigall, L. G., Araujo, R. M., & Nachtigall, G. R. (2017). Use of Images of Leaves and Fruits of Apple Trees for Automatic Identification of Symptoms of Diseases and Nutritional Disorders. *International Journal of Monitoring and Surveillance Technologies Research*, *5*(2), 1–14. doi:10.4018/IJMSTR.2017040101

Nagesh, K., Sumathy, R., Devakumar, P., & Sathiyamurthy, K. (2017). A Survey on Denial of Service Attacks and Preclusions. *International Journal of Information Security and Privacy*, *11*(4), 1–15. doi:10.4018/IJISP.2017100101

Nanda, A., Popat, P., & Vimalkumar, D. (2018). Navigating Through Choppy Waters of PCI DSS Compliance. In M. Gupta, R. Sharman, J. Walp, & P. Mulgund (Eds.), *Information Technology Risk Management and Compliance in Modern Organizations* (pp. 99–140). Hershey, PA: IGI Global. doi:10.4018/978-1-5225-2604-9.ch005

Newton, S. (2017). The Determinants of Stock Market Development in Emerging Economies: Examining the Impact of Corporate Governance and Regulatory Reforms (I). In M. Ojo & J. Van Akkeren (Eds.), *Value Relevance of Accounting Information in Capital Markets* (pp. 114–125). Hershey, PA: IGI Global. doi:10.4018/978-1-5225-1900-3.ch008

Nidhyananthan, S. S. A., J. V., & R., S. S. (2018). Wireless Enhanced Security Based on Speech Recognition. In C. Pradhan, H. Das, B. Naik, & N. Dey (Eds.), Handbook of Research on Information Security in Biomedical Signal Processing (pp. 228-253). Hershey, PA: IGI Global. doi:10.4018/978-1-5225-5152-2.ch012

Norri-Sederholm, T., Huhtinen, A., & Paakkonen, H. (2018). Ensuring Public Safety Organisations' Information Flow and Situation Picture in Hybrid Environments. *International Journal of Cyber Warfare & Terrorism*, *8*(1), 12–24. doi:10.4018/IJCWT.2018010102

Nunez, S., & Castaño, R. (2017). Building Brands in Emerging Economies: A Consumer-Oriented Approach. In Rajagopal, & R. Behl (Eds.), Business Analytics and Cyber Security Management in Organizations (pp. 183-194). Hershey, PA: IGI Global. doi:10.4018/978-1-5225-0902-8.ch013

Odella, F. (2018). Privacy Awareness and the Networking Generation. *International Journal of Technoethics*, *9*(1), 51–70. doi:10.4018/IJT.2018010105

Related References

Ojo, M., & DiGabriele, J. A. (2017). Fundamental or Enhancing Roles?: The Dual Roles of External Auditors and Forensic Accountants. In M. Ojo & J. Van Akkeren (Eds.), *Value Relevance of Accounting Information in Capital Markets* (pp. 59–78). Hershey, PA: IGI Global. doi:10.4018/978-1-5225-1900-3.ch004

P, P., & Subbiah, G. (2016). Visual Cryptography for Securing Images in Cloud. In S. Geetha, & A. Phamila (Eds.), *Combating Security Breaches and Criminal Activity in the Digital Sphere* (pp. 242-262). Hershey, PA: IGI Global. doi:10.4018/978-1-5225-0193-0.ch015

Pandey, S. (2018). An Empirical Study of the Indian IT Sector on Typologies of Workaholism as Predictors of HR Crisis. In V. Ahuja & S. Rathore (Eds.), *Multidisciplinary Perspectives on Human Capital and Information Technology Professionals* (pp. 202–224). Hershey, PA: IGI Global. doi:10.4018/978-1-5225-5297-0.ch011

Pattabiraman, A., Srinivasan, S., Swaminathan, K., & Gupta, M. (2018). Fortifying Corporate Human Wall: A Literature Review of Security Awareness and Training. In M. Gupta, R. Sharman, J. Walp, & P. Mulgund (Eds.), *Information Technology Risk Management and Compliance in Modern Organizations* (pp. 142–175). Hershey, PA: IGI Global. doi:10.4018/978-1-5225-2604-9.ch006

Prachi. (2018). Detection of Botnet Based Attacks on Network: Using Machine Learning Techniques. In G. Shrivastava, P. Kumar, B. Gupta, S. Bala, & N. Dey (Eds.), *Handbook of Research on Network Forensics and Analysis Techniques* (pp. 101-116). Hershey, PA: IGI Global. doi:10.4018/978-1-5225-4100-4.ch007

Pradhan, P. L. (2017). Proposed Round Robin CIA Pattern on RTS for Risk Assessment. *International Journal of Digital Crime and Forensics*, 9(1), 71–85. doi:10.4018/IJDCF.2017010105

Prentice, S., & Taylor, P. J. (2018). Psychological and Behavioral Examinations of Online Terrorism. In J. McAlaney, L. Frumkin, & V. Benson (Eds.), *Psychological and Behavioral Examinations in Cyber Security* (pp. 151–171). Hershey, PA: IGI Global. doi:10.4018/978-1-5225-4053-3.ch009

Priyadarshini, I. (2017). Cyber Security Risks in Robotics. In R. Kumar, P. Pattnaik, & P. Pandey (Eds.), *Detecting and Mitigating Robotic Cyber Security Risks* (pp. 333–348). Hershey, PA: IGI Global. doi:10.4018/978-1-5225-2154-9.ch022

R., A., & D., E. (2018). Cyber Crime Toolkit Development. In G. Shrivastava, P. Kumar, B. Gupta, S. Bala, & N. Dey (Eds.), *Handbook of Research on Network Forensics and Analysis Techniques* (pp. 184-224). Hershey, PA: IGI Global. doi:10.4018/978-1-5225-4100-4.ch011

Raghunath, R. (2018). Research Trends in Forensic Sciences: A Scientometric Approach. In J. Jeyasekar & P. Saravanan (Eds.), *Innovations in Measuring and Evaluating Scientific Information* (pp. 108–124). Hershey, PA: IGI Global. doi:10.4018/978-1-5225-3457-0.ch008

Ramadhas, G., Sankar, A. S., & Sugathan, N. (2018). The Scientific Communication Process in Homoeopathic Toxicology: An Evaluative Study. In J. Jeyasekar & P. Saravanan (Eds.), *Innovations in Measuring and Evaluating Scientific Information* (pp. 163–179). Hershey, PA: IGI Global. doi:10.4018/978-1-5225-3457-0.ch011

Ramani, K. (2018). Impact of Big Data on Security: Big Data Security Issues and Defense Schemes. In G. Shrivastava, P. Kumar, B. Gupta, S. Bala, & N. Dey (Eds.), *Handbook of Research on Network Forensics and Analysis Techniques* (pp. 326–350). Hershey, PA: IGI Global. doi:10.4018/978-1-5225-4100-4.ch018

Ramos, P., Funderburk, P., & Gebelein, J. (2018). Social Media and Online Gaming: A Masquerading Funding Source. *International Journal of Cyber Warfare & Terrorism*, 8(1), 25–42. doi:10.4018/IJCWT.2018010103

Rao, N., & Srivastava, S., & K.S., S. (2017). PKI Deployment Challenges and Recommendations for ICS Networks. *International Journal of Information Security and Privacy*, 11(2), 38–48. doi:10.4018/IJISP.2017040104

Rath, M., Swain, J., Pati, B., & Pattanayak, B. K. (2018). Network Security: Attacks and Control in MANET. In G. Shrivastava, P. Kumar, B. Gupta, S. Bala, & N. Dey (Eds.), *Handbook of Research on Network Forensics and Analysis Techniques* (pp. 19–37). Hershey, PA: IGI Global. doi:10.4018/978-1-5225-4100-4.ch002

Ricci, J., Baggili, I., & Breitinger, F. (2017). Watch What You Wear: Smartwatches and Sluggish Security. In A. Marrington, D. Kerr, & J. Gammack (Eds.), *Managing Security Issues and the Hidden Dangers of Wearable Technologies* (pp. 47–73). Hershey, PA: IGI Global. doi:10.4018/978-1-5225-1016-1.ch003

Rossi, J. A. (2017). Revisiting the Value Relevance of Accounting Information in the Italian and UK Stock Markets. In M. Ojo & J. Van Akkeren (Eds.), *Value Relevance of Accounting Information in Capital Markets* (pp. 102–113). Hershey, PA: IGI Global. doi:10.4018/978-1-5225-1900-3.ch007

Rowe, N. C. (2016). Privacy Concerns with Digital Forensics. In R. Cropf & T. Bagwell (Eds.), *Ethical Issues and Citizen Rights in the Era of Digital Government Surveillance* (pp. 145–162). Hershey, PA: IGI Global. doi:10.4018/978-1-4666-9905-2.ch008

Sabillon, R., Serra-Ruiz, J., Cavaller, V., & Cano, J. J. (2017). Digital Forensic Analysis of Cybercrimes: Best Practices and Methodologies. *International Journal of Information Security and Privacy*, *11*(2), 25–37. doi:10.4018/IJISP.2017040103

Sample, C., Cowley, J., & Bakdash, J. Z. (2018). Cyber + Culture: Exploring the Relationship. In J. McAlaney, L. Frumkin, & V. Benson (Eds.), *Psychological and Behavioral Examinations in Cyber Security* (pp. 64–79). Hershey, PA: IGI Global. doi:10.4018/978-1-5225-4053-3.ch004

Sarıgöllü, S. C., Aksakal, E., Koca, M. G., Akten, E., & Aslanbay, Y. (2018). Volunteered Surveillance. In J. McAlaney, L. Frumkin, & V. Benson (Eds.), *Psychological and Behavioral Examinations in Cyber Security* (pp. 133–150). Hershey, PA: IGI Global. doi:10.4018/978-1-5225-4053-3.ch008

Shahriar, H., Clincy, V., & Bond, W. (2018). Classification of Web-Service-Based Attacks and Mitigation Techniques. In Y. Maleh (Ed.), *Security and Privacy Management, Techniques, and Protocols* (pp. 360–378). Hershey, PA: IGI Global. doi:10.4018/978-1-5225-5583-4.ch015

Shet, S., Aswath, A. R., Hanumantharaju, M. C., & Gao, X. (2017). Design of Reconfigurable Architectures for Steganography System. In N. Dey, A. Ashour, & S. Acharjee (Eds.), *Applied Video Processing in Surveillance and Monitoring Systems* (pp. 145–168). Hershey, PA: IGI Global. doi:10.4018/978-1-5225-1022-2.ch007

Shrivastava, G., Sharma, K., Khari, M., & Zohora, S. E. (2018). Role of Cyber Security and Cyber Forensics in India. In G. Shrivastava, P. Kumar, B. Gupta, S. Bala, & N. Dey (Eds.), *Handbook of Research on Network Forensics and Analysis Techniques* (pp. 143–161). Hershey, PA: IGI Global. doi:10.4018/978-1-5225-4100-4.ch009

Singh, N. (2016). Cloud Crime and Fraud: A Study of Challenges for Cloud Security and Forensics. In S. Geetha & A. Phamila (Eds.), *Combating Security Breaches and Criminal Activity in the Digital Sphere* (pp. 68–84). Hershey, PA: IGI Global. doi:10.4018/978-1-5225-0193-0.ch005

Singh, N., Mittal, T., & Gupta, M. (2018). A Tale of Policies and Breaches: Analytical Approach to Construct Social Media Policy. In M. Gupta, R. Sharman, J. Walp, & P. Mulgund (Eds.), *Information Technology Risk Management and Compliance in Modern Organizations* (pp. 176–212). Hershey, PA: IGI Global. doi:10.4018/978-1-5225-2604-9.ch007

Singh, R., & Jalota, H. (2018). A Study of Good-Enough Security in the Context of Rural Business Process Outsourcing. In J. McAlaney, L. Frumkin, & V. Benson (Eds.), *Psychological and Behavioral Examinations in Cyber Security* (pp. 239–252). Hershey, PA: IGI Global. doi:10.4018/978-1-5225-4053-3.ch014

Sivasubramanian, K. E. (2018). Authorship Pattern and Collaborative Research Productivity of Asian Journal of Dairy and Food Research During the Year 2011 to 2015. In J. Jeyasekar & P. Saravanan (Eds.), *Innovations in Measuring and Evaluating Scientific Information* (pp. 213–222). Hershey, PA: IGI Global. doi:10.4018/978-1-5225-3457-0.ch014

Somasundaram, R., & Thirugnanam, M. (2017). IoT in Healthcare: Breaching Security Issues. In N. Jeyanthi & R. Thandeeswaran (Eds.), *Security Breaches and Threat Prevention in the Internet of Things* (pp. 174–188). Hershey, PA: IGI Global. doi:10.4018/978-1-5225-2296-6.ch008

Sonam, & Khari, M. (2018). Wireless Sensor Networks: A Technical Survey. In G. Shrivastava, P. Kumar, B. Gupta, S. Bala, & N. Dey (Eds.), *Handbook of Research on Network Forensics and Analysis Techniques* (pp. 1-18). Hershey, PA: IGI Global. doi:10.4018/978-1-5225-4100-4.ch001

Soni, P. (2018). Implications of HIPAA and Subsequent Regulations on Information Technology. In M. Gupta, R. Sharman, J. Walp, & P. Mulgund (Eds.), *Information Technology Risk Management and Compliance in Modern Organizations* (pp. 71–98). Hershey, PA: IGI Global. doi:10.4018/978-1-5225-2604-9.ch004

Sönmez, F. Ö., & Günel, B. (2018). Security Visualization Extended Review Issues, Classifications, Validation Methods, Trends, Extensions. In Y. Maleh (Ed.), *Security and Privacy Management, Techniques, and Protocols* (pp. 152–197). Hershey, PA: IGI Global. doi:10.4018/978-1-5225-5583-4.ch006

Srivastava, S. R., & Dube, S. (2018). Cyberattacks, Cybercrime and Cyberterrorism. In G. Shrivastava, P. Kumar, B. Gupta, S. Bala, & N. Dey (Eds.), *Handbook of Research on Network Forensics and Analysis Techniques* (pp. 162–183). Hershey, PA: IGI Global. doi:10.4018/978-1-5225-4100-4. ch010

Stacey, E. (2017). Contemporary Terror on the Net. In *Combating Internet-Enabled Terrorism: Emerging Research and Opportunities* (pp. 16–44). Hershey, PA: IGI Global. doi:10.4018/978-1-5225-2190-7.ch002

Sumana, M., Hareesha, K. S., & Kumar, S. (2018). Semantically Secure Classifiers for Privacy Preserving Data Mining. In Y. Maleh (Ed.), *Security and Privacy Management, Techniques, and Protocols* (pp. 66–95). Hershey, PA: IGI Global. doi:10.4018/978-1-5225-5583-4.ch003

Suresh, N., & Gupta, M. (2018). Impact of Technology Innovation: A Study on Cloud Risk Mitigation. In M. Gupta, R. Sharman, J. Walp, & P. Mulgund (Eds.), *Information Technology Risk Management and Compliance in Modern Organizations* (pp. 229–267). Hershey, PA: IGI Global. doi:10.4018/978-1-5225-2604-9.ch009

Survey, A. K. Balasubramanian & M. Rajakani (Eds.), *Algorithmic Strategies for Solving Complex Problems in Cryptography* (pp. 111–123). Hershey, PA: IGI Global. doi:10.4018/978-1-5225-2915-6.ch009

Tank, D. M. (2017). Security and Privacy Issues, Solutions, and Tools for MCC. In K. Munir (Ed.), *Security Management in Mobile Cloud Computing* (pp. 121–147). Hershey, PA: IGI Global. doi:10.4018/978-1-5225-0602-7. ch006

Thackray, H., & McAlaney, J. (2018). Groups Online: Hacktivism and Social Protest. In J. McAlaney, L. Frumkin, & V. Benson (Eds.), *Psychological and Behavioral Examinations in Cyber Security* (pp. 194–209). Hershey, PA: IGI Global. doi:10.4018/978-1-5225-4053-3.ch011

Thandeeswaran, R., Pawar, R., & Rai, M. (2017). Security Threats in Autonomous Vehicles. In N. Jeyanthi & R. Thandeeswaran (Eds.), *Security Breaches and Threat Prevention in the Internet of Things* (pp. 117–141). Hershey, PA: IGI Global. doi:10.4018/978-1-5225-2296-6.ch006

Thota, C., Manogaran, G., Lopez, D., & Vijayakumar, V. (2017). Big Data Security Framework for Distributed Cloud Data Centers. In M. Moore (Ed.), *Cybersecurity Breaches and Issues Surrounding Online Threat Protection* (pp. 288–310). Hershey, PA: IGI Global. doi:10.4018/978-1-5225-1941-6.ch012

Thukral, S., & Rodriguez, T. D. (2018). Child Sexual Abuse: Intra- and Extra-Familial Risk Factors, Reactions, and Interventions. In R. Gopalan (Ed.), *Social, Psychological, and Forensic Perspectives on Sexual Abuse* (pp. 229–258). Hershey, PA: IGI Global. doi:10.4018/978-1-5225-3958-2.ch017

Tidke, S. (2017). MonogDB: Data Management in NoSQL. In S. Tamane, V. Solanki, & N. Dey (Eds.), *Privacy and Security Policies in Big Data* (pp. 64–91). Hershey, PA: IGI Global. doi:10.4018/978-1-5225-2486-1.ch004

Tierney, M. (2018). #TerroristFinancing: An Examination of Terrorism Financing via the Internet. *International Journal of Cyber Warfare & Terrorism*, *8*(1), 1–11. doi:10.4018/IJCWT.2018010101

Topal, R. (2018). A Cyber-Psychological and Behavioral Approach to Online Radicalization. In J. McAlaney, L. Frumkin, & V. Benson (Eds.), *Psychological and Behavioral Examinations in Cyber Security* (pp. 210–221). Hershey, PA: IGI Global. doi:10.4018/978-1-5225-4053-3.ch012

Tripathy, B. K., & Baktha, K. (2018). Clustering Approaches. In *Security, Privacy, and Anonymization in Social Networks: Emerging Research and Opportunities* (pp. 51–85). Hershey, PA: IGI Global. doi:10.4018/978-1-5225-5158-4.ch004

Tripathy, B. K., & Baktha, K. (2018). De-Anonymization Techniques. In *Security, Privacy, and Anonymization in Social Networks: Emerging Research and Opportunities* (pp. 137–147). Hershey, PA: IGI Global. doi:10.4018/978-1-5225-5158-4.ch007

Tripathy, B. K., & Baktha, K. (2018). Fundamentals of Social Networks. In *Security, Privacy, and Anonymization in Social Networks: Emerging Research and Opportunities* (pp. 1–22). Hershey, PA: IGI Global. doi:10.4018/978-1-5225-5158-4.ch001

Tripathy, B. K., & Baktha, K. (2018). Graph Modification Approaches. In *Security, Privacy, and Anonymization in Social Networks: Emerging Research and Opportunities* (pp. 86–115). Hershey, PA: IGI Global. doi:10.4018/978-1-5225-5158-4.ch005

Tripathy, B. K., & Baktha, K. (2018). Social Network Anonymization Techniques. In *Security, Privacy, and Anonymization in Social Networks: Emerging Research and Opportunities* (pp. 36–50). Hershey, PA: IGI Global. doi:10.4018/978-1-5225-5158-4.ch003

Tsimperidis, I., Rostami, S., & Katos, V. (2017). Age Detection Through Keystroke Dynamics from User Authentication Failures. *International Journal of Digital Crime and Forensics, 9*(1), 1–16. doi:10.4018/IJDCF.2017010101

Wadkar, H. S., Mishra, A., & Dixit, A. M. (2017). Framework to Secure Browser Using Configuration Analysis. *International Journal of Information Security and Privacy, 11*(2), 49–63. doi:10.4018/IJISP.2017040105

Wahlgren, G., & Kowalski, S. J. (2018). IT Security Risk Management Model for Handling IT-Related Security Incidents: The Need for a New Escalation Approach. In Y. Maleh (Ed.), *Security and Privacy Management, Techniques, and Protocols* (pp. 129–151). Hershey, PA: IGI Global. doi:10.4018/978-1-5225-5583-4.ch005

Wall, H. J., & Kaye, L. K. (2018). Online Decision Making: Online Influence and Implications for Cyber Security. In J. McAlaney, L. Frumkin, & V. Benson (Eds.), *Psychological and Behavioral Examinations in Cyber Security* (pp. 1–25). Hershey, PA: IGI Global. doi:10.4018/978-1-5225-4053-3.ch001

Xylogiannopoulos, K. F., Karampelas, P., & Alhajj, R. (2017). Advanced Network Data Analytics for Large-Scale DDoS Attack Detection. *International Journal of Cyber Warfare & Terrorism, 7*(3), 44–54. doi:10.4018/IJCWT.2017070104

Yan, W. Q., Wu, X., & Liu, F. (2018). Progressive Scrambling for Social Media. *International Journal of Digital Crime and Forensics, 10*(2), 56–73. doi:10.4018/IJDCF.2018040104

Yang, L., Gao, T., Xuan, Y., & Gao, H. (2016). Contrast Modification Forensics Algorithm Based on Merged Weight Histogram of Run Length. *International Journal of Digital Crime and Forensics*, 8(2), 27–35. doi:10.4018/IJDCF.2016040103

Yassein, M. B., Mardini, W., & Al-Abdi, A. (2018). Security Issues in the Internet of Things: A Review. In S. Aljawarneh & M. Malhotra (Eds.), *Critical Research on Scalability and Security Issues in Virtual Cloud Environments* (pp. 186–200). Hershey, PA: IGI Global. doi:10.4018/978-1-5225-3029-9.ch009

Yassein, M. B., Shatnawi, M., & l-Qasem, N. (2018). A Survey of Probabilistic Broadcast Schemes in Mobile Ad Hoc Networks. In S. Aljawarneh, & M. Malhotra (Eds.), *Critical Research on Scalability and Security Issues in Virtual Cloud Environments* (pp. 269-282). Hershey, PA: IGI Global. doi:10.4018/978-1-5225-3029-9.ch013

Yue, C., Tianliang, L., Manchun, C., & Jingying, L. (2018). Evaluation of the Attack Effect Based on Improved Grey Clustering Model. *International Journal of Digital Crime and Forensics*, 10(1), 92–100. doi:10.4018/IJDCF.2018010108

Zhang, P., He, Y., & Chow, K. (2018). Fraud Track on Secure Electronic Check System. *International Journal of Digital Crime and Forensics*, 10(2), 137–144. doi:10.4018/IJDCF.2018040108

Zhao, J., Wang, Q., Guo, J., Gao, L., & Yang, F. (2016). An Overview on Passive Image Forensics Technology for Automatic Computer Forgery. *International Journal of Digital Crime and Forensics*, 8(4), 14–25. doi:10.4018/IJDCF.2016100102

Zhao, X., Zhu, J., & Yu, H. (2016). On More Paradigms of Steganalysis. *International Journal of Digital Crime and Forensics*, 8(2), 1–15. doi:10.4018/IJDCF.2016040101

Zhou, L., Yan, W. Q., Shu, Y., & Yu, J. (2018). CVSS: A Cloud-Based Visual Surveillance System. *International Journal of Digital Crime and Forensics*, 10(1), 79–91. doi:10.4018/IJDCF.2018010107

Zhu, J., Guan, Q., Zhao, X., Cao, Y., & Chen, G. (2017). A Steganalytic Scheme Based on Classifier Selection Using Joint Image Characteristics. *International Journal of Digital Crime and Forensics*, 9(4), 1–14. doi:10.4018/IJDCF.2017100101

Zoughbi, S. (2017). Major Technology Trends Affecting Government Data in Developing Countries. In S. Zoughbi (Ed.), *Securing Government Information and Data in Developing Countries* (pp. 127–135). Hershey, PA: IGI Global. doi:10.4018/978-1-5225-1703-0.ch008

Zubairu, B. (2018). Security Risks of Biomedical Data Processing in Cloud Computing Environment. In C. Pradhan, H. Das, B. Naik, & N. Dey (Eds.), *Handbook of Research on Information Security in Biomedical Signal Processing* (pp. 177–197). Hershey, PA: IGI Global. doi:10.4018/978-1-5225-5152-2.ch009

About the Author

Ananda Mitra is a Professor of Communication at Wake Forest University; his research and teaching interests include media, technology, culture, data collection, data management, and issues surrounding Indian culture. He is also credited with the invention of the idea of narbs and his principal research, writing, and practical concerns are in the ways in which technology is constantly reshaping our everyday life practices and calling into question how we live our life within a constantly changing global space. He uses the theoretical approach of the primacy of mediated narratives in contemporary life as reported at themediawatch.com. He was educated at the Indian Institute of Technology (Kharagpur), Wake Forest University, and the University of Illinois at Urbana-Champaign. He is the owner of an independent research agency called Management Learning Laboratories that specializes in applying technology to the collection, management, and visualization of data.

Index

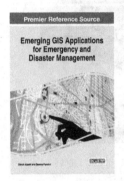
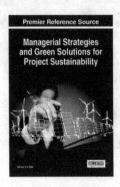

Printed in the United States
by Baker & Taylor Publisher Services